VULNERABILITY

D1566642

Gender in Law, Culture, and Society

Series Editor
Martha Albertson Fineman, Emory University School of Law, USA

Gender in Law, Culture, and Society will address key issues and theoretical debates related to gender, culture, and the law. Its titles will advance understanding of the ways in which a society's cultural and legal approaches to gender intersect, clash, and are reconciled or remain in tension. The series will further examine connections between gender and economic and political systems, as well as various other cultural and societal influences on gender construction and presentation, including social and legal consequences that men and women uniquely or differently encounter. Intended for a scholarly readership as well as for courses, its titles will be a mix of single-authored volumes and collections of original essays that will be both pragmatic and theoretical. It will draw from the perspectives of critical and feminist legal theory, as well as other schools of jurisprudence. Interdisciplinary, and international in scope, the series will offer a range of voices speaking to significant questions arising from the study of law in relation to gender, including the very nature of law itself.

Other titles in the series

Sister Wives, Surrogates and Sex Workers
Outlaws by Choice?
Angela Campbell
ISBN 9781409435211

Exploring Masculinities
Feminist Legal Theory Reflections
Edited by Martha Albertson Fineman and Michael Thomson
ISBN 9781472415110

Feminism, Law and Religion
Edited by Marie A. Failinger, Elizabeth R. Schiltz and Susan J. Stabile
ISBN 978 409444190

Critical Queer Studies
Law, Film, and Fiction in Contemporary American Culture
Casey Charles
ISBN 9781409444060

Vulnerability
Reflections on a New Ethical Foundation for Law and Politics

Edited by

MARTHA ALBERTSON FINEMAN
Emory University, USA

ANNA GREAR
Cardiff Law School, UK and
University of Waikato, New Zealand

ASHGATE

Published by
Ashgate Publishing Limited
Wey Court East
Union Road
Farnham
Surrey, GU9 7PT
England

Ashgate Publishing Company
110 Cherry Street
Suite 3–1
Burlington, VT 05401–3818
USA

www.ashgate.com

British Library Cataloguing in Publication Data
A catalogue record for this book is available from the British Library

The Library of Congress has cataloged the printed edition as follows:
Fineman, Martha.
     Vulnerability : reflections on a new ethical foundation for law and politics / by Martha
     Albertson Fineman and Anna Grear.
          pages cm – (Gender in law, culture, and society)
     Includes bibliographical references and index.
     ISBN 978–1–4724–2162–3 (hardback : alk. paper) — ISBN 978–1–4724–2163–0
     (pbk. : alk. paper) – ISBN 978–1–4724–2164–7 (ebook) – ISBN 978–1- 4724–2165–4
     (epub)
     1. Law—Philosophy. 2. Vulnerability 3. Law and ethics. 4. Sociological
     jurisprudence. I. Grear, Anna, 1959–
     II. Title.
     K247.6.F56 2013
     174'.3–dc23
     2013019289

ISBN 9781472421623 (hbk)
ISBN 9781472421630 (pbk)
ISBN 9781472421647 (ebk – PDF)
ISBN 9781472421654 (ebk – ePUB)

Printed in the United Kingdom by Henry Ling Limited,
at the Dorset Press, Dorchester, DT1 1HD

Contents

Notes on Contributors

Alison Assiter
Professor of Feminist Theory at the University of the West of England. Alison has written a number of books and articles including *Althusser and Feminism*, Pluto Press, 1990; *Enlightened Women*, Routledge, 1996; *Revisiting Universalism*, Macmillan, 2003 and, more recently, *Kierkegaard, Metaphysics and Political Theory*, Continuum, 2009. Her present interests include political and feminist philosophy and the philosophy of Kant and Kierkegaard.

Helen Carr
Reader at Kent Law School. Helen's research is concerned with social welfare and the limits of human rights, in particular in the areas of housing and adult social care. Currently, her focus is gender and the politics of austerity and welfare reform. She is co-authoring a book on homelessness with Professor Caroline Hunter. She is a solicitor and sits as a judge with the Residential Property Tribunal.

Morgan Cloud
Charles Howard Candler Professor of Law at Emory University. Morgan's scholarship ranges across disciplines, including constitutional law, criminal law, and legal history. He has taught and lectured at universities throughout the United States and Europe.

Sean Coyle
Chair of English Laws, University of Birmingham, and was previously Reader in Jurisprudence, University College London. Sean writes in legal and political philosophy, examining the nature of law and justice as a theologico-political problem. His latest book, *Dimensions of Politics and English Jurisprudence*, was published by Cambridge University Press in 2013.

Rachel Anne Fenton
Senior Lecturer in Law at Bristol Law School, University of the West of England. Rachel's teaching and research interests lie in the fields of medical law, gender, and sexual violence with a particular focus on assisted reproduction, rape, and sexual assault. She also writes about Italian law in these areas. She is co-editor of *Gender, Sexualities and Law*, Routledge, 2011.

Martha Albertson Fineman
Robert W. Woodruff Professor of Law at Emory University. A leading authority on family law and feminist jurisprudence, Martha is the founding director of

the Feminism and Legal Theory Project, an interdisciplinary scholarly project she began at the University of Wisconsin in 1984. Since 2007, she also directs Emory's Vulnerability and the Human Condition Initiative, an interdisciplinary project housed in the Laney Graduate School. Her scholarly work focuses on various aspects of the legal regulation of intimacy and on the social, cultural, and legal implications of human dependency and vulnerability.

Anna Grear
Reader in Law, Cardiff University and Adjunct Associate Professor of Law, University of Waikato, New Zealand. Anna is a Global Affiliate of the Vulnerability and Human Condition Initiative. Her work focuses upon the law's construction of the human and of the human relationship with the world, broadly understood, with a particular emphasis upon the environment and globalization. Anna's scholarship is best known for its critical deconstruction of corporate human rights claims and for her related explorations of legal rights subjectivity. Anna's 2010 monograph, *Redirecting Human Rights: Facing the Challenge of Corporate Legal Humanity*, has been welcomed as constituting "a new ground of contestation" and marking a fresh start "towards understanding the ontology of human rights." Anna is also Director of the Global Network for the Study of Human Rights and the Environment and founder and co-editor in chief of the *Journal of Human Rights and the Environment*.

Susan Kuo
Associate Professor at the University of South Carolina School of Law. Susan's current research focuses on social justice issues in disaster law and policy, and she has particular expertise concerning riots and mob violence. She has also written about criminal law and procedure, privacy, and legal education. She teaches or has taught a variety of courses, including Criminal Law, Criminal Procedure, Federal Courts, Conflict of Laws, Civil Procedure, Law and Social Justice, and Race and the Law. Prior to entering into teaching, she was a Special Assistant United States Attorney with the United States Attorney's Office in Atlanta, Georgia. She also completed two federal judicial clerkships, one with Judge Eugene E. Siler, Jr. of the United States Court of Appeals for the Sixth Circuit and the other with Judge Robert H. Hall of the United States District Court for the Northern District of Georgia.

Benjamin Means
Associate Professor at the University of South Carolina School of Law. Graduated *cum laude* from Dartmouth College, and *magna cum laude* from Michigan Law School, where he was an articles editor for the *Michigan Law Review*. Prior to joining the faculty at the University of South Carolina, Benjamin practiced law at Davis Polk & Wardwell and Satterlee Stephens Burke & Burke LLP, both in New York City, where he represented clients including JPMorgan Chase Bank, Moody's Investors Service, National Geographic, and the Thomson Corporation

in matters of corporate law and litigation. He also served as a law clerk to the Honorable Rosemary Pooler of the United States Court of Appeals for the Second Circuit. Benjamin's scholarship focuses on the governance of closely held business organizations. He teaches Business Associations, Business Crimes, Mergers and Acquisitions, and a seminar on Liberty Theory.

Ani B. Satz

Associate Professor of Law at Emory University, with faculty appointments at the Rollins School of Public Health and University Center for Ethics at Emory. Ani holds a J.D. from the University of Michigan and a Ph.D. in philosophy from Monash University in Melbourne, Australia, which she completed while a fellow at Princeton University. She teaches courses at the intersection of health, disability, and animal law and ethics. Ani's research focuses on the legal response to vulnerability and governmental obligations to those who are vulnerable. Her most recent scholarship addresses from a law and ethics perspective access to health care, disability discrimination, and the well-being of nonhuman animals.

Alexandra Timmer

Post-doctoral Researcher at the Netherlands Institute of Human Rights, Utrecht University. Formerly Ph.D. candidate at the Human Rights Center of Ghent University. Alexandra's research explores issues of equality and discrimination in the case law of the European Court of Human Rights. Together with her colleague Lourdes Peroni, she has also written an article on the concept of vulnerable groups in the case law of the ECtHR. Alexandra obtained an MA in History and an LLM from Leiden University, as well as a LLM from Columbia Law School. She is co-founder and regular contributor to the blog www.strasbourgobservers.com.

Acknowledgments

We would like to thank all of our contributors to this collection. We were particularly grateful for the wonderful discussions that this collaboration produced. We are also very appreciative of the technical help provided by Danny Kim of Emory Law School in helping us to get this volume ready for publication.

Introduction
Vulnerability as Heuristic—An Invitation to Future Exploration

Martha Albertson Fineman and Anna Grear

Vulnerability is a concept increasingly explored by a range of scholars. Key among these scholars is Martha Albertson Fineman, who developed a theory of vulnerability as an extension of her earlier critical work concerning dependency as a way of problematizing the core assumptions underlying the "autonomous" subject of liberal law and politics specifically in the context of US equality discourse. As Fineman's work has evolved, she has drawn together various other scholars—some of whom were already addressing vulnerability in different contexts and in different ways—in a nexus of ongoing and lively discussions concerning the power, limitations and promise of vulnerability as an heuristic tool through which to interrogate the core concepts and conclusions of liberal legal and political subjectivity and the structural arrangements they support.

In 2008 Fineman established the Vulnerability and the Human Condition Initiative (VHC) as an interdisciplinary theme of Emory University's Laney Graduate School. The Initiative was initially supported by joint contributions from Emory's Race and Difference Initiative and the Feminism and Legal Theory Project (which Fineman established in 1984 while at the University of Wisconsin). The VHC Initiative's webpages set forth its ambition to "carve out academic space within which scholars can imagine models of state support and legal protection that focus on the commonalities of the human condition—most centrally the universal vulnerability of human beings and the imperfection of the societal institutions created to address that vulnerability." The VHC Initiative's first public session took the form of a roundtable discussion with Bryan S. Turner and Peadar Kirby (both of whom were already working on concepts of vulnerability in relation to a sociology of human rights and a critical account of globalization respectively). It was at this event that Fineman distributed her 2008 paper "The Vulnerable Subject" for early discussion. Various workshops, programs, and publications have followed.

This coedited collection represents a continued engagement with that earlier work on vulnerability by presenting a series of reflections upon Fineman's current conception of the significance and implications of human vulnerability for social and legal policy. It is, in that sense, Fineman's vulnerability thesis "refracted" through various lenses. The collection brings together scholars who have thought about vulnerability in different ways and contexts prior to encountering Fineman's thesis, and scholars for whom Fineman's work was a first initiation or entry-point to thinking through a vulnerability lens. Every chapter in this collection, however, engages with Fineman's vulnerability thesis. The idea of the collection began with two roundtables held in the United Kingdom at Bristol Law School, University of the West of England in 2010 and 2011, and represents the fruit of those workshops and a research conversation between Fineman and Grear which resulted in a partnership between the VHC Initiative and the International Law and Human Rights Unit at Bristol Law School headed by Grear. In fact, it was Grear's interest in theorizing "embodied vulnerability" as a foundation of international human rights subjectivity that drew her into personal contact with Fineman in 2008.

The engagements with Fineman's vulnerability thesis offered here move from theoretical and philosophical contributions to rather more "situated" reflections addressing specific contexts. The collection begins with Fineman's own contribution laying out the broad cartography of her thesis—and thereafter is taken up in a range of ways by different scholars. Significantly, she rejects identity categories and "intersectionality" in creating a universal "vulnerable subject" defined by its shared and constant vulnerability. Fineman developed the concept of vulnerability and the idea of a vulnerable subject initially as a stealthily disguised human rights discourse, fashioned for an American audience. The concept has evolved from those early articulations, and she argues that it has some significant differences as an approach, particularly in that a focus on vulnerability is decidedly focused on exploring the nature of the human part, rather than the rights part, of the human rights trope.

In addition to emphasizing the universality and constancy of human vulnerability and using that to undermine the mythical (and equality destructive) autonomous liberal subject of neoliberal rhetoric, Fineman calls for a "responsive state." Beyond the mandate for state responsiveness, her approach is significant because addressing vulnerability brings the concept of "resilience" to the fore and brings the societal institutions through which resources and resilience are produced under scrutiny. The vulnerability thesis thus mediates between calls for regulatory state policies and contemporary calls for "individual responsibility" with regard to monitoring institutional actions. Vulnerability is posited as a fundamental characteristic that positions individuals in relation to each other as human beings and also suggests an appropriate relationship of shared responsibility as between state, societal institutions, and individuals.

In Fineman's vulnerability thesis there is no position of "invulnerability" (or independence and self-sufficiency starkly understood) and we have only resilience upon which to rely as we encounter life's challenges and opportunities. While vulnerability is universal, resilience is particular, found in the assets or resources an individual accumulates and dispenses over the course of a lifetime and through interaction with and access to society's institutions. Those institutions should operate in ways that do not unduly privilege some, while disadvantaging others. The nature of human vulnerability and the process of building resilience through institutions mandate the state to be active, involved, and responsive to vulnerability—monitoring institutions and better ensuring that the promise of equality of access and opportunity is realized.

In "Kierkegaard and Vulnerability," Assiter draws upon an important philosophical treatment of vulnerability in the work of Søren Kierkegaard to offer a metaphysic which might be read as underpinning Fineman's work. Assiter points to the dualistic metaphysic underlying liberal political theory, which is claimed, by various feminist theorists, to "govern" Western thought. Relatedly or not, she notes, there is also a clear dualism in classical social contract theory which positions the individual *political* subject (the subject of rights) in direct contradistinction to the private, familial, conjugal sphere. Importantly, in such a dualistic metaphysic, disembodiment plays a central role—relatedly constructing the disembodied political subject as being fundamentally invulnerable for important purposes and in an important sense. In particular, one implication of this, Assiter notes, is that in the context of ethical reasoning, the body-self (in other words, the vulnerable self) is to be transcended. In contrast to this disembodied, relatively invulnerable self, however, stands the conception of the "vulnerable self"—or, in Fineman's terms—the "vulnerable subject." Kierkegaard's philosophical account of the subject, for Assiter, "chimes with key features of Fineman's notion of the vulnerable self," for Kierkegaard's subject is both embodied and vulnerable.

Importantly, Assiter's Kierkegaardian subject is simultaneously responsible and vulnerable, free and finite. This subject is quintessentially vulnerable as a result of a natal fact: He/she is born, and dies. This subject is also fully capable of responsibility and is open to "infinite love." Assiter's Kierkegaardian subject is, then, a fundamentally relational self. This vulnerable self is not a victim, though—he/she can act, both individually and collectively. Nevertheless, he/she never transcends the vulnerability characterizing the condition of a *natural being*. For Kierkegaard, Assiter notes, "[e]thics begins with the actual." Assiter's exploration arguably provides a way of theorizing the vulnerable subject and locating it within a broader philosophical construction of both subjectivity and ethics. Her account of Kierkegaardian subjectivity chimes especially well with a vulnerability-centered ethics that insists, as the work of Fineman does, that substantive questions of relative positionality must form the heart of any responsible analysis of our legal and political life together.

Grear's argument in this collection has particular affinity with Assiter's Kierkegaardian point concerning the role of the actual in ethics—as well as the role of embodiment in relation to our conception of vulnerability and its implications. Grear argues in "Vulnerability, Advanced Global Capitalism and Co-symptomatic Injustice: Locating the Vulnerable Subject" that there is an urgent need for an "ethico-material turn" in law in the form of a greater degree of juridical responsiveness to the vulnerabilities inherent in bio- and socio-materiality.

For Grear, one of the most promising aspects of the growing scholarly interest in the concept of vulnerability concerns its potential for responsiveness to the complexity, affectability, and vulnerability of the living order and of the multiple beings interrelationally co-constituted by and within it. There is a need for law to face up to and embrace a certain nonnegotiability of *ethical* demand emerging from the implications of living materiality itself, notwithstanding the fact that the precise implications of such ethical demand remain, in large part, undecided.

In response to this central ethical challenge, Grear chooses to "locate" Fineman's vulnerable subject within the complex materialities of advanced global capitalism—which—along with the climate crisis –forms "an indispensable backdrop for any adequate exploration both of human and environmental vulnerability and of law's construction of subjectivity."

Grear's critique is directly addressed to core assumptions undergirding law's view of the paradigm legal actor—the "unencumbered self" (to borrow Schlag's evocative term)—the rational, property-owning actor at the heart of classic liberalism—and precisely the subject that Fineman's vulnerable subject seeks to replace. Grear locates this vulnerable subject (embodied and affectable) in the structural "unevenness" of the globalized world order, which she contrasts with the mythical "evenness" of the juridical plane implied by the formally equal actors at the heart of liberal legal theory. Arguing that structural advantage and the imposition of oppression can usefully be understood to be "co-symptomatic," Grear seeks to highlight (if not necessarily in directly causal terms) the dense and patterned imposition of well-practiced distributions of life and death in the global order. Co-symptomatic injustice, suggests Grear, can be read as being an inherent implication of the vulnerability thesis—one worth highlighting in the light of "the ethico-material urgencies of our age."

The theme of the relationship between ethics, actualities, and vulnerability is also clearly central to Coyle's contribution to this collection, "Vulnerability and the Liberal Order." Coyle takes the hesitancy of the Roman Catholic Church concerning capitalism as a context against which to reflect upon the "problem of vulnerability" by setting it in relation to the ambivalence of the market order with which liberalism is so closely associated. Coyle draws attention to both the new social freedoms associated with the market order and to new forms of vulnerability typifying it. There are at least two connections between Coyle's contribution and that of Grear: The decontextualized liberal self (central to Grear's analysis) makes an appearance in Coyle's analysis in the form of the liberal individual freed "from social structures" who in this freedom "also becomes a commodity," and the theme of the co-symptomatic is hinted at by Coyle's direct attention to the fact the very market forces distributing resources and creating wealth are also those producing new forms of wage slavery and poverty.

Coyle identifies the failure of both the conservative and socialist perspectives on the market adequately to respond to vulnerability. For him, both positions share a fundamental flaw: They portray vulnerability as a structural question with a political solution, overlooking the central fact that "vulnerability is fundamentally an embodied experience and not exclusively a structural one." Accordingly, both positions focus on the wrong kind of solution to a misperceived problem. Whether they fight vulnerability through class struggle (socialist "left" approaches) or through the market (conservative "right" approaches), both of these contemporary liberal political approaches overlook, moreover, the centrally important context of civil society.

While Coyle is sympathetic to Fineman's aims in her account of the need for a responsive state, he clearly has reservations. First, he seems concerned that the responsive state might place a chilling effect on civil society. Second, while sharing Fineman's concern that state and market alike should be made more accountable, Coyle is ultimately unable to share her faith that the state has a distinctive contribution stemming from its being "theoretically freed from the market and profit constraints placed on individual industries and businesses" and being in a "superior position [to implement] public values." Indeed, argues Coyle, both vulnerability and resilience are likely to be *best* understood when they are *detached* from politics and located in "civil society." For him, the progressive erosion of civil society needs to be seen as the fundamental context against which to understand vulnerability in liberal societies—especially the vulnerability of the most vulnerable.

For Coyle, the proper role of politics is not a kind of interventionism, but the creation of conditions under which civil society (and its basic instantiation of neighborly relations) flourishes. Coyle is concerned with civil society as the space for enacting or embodying justice at the basic level of respect for the dignity of other persons—through the operation of "intermediate communities … [giving] life to specific networks of solidarity." This approach suggests that, while the "needs of justice cannot be met without the state's involvement, [these are not] capable of systematic integration into society unless the community itself becomes more integrated, more responsive to the needs of others"—and that political responses cannot and must not replace or denude the distinctive contribution of civil society to the amelioration of vulnerabilities.

Morgan Cloud also reverts to Catholicism as a lens through which to view vulnerability in his "More than Utopia" chapter. Cloud views Fineman as writing in the utopian tradition and compares and contrasts her vision with that of Thomas More's *Utopia*. At the heart of the utopian project is an imagined society in which there is a more equal distribution of assets that ameliorates "the burdens and anxieties suffered by everyone, but particularly the disadvantaged members of society." Morgan notes that Fineman's ideas, unlike More's, arise not from religious precepts, but resonate in the "values and methods" of contemporary critical theory. It is the taking apart of ideological myths or "illusory absolutes" of liberal individualism and setting forth a more accurate understanding of the world that Cloud sees as the important and foundational task of the vulnerability thesis. It is a better device for explaining the human condition and thus for imagining a just society. The paradox of vulnerability as both universal and particular Cloud finds provides a "powerful secular model" for the reconstruction of a more just society. Cloud observes: "Vulnerability's universality makes it a powerful concept for social organization, but its particularity fuels Fineman's arguments for reconceiving our social values and institutions to support the poor, weak, the powerless, and the despised, just as More imagined happened in Utopia."

Cloud is ultimately skeptical about the transformative possibilities of any theory, including vulnerability theory. He notes that More was a pessimist and imagined severe constraints on human freedom or agency were necessary to rein in the "sinful nature of human beings." Perhaps echoing some of Coyle's fears, Cloud acknowledges that Fineman's proposals would lead to a more authoritarian state even as she has argued that state responsiveness need not be overreaching or authoritarian. Calling her a "human nature optimist," Cloud nonetheless realizes that the fact that Fineman lives in a constitutional democracy allows her more support for optimism than More's experiences in an authoritarian sixteenth-century monarchy could allow him. Cloud finds such optimism a potential weakness in the vulnerability thesis, one that obscures the strength of the competing values, myths, and theories rooted in the individualism and acquisitiveness that he finds are fundamental and define contemporary society.

Cloud's speculations about the limitations on altruism in human nature and Coyle's conclusion concerning the imperative need for the rejuvenation of civil society and for a richer sense of "networks of solidarity" are addressed in part by the argument offered by Kuo and Means. In "After the Storm: The Vulnerability and Resilience of Locally Owned Business," Kuo and Means extend Fineman's conception of the "vulnerable subject" to locally owned businesses, characterizing these—in essence—as relational communities which cannot survive "without the support of the community." Their analysis frays the edges of assumptions concerning market economies and the power of corporate entities, and points directly to the vulnerability of locally owned businesses as important nodes in a web of local social and economic relationships. This chapter highlights that institutions (including the state) should be conceived of as vulnerable. The particular nature of a local business as a form of vulnerable subject renders them particularly susceptible to disaster harms but also makes them key actors in post-disaster recovery, since the very dependency and interconnectivity that deepen their vulnerability is also the interdependency and connection that fosters resilience. Importantly, this resilience works in two directions—a fact richly suggesting the role of small businesses as elements of the kind of relational civil society that Coyle defends. Locally owned businesses, contend Kuo and Means, "reduce a community's vulnerability to disaster, not only by contributing to the local economy, but also by helping to create and sustain social capital." Because local business owners have a core investment in the life of a particular local community, disaster recovery plans should explicitly respond to the role that "locally owned businesses play in supporting, and sometimes spearheading, recovery."

Kuo and Means conclude that the laws, regulations, and policies concerning disaster response reveal the possibilities inherent in "[richly theorizing] a concept of vulnerability [and developing] a more complex subject around which to build social policy and law," as Fineman has suggested. Disaster discourse, to some extent, routinely makes vulnerability central to its analysis. As Kuo and Means note, it equally reflects the fact that the sources for resilience are diverse and should be supported: "Comprehensive disaster planning proceeds on the assumption that everyone is susceptible to harm and, at the same time, that a community contains many potential sources of resilience and recovery." These include locally owned businesses, which contribute to "the longer-term recovery of afflicted communities by building and supporting social networks that help individuals in a community cope with shared vulnerability."

Carr refracts Fineman's conception of the vulnerable subject through the lens of UK housing law—another particular socio-regulatory context—and reflects upon Fineman's claim that a "vulnerability analysis may ultimately prove more theoretically powerful [than the concept of dependency] in making wide-reaching claims for broader manifestations of social responsibility." In "Housing the Vulnerable Subject: The English Context," Carr applies Fineman's analysis to contemporary debates concerning English welfare provision with a particular eye on those policies that question the future role of social housing. Carr focuses on the British state's responses to an ongoing housing crisis in the UK and demonstrates the way in which an initial, and ambivalent, post-World War II commitment to the state provision of rental housing has been replaced by a policy of assisting citizens to achieve autonomy via home ownership. This is a context in which the state's social obligations, previously taken for granted, have become questionable in a reconfiguration of welfare—particularly in England.

Carr analyzes the relevance of Fineman's vulnerability thesis for contemporary arguments about the allocation of housing resources in England: first, in the context of those who are threatened with repossession by their mortgagee and may become homeless, and, second, in relation to the state provision of life tenancies for some citizens. Carr concludes that both these contexts, and the shifts characterizing them, present particular manifestations of broader shifts from "social to economic rationalities." This eroding of the social in favor of the dominance of economic rationality implies, for Carr, that "Fineman's work can be used more generally to disrupt these trends." Carr argues that Fineman's analysis of the responsive state provides us with the conceptual tools to reimagine the role of the state and to rebut the prevalent neoliberal logic.

This returns us, as it were, to Fineman's call for vigilance in "ensuring that the distribution of [assets necessary for resilience] is accomplished with attention to public values or objectives beyond private or profit motivation, including that of equality or justice" (Fineman 2012). Such an analysis, suggests Carr, allows "structural inequality back into the political equation and provides the possibility for ethical scrutiny of legislative activity." Carr, in this sense, takes a rather different route than do Kuo and Means or Coyle. Her focus is upon the state as responsive provider. She emphasizes the importance of rendering the state transparent in its conferral of privileges—which, in the context of her analysis, implies that a decision to withdraw the privilege of a "tenancy for life" from a tenant would require justification taking into account the paucity of other assets available to provide the council tenant with resilience. Carr concludes that Fineman's theoretical contribution potentially disrupts the neoliberal consensus "that equality of opportunity is a more than sufficient basis for social provision."

Fineman's work, in Carr's view, also reveals the ultimately economic character of contemporary interventions that purport to be social interventions. Ultimately, Carr concludes, Fineman's work gives scope for the reimagination "of an active state in non-authoritarian terms (Fineman 2012)." The implied relationship between state and economy in Carr's account, however, may not entirely convince some that the responsive state would remain suitably restrained—even as a nonauthoritarian state. While Carr reads Fineman's work as giving "substance to the desire for a meaningful collective life, which, for Harvey, poses the greatest threat to the neoliberal project," other commentators would doubtless wish to explore further, with both Fineman and Carr, the meaning of "collective life" and the assumptions underpinning the term concerning the precise relationship between the state and the networks of "civil society." Carr, meanwhile, seems relatively committed to the idea that the responsive state is the key structure for resisting market pressure and the strictures of neoliberal closures.

Market pressure and the dangers of neoliberal global trends form an important component of Fenton's chapter reflecting upon the vulnerable, infertile subject. Fenton sets out to explore infertility and the provision of Assisted Reproductive Technologies (ARTs) through the framework of Fineman's vulnerability thesis, adopting UK fertility treatment provision as her lens for doing so. She argues that a post-autonomy and post-identity analysis along the lines of Fineman's thesis exposes the state's inadequacy in addressing the embodied vulnerability of the infertile and the ways in which this inadequacy exacerbates unequal distributions of privilege and disadvantage.

Fenton's argument also calls upon the role of actualities in the determination of ethical and legal dilemmas surrounding access to fertility treatment provision. She fundamentally endorses Fineman's argument by suggesting that substantive equality can be achieved only by moving beyond autonomy and merely formal equality to an examination of the actual opportunities of access to ART provision. It is in the light of this more substantive, context-sensitive analysis, Fenton argues, that the UK state is revealed as unresponsive to infertility and that genuine equality is exposed as an illusion. Fenton is not just focused upon the UK context, however. She argues that the inadequacies of UK ART provision reach far beyond the limits of the jurisdiction, to shore up global fertility markets in ways perpetuating privilege and disadvantage along global geographic trajectories.

Fenton also draws upon Grear's concern with the trajectories of socio-material oppression under conditions of advanced economic globalization, and, like Grear, focuses the vulnerability thesis upon the global relationalities now characterizing a range of dense interpenetrations, normative, political, social and economic. In this sense, Fenton's work also draws attention to the unevenness of the global field. Hers is a call for states to respond to the deep structural inequalities characterizing neoliberal globalization—and she draws direct attention to the fact that the savage corollary of inequality and unethical legislative behavior in the UK (and other nation states) is "the bolstering of an unregulated global market in which reproductive material can be bought and sold regardless of home state ethics and commodification concerns, and in which the exploitation of the conception-pursuer and the globally socio-economically disempowered is probable if not inevitable."

Fenton recognizes that there may be limitations to the use of the vulnerability thesis in this context, emphasizing that the thesis cannot "address with easy solutions the many ethical nuances which the area of assisted reproduction raises." The thesis has the virtue, however, of being a measure against which to begin theorization—minimally ensuring recognition of our universal embodied vulnerability as an important actuality that state policy, ethics, and law need to take into account. Accordingly, in the final analysis, Fenton emphasizes the intimate relationship between the vulnerability thesis and an ethics and law responsive to actual, embodied conditions—not just to structural concerns.

The power of universal embodied vulnerability as an indispensable *minima* informing law's ethical response to lived actualities is also a theme amply reflected in Timmer's contribution to this collection, which draws richly upon Fineman's vulnerability thesis in direct conversation with the work of scholars who have theorized vulnerability in relation to human rights theories, including Turner and Grear.

Timmer explores the "quiet revolution" taking place within the case law of the European Court of Human Rights (ECtHR) concerning the increasing deployment of "vulnerability reasoning" in respect of including "marginalized people into the legal tests used by the EctHR." Her aim is to analyze tensions and the synergies between Fineman's vulnerability approach and the Court's vulnerability case law in order to draw out the potential and implications of the Court's reasoning (and its limits) with respect to human rights. Timmer's ultimate conclusion is that the Court has not fully embraced an approach to vulnerability consistent with Fineman's vulnerability thesis. This is despite the increasing appeal made by the Court to the concept of vulnerability.

Timmer suggests that, while vulnerability scholars embrace vulnerability because of its potential to emphasize (and transform) the notion of the universal, the ECtHR turns to vulnerability for its "ability to capture the particular." Timmer rightly notes that the universal and the particular are not necessarily at odds. Indeed, it might be surprising if they were, and Timmer's position is shared by theorizations of vulnerability: Fineman's work (2008 and 2010), for example, clearly emphasizes the ability of vulnerability to respond to both the universal and the particular, while Grear has argued (2010) that "embodied vulnerability" brings universality and particularity into a new and intimate theoretical reconciliation (with particular reference—in context—to human rights law and its difficulties in reconciling the universal and the particular). Timmer's careful analysis of the ECtHR case law leads her to the conclusion that "the Court's focus on specific vulnerability can go hand in hand with universal vulnerability as the (implicit) presupposition of human rights law." This, however, does not imply that the Court's reasoning reflects an acceptance of the more radical implications of the universal vulnerability at the heart of Fineman's thesis. Indeed, Timmer does not argue that the Court's quiet revolution amounts to the full embrace of a position on all fours with Fineman's vulnerable subject and its implications.

In fact, Timmer's analysis reveals that, when vulnerability is explicitly appealed to in the Court's jurisprudence, it "functions as a prioritization or as an extension/specification tool … [and as] an important judicial concept that helps create a more inclusive human rights law: in other words, a human rights law that is more responsive to the needs of vulnerable people." This is a position that need not depart, entirely, from the liberal framework of the autonomous invulnerable self and its vulnerable "others," and Timmer's account is not naive concerning the struggle associated with evolution taking place in the ECtHR jurisprudence. Recognizing that Fineman's articulation of the vulnerability thesis asserts that institutions (including the state) should also be seen as vulnerable, she argues:

> the work of Fineman and Grear enables us to see that the Court struggles between a liberal subject approach and a vulnerability approach. Somewhat ironically, their thesis also helps us to see why the Court is attacked by critics in the process. The vulnerability thesis thus predicts its own limits in the ECtHR context: as a social institution the Court is vulnerable in and of itself, which is a reality that the Court will have to take seriously in order to survive as a supranational human rights court.

Accordingly, "vulnerability is a concept to keep an eye on": If the vulnerability thesis suggests an alternative foundation upon which to restructure societal institutions, it also has transformative potential with regard to the way in which we understand, imagine, and construct the foundations of law—and, in particular, "invites a reimagining of the human of human rights law."

Satz extends the logical implications of the vulnerability thesis to explore and defend the notion of the nonhuman animal as an instance of the vulnerable subject. In "Animals as Vulnerable Subjects: Beyond Interest-Convergence, Hierarchy, and Property," Satz offers a thoughtful examination of the subject-positionality of nonhuman animals in a regulatory paradigm in which their inherent worth and capacities are muted beneath anthropocentric concerns and human interests. Satz argues that "[h]uman relations with domestic animals—companion, factory farm, and laboratory animals—are based on contradiction" and that this is problematically revealed by the numerous contradictions characterizing "a sprawling body of law regulating human use of animals as property." Indeed, to Satz so invidious are the contradictions and level of dependency characterizing the lives of domestic animals (a violently exploited category of being) that domestic animals should be understood to be the most vulnerable of all vulnerable subjects.

Satz rejects the current assumptions undergirding legal regulation and much legal scholarship concerning the protection of animals. First, she points to the unacceptability (and radical insufficiency) of "interest-convergence" approaches to the protection of nonhuman animals whereby their protection coincides with, and is governed and shaped by, human interests. Secondly, Satz argues that current legal scholarship, in attempting to address the problems presented by interest-convergence approaches, fails to move beyond a set of problems implicit in rights and interest-based approaches. Such legal scholarship cannot transcend two fundamental problems: the "hierarchy problem" (the higher functioning of humans means that human interests always trump those of animals) and the equally problematic tendency for such scholarship to stay locked in the conceptual quagmire concerning the categorization of animals as "persons" rather than as "property" (which, Satz concludes, merely has the effect of postponing the problem to a further calculation of relative worth between "persons").

Current law and scholarship, in short, fail to provide mechanisms capable of protecting animals from human abuse (most especially from the routinized, regulated forms of abuse characterized by the industrial and/or scientific exploitation of animals as flesh-food and/or experimental living material). Against this failure, Satz proposes a "new legal paradigm for the regulation of human interaction with domestic animals based on the principle of equal protection that 'like beings should be treated alike'." She combines the insights of vulnerability theorists with the equal protection principle and an application of Sen's capability theory in order to lay the foundations for the recognition of the "equal claims of human and non-human animals to protections against suffering." In Satz's approach, therefore, the universality and particularly of vulnerability and resilience so characteristic of Fineman's vulnerability thesis find a novel and important application through a "non-discrimination" framework applied to nonhuman animals.

With Satz's contribution, this edited collection returns to the central ethical impulse animating vulnerability theory: the question of embodied life and its ethical implications in *lived* situations in which highly selective forms of vulnerability (and putative "invulnerability") are deployed (sometimes imposed) in order to disguise their structural production. The question of embodied life—and the politics of embodied life—should be understood as being central to a vulnerability-responsive critique of juridical, economic, and political closures enacted in the service of regimes of property, rights, and personhood (including state–private relations) predicated upon the mastery of the "autonomous human subject." The contributions in this collection point toward the emergence of an increasingly nuanced, embodiment-centered critical perspective informing scholarship in a range of areas. The reflections upon the vulnerability thesis offered here suggest that the rich heuristic value of the tropes of the vulnerable subject, resilience, and the responsive state have significant implications and await future exploration and critique. We welcome the prospect of those further engagements.

Chapter 1

Equality, Autonomy, and the Vulnerable Subject in Law and Politics

Martha Albertson Fineman

Introduction[1]

My development of the concept of vulnerability and the idea of a vulnerable subject began as a stealthily disguised human rights discourse, fashioned for an American audience. The concept has evolved from those early articulations and I now think it has some significant strength as an independent universal approach to justice, one that focuses on exploring the nature of the human, rather than the rights, part of the human rights trope. Vulnerability is inherent in the human condition and inevitably descriptive of the institutions we build in response to that vulnerability, including the state. Therefore, while the focus of this chapter is the United States, the points made are relevant for any system that seeks justice, particularly those that address discrimination as a primary cause of social, economic, and political inequalities and systems in which individual liberty or autonomy is seen as a paramount virtue and privileged over equality.

The chapter begins with a discussion of the limitations of equality as it is understood in the United States as formal in nature, filtered through a robust conception of autonomy or liberty to mean little more than a mandate for sameness of treatment. I set out an alternative vision for justice by developing the concepts of vulnerability and resilience and articulating an argument for a responsive state—a state built around the recognition of the vulnerable subject. Vulnerability is posited in this argument as the characteristic that positions us in relation to each other as human beings, as well as forming the basis for a claim that the state must be more responsive to that vulnerability.

---

1 This chapter is based on three of my articles: "The Vulnerable Subject," 20 *Yale Journal of Law and Feminism* 1 (2008); "The Vulnerable Subject and the Responsive State," 60 *Emory Law Journal* 251 (2010); and "Beyond Identities: The Limits of an Anti-discrimination Approach to Equality," 92 *Boston University Law Review* 1713 (2012).

Equal Protection of Law

Equal protection law under the United States Constitution requires that, in order to be treated equally, individuals must be treated the same. This sameness of treatment version of equality positions discrimination as the major impediment to achieving equality. Its methodology is comparative: A person or group of persons asserts that they are inappropriately being treated differently from another person or group of persons and that person or group is legally indistinguishable from them. However, this comparison ignores most contexts, as well as differences in circumstances and abilities on the part of those whose treatment is compared. While differences may come into the discussion as a defense, since some distinctions can operate as a justification for different or discriminatory treatment, basically an equivalence of position and possibilities are presumed. Such a narrow approach to equality is ineffective in combating the forces that have resulted in the growing inequality in wealth, position, and power experienced in the United States over the past few decades.

Profound inequalities are tolerated—even justified—by reference to "individual responsibility" and warnings about the addictive dependency of social welfare provisions. The state is not mandated to respond to those inequalities, nor does it have to establish mechanisms to ensure more equitable distributions of either social goods or responsibilities between individuals, groups, and institutions. Quite the opposite: The state is restrained from intervening to readjust relationships or reorder responsibilities between and among individuals, groups, and institutions. State interference with an assumed meritocracy and a market constructed as "free" would be in violation of the principles of individual liberty and autonomy and an encroachment on freedom of contract.

Of course, the state has intervened in response to social movements and political pressures at certain points in American history. During the mid-twentieth-century major civil rights struggles in American society led to interpretations of the Constitution and the development of equal protection legislation that offered special, heightened judicial scrutiny to distinctions drawn along the lines of some personal characteristics or social categories, such as race, gender, and ethnicity. However, it was not discrimination in general that was prohibited, only discrimination directed at a few groups within society who were able to successfully mobilize the political and legal systems and press for inclusion and protection. A person who cannot claim membership in one of the favored identity groups is relatively unprotected under a review standard that asks only if the legislation or classification is "arbitrary." In the United States, a person can be fired from employment on a whim, for any reason whatsoever,[2] or be denied housing or access to goods and services, as long as the dismissal or denial is not the result of prohibited identity-based discrimination.

---

2   The exception would be if he or she had statutory tenure or a contract that specified the terms and length of employment.

It is not surprising that an approach to inequality that protects only some has generated a politics of resentment and backlash on the part of those who fall outside of the protected groupings. Ironically, it doesn't always work to the benefit of those who are favored either. Discrimination cases are hard to win and those that are successful are overturned on appeal at a rate higher than other cases (Fineman 2013).

In addition, one protected group can be perversely pitted against another in a zero-sum political game resulting in harmful or compromised policies. The focus on equality as antidiscrimination divides those who may otherwise be allies in a struggle for a more just society by casting them as competitors in a struggle over just whose oppression should count.[3] Legal and political battles revolve around the question of whether a specific group seeking protection can be determined to constitute a "discrete and insular minority" and whether they can show a lengthy history of exclusion and animus thus allowing an analogy to groups historically protected. This is what is now unfolding with lesbians and gay men who are fighting for marriage equality by arguing that their exclusion from the institution is discrimination based on animus. In doing so, they reference the miscegenation statues that prohibited interracial marriage until they were struck down in the 1960s as violating equal protection by the Supreme Court. This analogy has generated substantial resentment and resistance on the part of some religious African American groups and others who do not place marriage equality on the same scale as the civil rights struggles over racial oppression. Such resentment is the troubling legacy of our narrow identity-based antidiscrimination approach to equality. Few groups are protected and those who are may not want to see that protection diluted by what they view as lesser claims to the civil rights mantle.

From my perspective, however, the most troubling aspects of organizing equality discourse around identity characteristics is that it distorts our understanding of a variety of social problems and takes only a limited view of what should constitute governmental responsibility in regard to social justice issues. Identity categories have become proxies for problems such as poverty or the failure of public educational systems. The focus only on certain groups in regard to these problems

---

3   In being critical of contemporary equality thinking in the United States, I am not suggesting that discrimination based on race or gender is no longer a problem and should not be addressed by law. I focus on the insufficiency of identity-focused equality to place in context my argument that we must not stop with the incorporation of antidiscrimination measures, but also move beyond them to a more robust ideal of equality. Certainly, one lamentable consequence of this equal protection doctrine is that it predominantly protects against de jure discrimination (where laws facially disadvantage a protected class), rather than reaching situations of de facto discrimination. Another objection is that entrenched and privileged interests are the ones that benefit when political and legal organization around identity can effectively be manipulated to displace or eclipse concern for the welfare of all members of American society.

obscures the institutional, social, and cultural forces that distribute privilege and disadvantage in systems that transcend identity categories.

In fact, nestled safely within the rhetoric of "individual responsibility" and "autonomy," discrimination doctrine enshrines the notions that America generally provides for an equality of access and opportunity. Impermissible discrimination is cast as the discoverable and correctable exception to an otherwise just and fair system in which individuals are at liberty to compete on equal terms.

What then happens to those who fail in this system? Typically, they have been herded together by sociologists, political scientists, public health practitioners, pundits, and others who study them as members of designated "vulnerable populations." The political and legal response to such populations is surveillance and regulation. The response can be punitive and stigmatizing, as it is with prisoners, youth deemed "at risk," or single mothers in need of welfare assistance. It can also be paternalistic and stigmatizing, as are the responses to those deemed "deserving," such as the elderly, children, or individuals with disabilities. What these "populations" have in common is that they are stigmatized. Their perceived vulnerability marks them as lesser, imperfect, and deviant, and places them somehow outside of the protection of the social contract as it is applied to others (Fineman 2012).

Interestingly, sometimes protected identity groups end up being labeled as a vulnerable population. For example, the Urban Institute Health Policy Center defines "vulnerable populations" as "groups that are not well integrated into the health care system" and continues: "Commonly cited examples of vulnerable populations include racial and ethnic minorities, the rural and urban poor, undocumented immigrants, and people with disabilities or multiple chronic conditions."

The conception that the label of vulnerability belongs only to certain groups or "populations" is not only misleading and inaccurate, it is also pernicious. In the first place, clustering individuals into what is conceptualized as a cohesive population based on one or two shared characteristics masks significant differences among individuals and this is true whether those characteristics are identity based (such as race or gender) or status based (such as poor or immigrant). In addition, asserting that a group has significant differences from the general population obscures the similarities between members of the group and members of the larger society. Such groupings are both over- and under-inclusive.

However, perhaps the most insidious effect of segmenting society and designating only some as constituting vulnerable subpopulations is that such a designation suggests that some of us are not vulnerable. Those who stand outside of the constructed vulnerability populations are thus fabricated as invulnerable. Anyone who has ever tended a child, responded to an accident or emergency, experienced a natural disaster, been the victim of a crime, fell ill or been injured, or experienced many other routine life experiences of vulnerability knows there is no such thing as invulnerability. Yet, American political and legal culture continues to perpetuate this fiction through its adherence to an ideology of individual autonomy and self-sufficiency in which the state is restrained.

Defining the Political–Legal Subject

The Western legal tradition is built on liberal notions of the political and legal subject, in which the appropriate relationships among the state, societal institutions, and individuals are constructed in the shadow of individual liberty or autonomy. The liberal political and legal subject thus defined has the attributes necessary to function fully and independently. This liberal subject is a competent social actor capable of playing multiple and concurrent adult (formerly all-male) societal roles: the employee, the employer, the spouse, the parent, the consumer, the manufacturer, the citizen, the taxpayer, and so on. This liberal subject informs our economic, legal, and political principles. It is indispensable to the prevailing complementary ideologies of personal responsibility and the noninterventionist or restrained state.

Our primary metaphor for examining social and institutional relationships (outside of the family) is that of contract. Society is constituted through a social contract, and autonomous and independent individuals interact with the state and its institutions, as well as with each other, through processes of negotiation, bargaining, and consent. Society is conceived as a collection of self-interested individuals, each of whom has the capacity to manipulate and manage their independently acquired and overlapping resources. Importantly, rather than being dependent on or asserting entitlement to the provision of socioeconomic goods by the state, the liberal subject demands only the autonomy that will enable him to provide for himself and his family. His demand for liberty is refined as the freedom to make choices, the right to contract. Significantly, this demand for liberty on the part of the individual effectively operates as a restraint on the state, which is deterred from interference with individual liberty, even for the purpose of ensuring greater social equality.

The image of the human being encapsulated in the liberal subject is reductive and fails to reflect the complicated nature of the human condition. A vulnerability analysis asks us (and our economists, philosophers and politicians) to embrace a more complex reality by bringing human dependency and vulnerability back into the center of the inquiry into what it means to be human. A vulnerability approach replaces the liberal subject with the "vulnerable subject." The vulnerable subject is the embodiment of the realization that vulnerability is a universal and constant aspect of the human condition. Dependency and vulnerability are not deviant, but natural and inevitable.

Dependency

Dependency is not a characteristic typically associated with the liberal subject. If visible in liberal discourse, dependency is stigmatized. The preferred accommodation for dependency is to hide it within the private family. This family is the mechanism by which we privatize dependency and insulate policy and political discussions from having to grapple seriously with its significant societal implications. Burying dependency within the family is necessary to the construction of simplistic solutions to widespread poverty and inequality that rely on individual responsibility and assume both the desirability and the availability of a position of independence and self-sufficiency for individual and family alike, an ideology of autonomy that bears little relationship to the human condition.[4]

In *The Autonomy Myth: A Theory of Dependency*, I argued against such a simplistic approach to dependency and the stigmatization that often accompanies it, particularly in political discourse. Suggesting that we need a more complex and nuanced understanding of what is now encompassed by the single term "dependency," I noted that, in one form, dependency is inevitable; it is developmental and biological in nature. All of us are dependent on others as infants and many will become dependent as we age, are taken ill, or become disabled.

But recognizing the inevitability of biological or developmental dependency does not exhaust the term. Indeed, there is a second form of dependency that needs to be discussed in relation to, but separate from, inevitable dependency.[5] I labeled this form of dependency "derivative" to reflect the very simple—but often overlooked—fact that those who care for inevitable dependents are themselves dependent on resources in order to accomplish that care successfully. This form of dependency is not inevitable, nor is it universally experienced. Rather, derivative dependency is socially imposed through our construction of institutions such as the family, with roles and relationships traditionally defined and differentiated along gendered lines. Hence, we find an historic difference in expectations and aspirations attached to dichotomous pairings within the family, such as husband or wife, father or mother, and son or daughter. It has proven difficult to progress toward gender equality given this set of institutional arrangements and the persistence of traditional family relationships.

I argued for a more collective and institutionally shared approach to dependency—a reallocation of primary responsibility for dependency that would place some obligation on other societal institutions to share in the burdens of dependency, particularly those associated with the market and the state. This

---

4 Notions of what constitutes the "private," as contrasted with the "public," contribute to the vitality of this ideology by placing the family conceptually outside of state intervention or regulation barring extraordinary abuses or major failings on the part of individual families. Of course, the "private" family is a myth comparable to that of individual autonomy. The legal family is both constructed and dissolved by law and legal processes. The state through law privileges certain social entities as family and gives them both subsidy and protections not afforded to other entities. The family is also conceived as having unique bonds of affiliation and responsibility to members that place intra-family relationships on a "unique" level, thus furthering the perception that it is a private space ideally free of state intervention.

5 There are actually many different, though sometimes related, forms of dependency, such as economic, psychological, or emotional dependency. I limit my discussion to inevitable and derivative dependency inherent in the care work that takes place in the family and is essential to the reproduction of society and its institutions.

reallocation of responsibility seemed particularly appropriate since both state and market institutions reaped the benefits that care work produced in the form of the reproduction and regeneration of society.

While many commentators recognized the strength of the arguments I made, others were less convinced that dependency was centrally relevant to larger questions of liberal social policy and law. Because what I called inevitable dependency is understood as episodic and as shifting in degree over the lifetime of an individual, many mainstream political and social theorists can and often do conveniently ignore it in spinning out their theories about justice, efficiency, or liberty. In their hands, this form of dependency, if acknowledged at all, is merely a stage that the liberal subject has long ago transcended or left behind, and is, therefore, of no pressing theoretical interest as they develop their grand theoretical explorations in legal and political theory—it can be left to those of us who focus on more mundane and uninteresting things, such as the family.[6] As for derivative dependency, that is conveniently dismissed by reference to the liberal contractarian construction of individual "choice." Those who take up the caretaking role have chosen to do so and should not then complain about their situation or expect others to subsidize their choices.

In addition, the division between the public and the private has real tenacity for traditional legal theorists. In spite of decades of critical commentary showing the distinctions do not hold up, prominent American scholars continue to deal with dependency by relegating the burden of caretaking to the family, which is conceptualized as located within a zone of privacy, beyond the scope of state concern barring extraordinary family failures such as abuse or neglect. Thus largely rendered invisible within the family, dependency can be comfortably and mistakenly assumed to be adequately managed for the vast majority of people. To confront that misconception, I built on the insights of my earlier work and developed the concept of vulnerability and the idea of the "vulnerable subject." This construct supports an argument for a "responsive state"—a state that recognizes that it and the institutions it brings into being through law are the means and mechanisms whereby individuals accumulate the resilience or resources that they need to confront the social, material, and practical implications of vulnerability. As such, a responsive state also recognizes that it has a responsibility to monitor the activities of its institutions to ensure that they function in an appropriate, egalitarian manner. This progression from vulnerability to state responsiveness incorporates the realities of human dependency. However, since it is not only universal, but also constant, vulnerability proves more theoretically powerful than the idea of dependency in arguing for a more just society.

---

6   This reaction reflects the traditional division between public and private that has allowed many mainstream scholars to elude difficult and potentially disruptive issues in their theorizing.

Vulnerability

Vulnerability on one level can be thought of as an heuristic device, forcing us to examine hidden assumptions and biases folded into legal, social, and cultural practices. Vulnerability is universal. Detached from specific subgroups or populations, placed at the core of our understanding of what it means to be human, vulnerability can form the foundation upon which to build ideas about appropriate social and state responsibility for all. In addition to its universality, there are several other characteristics that define the concept of vulnerability as I am using it.

A second integral feature of vulnerability is its constancy. Human vulnerability arises in the first place from our embodiment, which carries with it the imminent or ever-present possibility of harm, injury, and misfortune. Bodily harms can take a variety of forms and range from those that are mildly annoying to those that are catastrophically devastating and permanent in nature. Bodily harm can result accidentally or be caused by intentional actions.[7] Bodily harm can result from the unleashing of forces of nature, from the mere passage of time, or from the fact that we humans just exist in a world full of often unpredictable material realities (Fineman 2008: 9). While we can attempt to lessen risk or act to mitigate possible manifestations of our vulnerability, the possibility of harm cannot be eliminated.

Significantly, many forms of harm are beyond individual, or even human, control. The process of aging and death, for example, are clear internal, biological processes that show the limitations of human control over the consequences of our embodiment, which is constantly and universally vulnerable. There are external threats to our bodily well-being that are difficult to eliminate or even substantially decrease. We may suffer or succumb to disease, epidemics, resistant viruses, or other biologically based catastrophes. Our bodies are also vulnerable to external forces in our physical environment: We can be injured by errant weather systems that produce floods, droughts with famine, and fires. These are "natural" disasters, certainly beyond our individual control to prevent. More directly humanly manufactured disruptions in our environment, such as pollution or chemical spills, may also cause us harm.

In addition to describing the biological and constant nature of human vulnerability, as well as the possible internal and external causes of harms, it is important to realize that vulnerability is complex and can manifest itself in multiple forms. Our bodily vulnerability is compounded by the possibility that, should we succumb to illness or injury, there may be accompanying economic and institutional harms and disruption of existing social, economic, or family

---

7   It is important to recognize a range of vulnerabilities. Some manifestations of vulnerability are clearly beyond individual or even societal control, while others can be cast as "self-induced." The liberal subject, constructed in terms of individual autonomy, self-sufficiency, and personal responsibility, does not distinguish between vulnerabilities, suggesting that individuals bear primary responsibility for their vulnerabilities, regardless of their nature.

relationships. These harms are not located in the body, but can be catastrophic to the individual nonetheless, and illustrate how we all are also vulnerable to and dependent upon the vagaries of societal institutions.

It is also important to recognize that, in addition to the ways in which economic and institutional harms can accumulate in a vulnerable individual life, there may also be a basis for recognition of harm to social groupings based on shared characteristics. While the quality or nature of economic and institutional harms may not be different assessed from an individual perspective, there may be statistically relevant distinctions in a quantitative sense, both on an individual and a group basis. For example, economic and institutional harms suffered by individuals can also affect their families when the burdens they generate are transferred from one generation to another. Further, negative economic and institutional harms may cluster around members of a socially or culturally determined grouping who share certain societal positions or have suffered discrimination based on constructed categories used to differentiate one class of persons from another, such as race, gender, ethnicity, or religious affiliation.

Universality and Particularity

The recognition that vulnerability varies across individual experiences reveals a final and somewhat paradoxical point about vulnerability: While it must initially be understood as universal and constant when considering the general human condition, vulnerability must be simultaneously understood as particular, varied, and unique on the individual level. Two forms of individual difference are relevant. The first form of difference is physical: mental, intellectual, and other variations in human embodiment. The second is social and constructed, resulting from the fact that individuals are situated within overlapping and complex webs of economic and institutional relationships.

Differences in embodiment   The variations in human embodiment are not socially neutral, and historically reactions to some of these variations have led to the creation of hierarchies, discrimination, and even violence. Individuals who have certain characteristics have been subordinated and excluded from many of the benefits of society; often because their differences are thought to indicate that they are dangerous, or are interpreted as inadequacy, inferiority, or weakness. These differences or variations are also the basis for segregation of some individuals into a "vulnerable population" category.

One appropriate legal response to this type of bias and/or exclusion is to improve and strengthen existing antidiscrimination measures, perhaps building complementary affirmative action and social welfare provisions to make up for past discrimination and reduce the probability of future disadvantage.

An equally important response to this category of embodied difference, however, is to recognize that individual experience of vulnerability varies according to the quality and quantity of resources we possess or can command. This shifts the focus to the second form of difference—that we are all differently situated within webs of economic, social, cultural, and institutional relationships. While society and its institutions cannot eradicate our vulnerability, it can and does mediate, compensate, and lessen our vulnerability through programs, institutions, and structures.

Status and institutional differences in resilience Differences are produced as a result of an individual's experiences within societal institutions and relationships over the life course. These differences structure options and create or impede opportunities. This focus of a vulnerability analysis is particularly significant because addressing this form of difference brings societal institutions into conversation with the vulnerable subject. This shifts our critical focus to the operation of societal institutions, including the state. This provides a much needed counterweight to the current assignment of dependence and vulnerability as solely a personal responsibility.

Societal institutions are theorized as having grown up around vulnerability. Our vulnerability and the need for connection and care it generates are what make us reach out and form society. It is the recognition and experience of human vulnerability that brings individuals into families, families into communities, and communities into societies, nation states, and international organizations.

The societal institutions we create should be seen as functioning in interlocking and overlapping ways, creating layered possibilities of opportunities and support, but also in configurations containing gaps and potential pitfalls. These institutions collectively form systems that can play an important role in lessening, ameliorating, and compensating for individual vulnerability, providing us with the resilience or resources with which to respond in specific times of crisis or opportunity.

Together and independently, these societal institutions provide us with "assets"—reservoirs of capabilities, advantages, or coping mechanisms that cushion us when we are facing misfortune, disaster, and violence, as well as constituting the resources that we will need if we are to take risks and avail ourselves of opportunities as they arise. Significantly, the counterpoint to vulnerability is not invulnerability, for that is impossible to achieve, but the resilience that comes from having some means with which to address and confront misfortune and opportunity. Our resources are accumulated and dissipated over the course of a lifetime in the processes of making decisions and responding and reacting to circumstances and situations as they arise. In times of both crisis and opportunity our accumulated resources define what are our realistic options—resources limit or enhance our individual ability to exercise autonomy or liberty, thus defining the scope and nature of our agency.

There are at least five different types of assets or resources that societal organizations and institutions can provide: physical assets, human assets, social assets, ecological or environmental assets, and existential assets. Physical assets are physical or material goods that determine our present economic quality of life and provide the material basis for accumulation of additional sustainable resources in the form of savings and investments. Certainly, tax and inheritance laws impact the distribution of physical assets and are part of this system, but so also are banking rules and regulations and credit policies.

Like physical assets, human assets also affect material well-being. Defined as "innate or developed abilities to make the most of a given situation," human assets provide on an individual level for the accumulation of human capital or "capabilities." They are dependent on our general health and on education systems. Human assets are also provided in employment systems. They are those goods that contribute to the development of a human being, allowing participation in the market and making possible the accumulation of material resources that help bolster individuals' resilience in the face of vulnerability.

Social assets are networks of relationships from which we gain support and strength. The family is a major institution providing social assets, particularly for the young. Social assets are conferred through other associations, such as political collectives in which individuals bolster their resilience by joining together to address vulnerabilities generated by the market. These collectives historically included trade unions and political parties. In recent decades, a sense of community organized around identity characteristics, such as race, ethnicity, and gender, has constituted powerful networks of affiliation and belonging.

Ecological assets can be conferred through our position in relation to the physical or natural environments in which we find ourselves. We live in the context of external factors and sets of physical conditions that interact with us and profoundly influence our needs, as well as shaping the circumstances of our well-being. The natural environment has been greatly altered and affected by human activity and institutions, only some of which is beneficial, and laws, regulations, and agencies have grown up around efforts to protect natural resources from further deterioration.

Existential resources are provided by systems of belief or aesthetics, such as religion, culture, or art. These resources can help us to understand our place within the world and allow us to see meaning and beauty in our existence. Governmental policies subsidize religious and cultural entities through tax policy and by more direct means.

Our experiences with asset-conferring institutions are often concurrent and interactive, but also can be sequential. For example, the relationships between the educational system and the employment and social security system are sequential. Collectively, they provide for the accumulation of resources, creating assets for use in the present and preserving possibilities and opportunities for the future.

Significantly, the failure of one system in a sequence, such as a failure to receive an adequate education, affects future prospects. Often, it is impossible to fully compensate for such failures given that the systems further down the line are constructed in reliance on the individual having successfully fulfilled the earlier steps. Someone who misses out on education typically will have fewer options and opportunities in the workplace, which will make for a more precarious retirement and fewer savings.

On the other hand, and also important, is the fact that sometimes privileges conferred in one concurrent system can compensate for, or even cancel out, disadvantages encountered in others. For example, a good early start in regard to education, such as that provided by Head Start, may trump poverty as a predictor of success later in school. This may be particularly likely when it is coupled with the advantages a social or relational system, such as a supportive family and progressive social network, can provide.

In sum, society's institutions interact in ways that actually produce (or fail to produce) social, political, and economic resilience. They can confer privilege or disadvantage, and an initial privilege or disadvantage may determine if an individual is able to benefit from other systems fully. Because this is true, the impact of privileges and disadvantages is cumulative and may have significant and more profound effects than the isolated gains or losses associated with any single indicator would suggest.

Resilience is not something we are born with. It is produced over time within social structures and under societal conditions over which individuals may have little control. This fact alone demonstrates that individual failure or success must be understood in terms broader than just individual responsibility. Success and failure are socially structured and intricately dependent on an individual's interactions within the institutions and political structures society has constructed. And this fact of primary and inevitable dependence on societal institutions is true whether those institutions are deemed public or private or are labeled as "family," "market," or "state" entities.

The Responsive State

How should our understanding of human vulnerability and the role of institutions in building resilience inform our notion of what constitutes a just and responsive state? The neoliberal restrained state ideology, which asserts that the state should privilege liberty in the form of autonomy for the individual and freedom for the market, ignores the significance of the fact that the state actually creates not only institutions as legitimate entities, but also the conditions under which they operate, all of which profoundly shape individual circumstances and experiences. Powerful, resource-giving institutions such as the family, corporations, schools, and financial institutions are constructs of the state. It is the legitimating authority of law and the regulatory machinery of the state that creates institutions such as marriage, defines the family, and mandates the corporate form. The state brings these entities into existence as legitimate institutions. The law both assigns content to and enforces the consequences of these institutions, most specifically through direct control over their formation and dissolution, but also through oversight and regulation. State mechanisms enforce "private" agreements (contracts) and provide security and structure. In fact, the state's regulation of the formation and dissolution of institutions is one of the primary ways it constitutes itself as an entity and establishes and expresses its monopoly over the legitimate means of coercion. The interrelationship between state and institution should make it clear that the choice is not one between an active or interventionist state on the one hand and an inactive or restrained state on the other. The state is always at least a residual actor in the formation and functioning of society and should accept some responsibility in regard to the effects and operation of those institutions it brings into being and helps to maintain.

If societal institutions are both vitally important to individuals and to society and also inextricably entangled with the state, their flaws, barriers, gaps, and potential pitfalls should be monitored and their operations adjusted when they are functioning in ways harmful to individuals and society. The values that should be applied in making such judgments and adjustments must be democratic and publicly oriented, reflecting norms of equality and open access and shared opportunity. This focus on the state's relationship to institutions might prompt us to reconceptualize the nature and scope of both individual and state responsibility.

In developing the vulnerability approach, I have come to see that one way of looking at the relationship between institutions and the state is to see that the state is actually responding to the vulnerability of its institutions. The vulnerability of corporate or business institutions to startup or ongoing production or operating costs is routinely evoked to justify subsidies, whether they take the form of tax policies, direct transfers, and investment, or are delivered through facilitating access to mechanisms of state authority, such as law or utilization infrastructures, and the convenience of having access to a publicly educated workforce. But these forms of responses to market vulnerability do not provoke calls for restraints on the state by the adherents of small government. Rather, the calls are to have the state adopt a policy of benign neglect with regard to the monitoring and regulation of the marketplace, while at the same time remaining active in giving subsidy and support.

One might appropriately ask: Is this duality of response reasonable? The answer most certainly would be "no" if we consider a different form of corporate vulnerability—the vulnerability to manipulation, misbehavior, and corruption that results from demands that the corporation produce hefty profits for shareholders and massive salaries for CEOs. The vulnerability of the corporation created by the fact that it is primarily a profit-driven entity actually provides a compelling argument for a much more attentive and responsive state than we currently have. Wasn't the lack of such a state a significant factor behind the practices that led to the Great Recession of 2008? Also compelling in the case for a more responsive state is the unavoidable realization that when corporations act primarily with a profit motive they can both intensify their own precariousness and generate hazards for society.

In regard to the last point, consider how the state responded to the increasingly vulnerable position of certain big businesses caused by the failing market during the recession. Their heightened vulnerability was met with loans to the auto industry and bailouts for the financial industry. At the same time, the heightened vulnerability of the individual mortgage holder created in the wake of the same crisis was ignored—his plight assigned to the realm of individual responsibility and the pleas for governmental aid deflected with cries of "moral hazard."

In other words, in recent history the state has blatantly played favorites, choosing vulnerable institutions over vulnerable individuals. This underscores the important recognition that the state itself is vulnerable and can be and has been abusive, overreaching, and authoritative. Like its institutions, the state is vulnerable to capture, corruption, and misdirection. Sometimes the misdirection comes from the outside, such as when powerful entrenched interests hijack even the most egalitarian impulses for their own purposes. Often state abuse is the result of flaws or weaknesses in the design or operation of state structures and practices. This is what we see currently in the corrupted legislative culture which actually provides incentives for repressive tactics, distortions of the truth, and democracy-frustrating partisanship.

But the fact remains that we need the state—we cannot do without it and the law, structures, and resources it provides. Further, it is important to remember that, although we may talk about "the state," it is not a monolith. The state is actually as a cluster of relationships, entities, and agencies reflecting and shaping public norms and values through law and policy. Those relationships include the relationship between citizen and state, as well as between state and institutions. In a responsive state, individuals realize that we, too, are part of the state. We do not—cannot—stand outside of the state and we have a responsibility to participate—to be vigilant in seeing that the state is working effectively and in an egalitarian manner.

Conclusion

Orienting the state to be responsive to the Vulnerable Subject would require dedication to a different set of values than those that informed the state built on an image of the Liberal Subject. Vulnerability's values would be more egalitarian and collective in nature, preferring connection and interdependence rather than autonomy and independence in both political and personal visions.

A responsive state would have to address the distortions that have arisen as a result of privileging liberty over equality and advantaging some in society at the expense of others. This would necessitate looking at existing structures of privilege, as well as at entrenched disadvantage. Institutions that serve to allocate society's resources unequally to the benefit of the few must be monitored and reformed. Politicians will tell us that this is an impossible task, when what they really mean is that it would place them in an uncomfortable position, particularly with those who are privileged.

It is important to conclude with the observation that a vulnerability approach does not mean that different treatment, even the conferral of privilege or advantage, is never warranted. It does mean that, where the state confers or tolerates institutional conferral of privilege or advantage, there is an affirmative obligation for there to be justifications for the disparate circumstances. Such privileging must be both transparent and explained. This type of process would certainly change political discourse and the terms under which legislators and legislation are judged.

Vulnerability analysis can be thought of as defining what constitutes ethical legislative behavior. It is an attempt to articulate a more self-conscious and aware egalitarian political culture; one that more robustly adheres to the all-American promise of equality of opportunity and equal access to the American Dream. It is those aspirations for substantive equality for the vulnerable subject that should form the ultimate ideals against which the state and its societal institutions and their actions are judged.

Chapter 2
Kierkegaard and Vulnerability

Alison Assiter

Kierkegaard and Vulnerability

Liberal political theory has been argued, by various feminist theorists, to depend upon a dualist metaphysic – broadly a divide between 'mind' and 'body' which may or may not reflect or coincide with other dualisms, such as those between the private and the public, reproduction and production, and the family and the state. The notion of individual responsibility implicit in this approach makes it difficult, as Fineman has noted, to accommodate state responsibility (Fineman, this volume, 17). Some feminists have even gone so far as to claim that Western thought is 'governed by' these kinds of dualisms (see Gatens 1996, 95). In classical social contract theory, the individual political subject – the subject of political and legal rights, the subject that enters into the contract, the citizen – is constructed in opposition to the private, conjugal and familial sphere (see Pateman 1989, for example). On certain versions of this kind of theory, the subject becomes literally disembodied. In some way, then, this subject is constructed as invulnerable. The needy, desiring and reproducing self – the vulnerable self – is to be transcended when the person operates as an ethical being.

In this chapter, I would like to suggest that the implicit metaphysic of Kierkegaard offers a theory that chimes with key features of Fineman's notion of the vulnerable self. Fineman's notion of the self seems to me to be an important one. En route, I will point out some advantages as well as some limitations of the work of a major philosopher whose work has inspired some significant feminist theorising of embodiment, that of Spinoza.

I would like to suggest that Kierkegaard offers a metaphysic that proposes a subject that is, in Martha Fineman's words, 'vulnerable' as a 'human' (Fineman, this volume, 13, 20–22). This subject, importantly, as Fineman has argued, cannot be hidden or ignored (Fineman, this volume, 17, 25–7 and also see Fineman 2004).

I would like to draw out something that resonates with Fineman's work that may not often be noted in the literature. This is that taking seriously the notion of the vulnerable self poses a problem for some readings of the self underlying both certain versions of liberal human rights thinking but also certain readings of a philosopher of embodiment – Baruch Spinoza. Specifically, as I will argue in the chapter, determinist readings of Spinoza not only under-emphasise human responsibility but they might also underplay the obverse of this notion – human vulnerability. I would like, in this chapter, in other words, to present a metaphysic that might helpfully be seen to underpin Fineman's work.

Descartes

Descartes (see Descartes 1968) is probably the most famous culprit when it comes to presenting an ontology of disembodiment. His self – the self that thinks and that exists as a thing that thinks – is constructed in opposition to mindless, mechanical matter. The body is conceived as a machine (although it is important to recognise that machines, for him, were objects of wonder and awe). Descartes compares his body variously to a watch, a cage, a prison and a swamp. His body is a 'mechanical configuration of limbs'. He – Descartes – can think, but bodies cannot think (Descartes 1968). Descartes wanted and set out to 'master nature'; this, indeed, became an Enlightenment optimistic claim. Human beings, again continuing the theme of invulnerability, might be able to control any natural disaster that could present itself. In a much earlier period, Plato, at least on some readings, had also seen the body, the self outside the control of the mind, as 'a source of countless distractions by reason of the mere requirement of food …' (Plato 1948, 66).

In so far as civilised society classically recognised embodiment, its citizens frequently possessed male bodies. The task – reproduction, another aspect of our vulnerability, which only women are able to perform – is excluded from civil society; from citizenship. Carole Patemen argued that liberalism is forged through the necessary subjection of women – of women's bodies (Pateman 1989).

A Spinozist Feminist Response to Descartes

One feminist response to this has been to use the work of Spinoza to offer a non-dualist metaphysic that is said to be beneficial for the position of women (see, for example, Gatens 1996 and Grosz 1994). Moira Gatens, for example, suggests that 'Spinoza insisted that mind and body are not two distinct substances but rather two ways in which the human understanding grasps that which exists' (Gatens 1996, 100). For Spinoza, therefore, reason, politics and ethics are always embodied. In some sense, therefore, there is a greater recognition, on the part of Spinoza than is the case with Descartes, of the feature of Fineman's thinking that emphasises 'embodiment' (Fineman, this volume, 20–22) that, as she also importantly points out, can lead to various forms of harm. These are forms of harm that would not affect a self, conceived, as it is implicitly in the metaphysic underlying much human rights discourse, as a rational mind. However, as I will argue in a moment, there is one crucial disadvantage of Spinoza's philosophy.

Importantly, for Gatens, an advantage of the Spinozist framework is that it allows us to think of human relations in terms of 'sociabilities and communities' (Gatens 1996, 110). For Spinoza, reason, desire and knowledge are 'embodied and dependent' (111). Moreover, the ethics or the reason produced by any collective body 'will always bear the marks of that bodies' genesis' (100). This kind of claim was also made by Schelling, who was influenced by Spinoza (see Grant 2006), as he grappled with Kant's transcendental framework, and with attempting to account for the various categories of thought which Kant appeared to take for granted – the division of the mind, for example, into sensibility, understanding and reason.

According to Spinoza, consciousness is to be understood as a mode of being. For Spinoza, by contrast to Descartes, there is only one substance. Body and mind are modal expressions of the attributes of substance. The latter are thought and extension. In his *Ethics*, Spinoza argues that there cannot be two things with every property in common. There cannot, in other words, be two absolutely identical things. He argues that there must also be a substance with all possible attributes – an infinite substance. God must exist because God is a substance and existence is part of the notion of substance.[1] If there are several substances, they will be distinguished from one another either by a difference in attribute or by a difference in their modifications. An attribute is what constitutes the essence of a substance and a 'modification' is that which exists in something other than itself (Spinoza, *Ethics*, Part 1. Defs. 4 and 5). But the attribute of being more than one will be a difference between substances. Therefore, there can be only one substance.

Whatever one makes of this argument, baldly put, it is a very influential statement of a monism and it stands as an important component of a position that can be taken to counter that of Descartes. In some sense, therefore, since it gives embodiment a central role, it gives greater recognition to the self as a vulnerable being that is dependent upon others and on the world outside it. Indeed, it might perhaps allow for the idea of the state as a responsible entity that engages with vulnerable humans who are linked with it (see Fineman 2004 again).

Reading Spinoza

The question of Spinoza's value for feminism and for the topic of this book stems crucially from the way in which one reads his works. In his own period, 'Spinozism' was feared and derided. In 1783 there occurred what appeared initially to be a personal dispute between two philosophers of the period – Friedrich Heinrich Jacobi and Moses Mendelssohn. The dispute was over the question of the commitment of a third philosopher – G.E. Lessing – to Spinozism (see Beiser 1987). If Lessing had indeed been seen at the time as a follower of Spinoza, then that was tantamount to his rejecting morality and religion, and any philosophy, of course, with this implication was to be both feared and most certainly rejected.

---

1 This argument was famously critiqued by Kant, who argued in the *Critique of Pure Reason* that 'existence is not a predicate or a determinate of a thing'. Existence is not an attribute of a thing in the sense in which redness or its smell are properties of the thing. Rather the thing's existence must be presupposed in order to attribute anything to it.

Jacobi represented himself as the true interpreter of Spinoza, in his *Werke* (Jacobi 1812). He believed that Spinoza's philosophy was tremendously important but that 'all philosophy' 'must end in Spinozistic fatalism' (MPW 187). Jacobi sees Spinoza's philosophy as the paragon of a philosophy grounded on reason (rather than that of Descartes) and yet he believed that it fell inevitably into an atheism and a fatalism. For Jacobi, Lessing's upholding of Spinozist pantheism was the inevitable end point of rationalist philosophy. What is important is that Jacobi represents Spinoza as 'the philosopher one must be persuaded by if one is consistent in one's commitment to reason' (Lord 2011, 23). Jacobi presents Spinoza as offering an account of Being as absolutely knowable, as distinct from Kant's denial that it is possible for finite and limited beings to know the nature of the ultimate 'noumenal' realm.

From the perspective of rationalist metaphysics, in the eighteenth century, then, Kant's ontology, in excluding God and the soul from being objects of knowledge, lacked absoluteness and objectivity (see Lord 2011, 24). In other words, Spinoza's contemporary critics saw him as a more extreme exponent of the notion of invulnerability – he became the ultimate rationalist, but he was worse than Descartes because he was also a fatalist and a determinist. So he might, in some way, recognise the dependence of individual selves on something outside them, but, rather than simply being dependent, they were fatalistically determined by this outside world and also by their wants and desires which would, somehow, be in conformity with their reason.

Now, whilst this is significant in locating humans within nature, an important limitation of this type of philosophy is clearly that it offers a diminished role for individual or collective human responsibility. If people are fatalistically determined by forces outside themselves, then it is difficult to be able to hold them responsible for what they do. The obverse of this, importantly, though, is that a form of determinism akin to the above reading of Spinoza also undermines individual vulnerability. A body governed by strict determinist forces is neither responsible nor vulnerable: it simply reacts to forces that affect it.

Thus, what is less often noted about this type of philosophy is that it also underplays two of the key aspects of vulnerability, as set out by Fineman. If individuals are fatalistically determined by the actions of other individuals, by their own natures or by forces stemming from social institutions such as the state, then these vulnerable individuals would be unable to react and to move to change the destructive social forces. Rather than being a *vulnerable* self, the self would become more like a victim or a pawn in the hands of other more powerful selves or institutions. It seems to me, therefore, that this illustrates one aspect of the significance of the word 'vulnerable' about the self, for it suggests a subject that is dependent and needy but that is also able to act perhaps collectively, to change these forms of dependence. A metaphysic that underplays this dimension of the subject, then, is less useful that one that emphasises it.

Contemporary Readings

Now there is much in the contemporary feminist literature on Spinoza, in the work of Elizabeth Grosz and others, that challenges the above reading of Spinoza and that offers an account that is more sympathetic to feminism and to the notion of the vulnerable self. So, for example, Gatens offers a reading that stresses two things that are important. The first is – drawing on Hans Jonas' view – that reason, desire and knowledge are not transcendent of nature, but rather they are embodied and somehow dependent on corporeal affects. Furthermore, bodies, for Spinoza, contrary to the above perspective, are, in Gatens' words, 'radically open to their surroundings' (Gatens 1996, 110). This, again, offers an important move in the direction of the kind of self advocated by Fineman, as positioned (Fineman, this volume, 22) by institutions around them. Elizabeth Grosz' reading, as well, emphasises a view of Spinoza, derived from that of Deleuze and Guattari, that focuses on the body's capacity to act and to be acted upon. She quotes from Deleuze and Parnett on Spinoza:

> Spinoza's question: *what is a body capable of?* What affects is it capable of? Affects are becomings: somewhere they awaken us to the extent they diminish our strength of action and decompose our relations (sadness), sometimes they make us stronger through augmenting our force, and make us enter into a faster and higher individual (joy). Spinoza never ceases to be astonished at the body: not of having a body but at what the body is capable of. Bodies are defined not by their genus and species but by what they can do, the affects they are capable of, in passion as in action. Such bodies, then, are capable of resisting the forces that shape them. They are also bodies that are acted upon and they can be acted upon in ways that strengthen them or, indeed, importantly, in ways that weaken them. (Grosz 1994, 169)

Gatens, as well, emphasises the active body in Spinoza. To a much greater degree, then, than is the case with the earlier readings, these feminist readings of Spinoza emphasise him as offering a view of the self as active but also as vulnerable. This is important, but it does not seem to me that it entirely circumvents the determinist reading of his work, which is difficult to avoid. Gatens does set out to suggest that there is a material in Spinoza's work that allows for responsibility. So, she writes: 'Human freedom, though not free will, amounts to the power that one possesses to assert and extend oneself, in the face of other (human and non-human) bodies that strive to do likewise' (Gatens 1996, 111). Virtue, she argues, consists in the power of any individual to continue in existence and all bodies possess this virtue, although in varying degrees. To some degree, then, this reading of Spinoza allows for the features of vulnerability in Fineman's work emphasised earlier.

The view of Gatens on Spinoza also resonates with those thinkers – perhaps some Schellingians – who want to argue that non-rational beings can be, in some sense, free. In other words, on this view, human beings would be continuous in their vulnerability, with the rest of the natural world. In so far, according to this view, as rationality is embodied, then one cannot rule out suggesting that it is in some sense 'in' all of nature. This view, indeed, does seem to me to deserve serious consideration (see Strawson 2006 for a defence of panpsychism) and it may be possible to read Spinoza this way, although it seems to me that this reading is difficult to reconcile with the clear determinist elements there are in his work. Gatens, however, doesn't want to go quite this far. She writes: 'Human virtue is qualitatively distinct from the virtue of other things in so far as it concerns the endeavour to increase one's power of existing in accordance with reason, which is a specifically human power' (Gatens 1996, 111).

Gatens accepts that Spinoza is indeed a determinist but she thinks that what is important about his view is that freedom only arises in a polity – in a collective context – and that each collective entity strives to increase its power, in an overall collective context. Freedom, then, is the capacity, collectively, to maximise our power and our interests.

This offers an important corrective to a pure Cartesian view of the self and of rationality, and indeed to a pure determinist Spinozist reading of the self. It offers, furthermore, a corrective over some aspects of a Kantian view of the self. It is difficult for Kant to account for the rationality of humans. Reason cannot account for itself. If it could, for every occurrence, there would have to be a reason why it is so and not otherwise. There would have to be a possible explanation for every worldly fact. Thought would have to be able to account for the unconditioned totality of things and for there being thus and not otherwise. If thought is to avoid an infinite regress, then there would have to be a 'reason that would prove capable of accounting for everything, including itself – a reason not conditioned by any other reason, and which only the ontological argument is capable of uncovering, since the latter secures the existence of X through the determination of X alone …' (Meillassoux 2008, 33). Meillassoux goes on to write that, if every variant of what he calls, following Kant, 'dogmatic metaphysics' is characterised by the thesis that 'at least one entity is absolutely necessary, then … it becomes clear how every entity is absolutely necessary. On this view, then, the self would possess an extreme kind of invulnerability – it would somehow wholly be able to control itself, which is clearly not possible.

Furthermore, the account derived from Spinoza also allows for collective agency and for collective action, which, particularly in the case of oppressed or vulnerable groupings, as noted by Fineman, is tremendously important.

However, it seems to me that freedom is not only about the capacity of the self to increase its power. It is also about the very ability of the self to be moral at all. There is, therefore, a very significant component both of freedom and of Fineman's conception of the self as vulnerable, which is omitted from Spinoza's picture, even in this importantly modified reading by Gatens. If one increases one's ability to act in accordance with a crucial feature of human nature – one's reason – and yet this reason is wholly determined by forces outside it, then the self becomes both a *victim* of these forces and unable to act in ways that significantly challenge them.

An illustration from Fineman's context would be that the individual would be shaped by the state in ways that would give her very little power to change that state. So it seems to me, therefore, that Spinoza's account, even as significantly and importantly read by Grosz and Gatens, does not allow for proper human responsibility and nor does it allow for vulnerability in Fineman's sense.

These crucial elements of the self that are left out of Spinoza's account, it seems to me, are implicit in Kant's view of the self and of freedom. However, it seems to me that the advantage of Kant's theory comes at a major cost. Kant's theory allows for individual responsibility, but it is responsibility for good. Kant separates out the free rational self from the phenomenal embodied self, and allows for human freedom in a way that certain readings of Spinoza do not, but this has two major and very significant disadvantages: it makes it difficult to see how an individual can be responsible for wrongdoing (see Assiter 2011 and 2013a) but also, again and in a different way, it underplays Fineman's characteristics of the self – the self as a vulnerable entity.

What is Important about Kant's View of Freedom?

Kant clearly doesn't want a simple compatibilist account of freedom. He thinks that determinism cannot be true because we could not account for human morality if it were true. If human beings were no different from the rest of nature, they could not possess freedom and nor could they be moral beings. This would be true, it seems to me, whether one adopted an individualist or a collectivist view of agency. Collective agency would no doubt have a different character from individual agency, yet, if one can show that individuals are genuinely free, then they would also be free within the collective and free to adopt collective decisions which would or might benefit them both as members of the collective and also as individuals.

Within the framework of transcendental idealism, free will is incompatible with determinate mechanist nature. Kant's Third Antinomy in the first *Critique* concerns the notion of causality according to freedom. Free will requires an originating spontaneity. In the *Groundwork of the Metaphysics of the Morals* (*G*), Kant argues that we cannot but act under the 'idea of freedom'. In the *Critique of Practical Reason* (*CPrR*), Kant begins with the fact of reason – with the existence of the moral law itself. This in some way 'determines' the will. The pure will, then, is determined by reason alone. This, once again, however, would be an account of the self as pure invulnerability – a self that would be wholly determined by its reason.

In the *Groundwork*, Kant sometimes writes as though he can prove the existence of reason in all of us (*G* 4 452). But he soon appears to realise that this would commit him to something to which he cannot be committed and that is that we know of our existence as reasoning beings. So he argues that the moral law and the reasoning being reciprocally imply one another (see, for example, *CPrR* 5 28).

Each can be deduced from the other. The moral law is the supreme practical law of rational beings. Thus, although he changed his view, he did not reject the picture that has the self as a moral and free being shaped by something other than determinist nature. In other words, the self would be in some way shaped by its own reason.

The will cannot be accommodated in nature and 'the inevitable consequence of obstinately insisting upon the reality of appearances is to destroy all freedom…' (*Critique of Pure Reason* [*CRP*] A537/B565). Transcendental freedom is a 'causality through which something takes place the cause of which is not itself determined, in accordance with necessary laws…' (*CPR* A446/B474). In the *Critique of Practical Reason*, Kant says that the moral law is the *ratio cognoscendi* of freedom. For, had not the moral law already been distinctly thought in our reason, we should never consider ourselves justified in assuming such a thing as freedom (*CPrR* 4n). 'Every being that cannot act otherwise than under the idea of freedom is just because of that really free in a practical respect; that is, all laws that are inseparably bound up with freedom hold for him just as if his will had been validly pronounced free in itself and in theoretical philosophy' (*G* 448).

It is undeniably the case for Kant that it is his principle of autonomy that is the basis for moral actions. Even in the third *Critique*, where he sometimes expresses a different view, he argues that the only thing of unconditional value is 'the human being who determines his ends through reason' (*Critique of Judgement* [*CPJ*] 5 233).

In the *Critique of Judgement*, Kant writes: 'The moral argument is not meant to provide any objective argument for the existence of God nor meant to prove to the doubter that there is a God; rather it is meant to prove that if his moral thinking is to be consistent, he must include the assumption of this proposition among the maxims of his practical reason' (*CPJ* 87, 4, 450-§1n). In this work, God becomes the super-sensible ground for the unity of freedom and mechanism. He writes; 'we must assume … the existence of a moral being as author of the world' (*CPJ*, § 87, p. 342).

Importantly, then, for Kant, by contrast with Spinoza, a very strong notion of freedom is a basic requirement of being able to be a moral being. Freedom, for him, must be grounded in something other than the phenomenal nature that is experienced by finite and rational beings. It cannot simply be accommodated as part of this nature. It cannot be seen to be part of our natures as vulnerable creatures.

It seems to me that there is something in this Kantian notion of freedom that is very important, and that a moral theory that operates broadly within a determinist framework cannot be satisfactory. However, given the very strong connection there is in Kant's work between freedom of the will and the moral law, it is difficult for him to give an account of freely doing wrong.

Furthermore, it is a theory that, because of its radical separation of the rational and free being from the embodied self, underplays the role played by human vulnerability in humanity's ability to act freely. It separates out the fragile, embodied nature of the self from the self as responsible and free.

I have suggested so far that there are some advantages of a Spinozist theory for accommodating crucial features of Fineman's vulnerable subject, but that there is something left out of it that is accommodated in a Kantian theory of free will. Kant's theory, however, omits another feature of the vulnerable self.

I would like to suggest, in the final part of this chapter, that Kierkegaard offers a theory that is compatible with the strong Kantian notion of freedom but that also proposes a non-dualist and embodied self at its core. This Kierkegaardian theory, furthermore, has the additional advantage over the Spinozist one, of offering a notion of the self as fundamentally a vulnerable self. I suggest, therefore, that Kierkegaard offers a theory that, of the three major thinkers considered so far, is most able to accommodate Fineman's notion of the self. This, it seems to me, is a significant strength of Kierkegaard's theory. In a sense, the Kierkegaardian self is a naturalist one, which, like that of Spinoza, is continuous with other natural objects, but it is not a determined self, and in this sense it takes something from Kant.

Kierkegaard

In his book *Kierkegaard and Kant: The Hidden Debt* (Green 1992) Ronald Green argues that there are many more similarities between Kant and Kierkegaard than most commentators suggest. One deep similarity is the centrality both accord to the notion of freedom. Kierkegaard, like Kant, accepts a strong libertarian account of freedom which could not coexist with any form of determinism.

Kierkegaard[2] (or his pseudonym Haufniensis) by contrast to Kant, begins his work that is inspired by Kant, *The Concept of Anxiety* (*CA*), by attempting to account for wrongdoing or evil. He has a picture of the self as fundamentally a natural and vulnerable being like other natural objects. *Either/Or*, importantly, begins with a crucial feature of human vulnerability – the fact of birth (Kierkegaard 1987, 19). Kierkegaard writes: 'Ethics begins with the actual' (*CA* 19). Human beings, for Kierkegaard are: 'a synthesis of the psyche and the body but also a synthesis of the temporal and the eternal… It is the … synthesis of the infinite and the finite (*SUD*, 127) (*CA* 85). The self, for Kierkegaard, is a finite self, whose life will end in death. In other words, it is a vulnerable self. But it is also a self that is capable of receiving absolute love from a God – the infinite – which is in some way outside it. In the *Eighteen Upbuilding Discourses* (*EUD*), Kierkegaard also compares the love God has for human beings to the natural love a father has for his children.

Kierkegaard (or now the pseudonym Victor Eremita) suggestively implies that the fantasy, expressed in the Don Juan myth, of an imaginary infinitely existing body and a perfectly rational will, stems from the same problematic assumptions: that the will and the body are radically separate and both are, in some way, invulnerable. In *Either/Or*, he talks about Don Juan and the Kantian rational self

---

2   Kierkegaard agreed with Leibniz that an 'indifferent will is an 'absurdity and a chimera' (JP. CA viii…) Kierkegaard was also critical of Descartes, writing: 'if I am to emerge from doubt into freedom, then I must enter in doubt in freedom'.

each embodying a form of determinism. One is determined by the notion of being a pure autonomous thing and the other by being pure body or pure sensuality.

Instead, in *CA*, which was clearly written after he had carefully read Kant's late work *Religion within the Limits of Mere Reason Alone* (see Green 1992), Kierkegaard gives an account of the origin of human freedom. He does so by means of a picture of the way in which sinfulness 'came into' Adam. Using a reading of Kierkegaard that is inspired by the influence of Schelling on him, I have suggested that he offers an account of how the capacity to reflect on our passions and desires and to enact some and not others – in other words, freedom – came into Adam (see Assiter 2013a). Adam may have existed alongside other natural objects with their powers and capacities. These natural objects possessed powers and capacities that were akin to our human conceptual apparatus but these powers and capacities were also different. The natural objects existing alongside Adam were not, in other words, purely inert mechanical things. Kierkegaard's model of causation, perhaps influenced by that of Schelling, is a non-mechanical one.

For Kant, nature could not function as a causal ground of freedom for two reasons. Firstly, phenomenal nature is set up in opposition to freedom. By contrast, for Kierkegaard, nature contains powers and capacities of its own that are capable of causally grounding human freedom. Secondly, for Kant, nature is coextensive with the phenomenal experience of rational and finite beings. But, for Kierkegaard, nature can function as the causal ground of freedom for natural beings might both pre-exist in a temporal sense and exist in a spatial sense outside the domain of limited and finite natural and rational beings. If nature exists outside the experience of limited and finite beings, then this nature, containing Adam but Adam prior to the experience of eating the fruit – in other words, Adam without freedom – might have existed. Freedom, if you like, evolved from other vulnerable and natural beings.

Kierkegaard, then, offers an account of the possible origin of a very strong Kantian notion of freedom. He therefore offers a metaphysic that might underpin a crucial component of Fineman's conception of the vulnerable self – which is that it is able to act individually and collectively. On the other hand, he further offers, like Spinoza, an implicit ontology of the self as a natural and vulnerable being shaped by forces around it, which is strongly at variance with the Kantian Enlightenment model. Unlike Spinoza (at least according to some readings), though, the model of causation he proposes is not a mechanical one. Matter is not inert. For him, matter, in a Schellingian fashion, is in some sense alive.

It is the combination of these two characteristics that seems to me to set Kierkegaard apart from all three philosophers – Descartes, Spinoza and Kant – and that suggests that Kierkegaard offers a metaphysic of the self that incorporates the two major components of vulnerability as set out by Fineman.

Kierkegaard's female characters, as outlined particularly in *Either/Or*, are embodied, vulnerable and emotional beings. To this extent, therefore, they offer a challenge to a humanism that would see the self as primarily a rational, invulnerable and autonomous thing. But the women are more than 'merely' natural beings; they are temporal beings, constituted partly by temporal flows that precede them and exist outside them. They are dynamic and relational beings. Moreover, they are positioned as dependent and as in some sense powerless. Despite this, however, the women of *Silhouettes*, particularly, offer a glimpse into the ultimate paradox that is the religious – for Kierkegaard, the paradox of the man made God. Thus, for Kierkegaard, one of the female characters – Marie – outlined in *Silhouettes*, represents an alternative ontological model to that of the Seeing Eye and that of a mechanical natural determinism.

Marie Baumarchais, discussed by Kierkegaard, or by Victor Eremita, in *Silhouettes* in *Either/Or*, is taken from Goethe's Clavigo. The real character Clavigo was a citizen of Madrid who seduced Lisette, the youngest sister of the French writer Baumarchais. Goethe transforms Lisette into Marie. Marie is seduced by Clavigo and then abandoned by him. She dies of despair.

The reference to God, in the text, suggests that Marie is seen as the paradigm ontological model: she is a victim; she has been wronged. Yet, for Kierkegaard, the relation between Marie and Clavigo exemplifies, in the moment of her passion, the relation between a self and God – or some kind of infinite ideal. In other words, she is never purely a victim: in the moment of her passion, she has the capacity to shape and influence her seducer. She is vulnerable but not wholly incapable of acting.

For Kierkegaard, although Marie is an extreme case, she both emphasises the passion of a relation between a self and a strong moral ideal and also provides a model of the self as a vulnerable and dependent being. All selves, by contrast to those of Kant, Spinoza and Descartes, are intrinsically dependent and needy and, in some way – as human finite, limited selves – never fully whole and autonomous, as is the Kantian 'person'. But Kierkegaard's vulnerable selves are also more phenomenologically persuasive than the Spinozist determined self.

In addition to the light they throw on an alternative ontology, Kierkegaard's female characters (and he clearly identified with some of them) can offer a glimpse of an alternative ethic to the liberal humanist one. They can offer an ethic based on love and sympathy. Kierkegaard's self is radically different from either the formal 'I think' that is presupposed by Kant in applying categories in the world or Kant's noumenal 'person' that is the subject of morality and to which Rawls refers approvingly in *A Theory of Justice* (Rawls 1971).[3] Kierkegaard's self is dependent, vulnerable, embodied and needy. So far, this may describe all human beings, in so far as they interrelate with others and with the natural world outside them, and in so far as their experience is temporal, flowing and sometimes repetitive. But, particularly in *Works of Love*, Kierkegaard stresses the importance of loving others; indeed of loving strangers. This, as I argued in my book *Kierkegaard,*

---

3   It is important to note that Battersby offers a different and interesting reading of the Kantian moral person, by reference to remarks of Kant about the females and by reference, also, to the Third Critique, in Battersby 2008.

Metaphysics and Political Theory (Assiter 2009), may offer an alternative ethic to that of the liberal humanist perspective.

In *Fear and Trembling*, Kierkegaard writes: 'Temporarily, finitude is all what it turns on' (*FT* 56). There are constant references, in Kierkegaard's work, to time, to finite human emotions and to the fact of death. We are not purely rational beings. We are intertwined with others. We are beings who are born, who live and who die. When he writes, in *The Sickness unto Death*, that the 'self is a relation that relates itself to itself or is the relations relating itself to itself in the relation; ... a human being is the synthesis of the infinite and the finite' and that the self is a 'derived relation' (*SD* 13), he is often read as claiming that the human is a derived self 'that owes its existence to God' (see, for example, Carlisle 2006,102). However, elsewhere (*UD*) he argues against theological voluntarism, so his view is clearly not that God shapes everything the self should do (*EUD* and see Assiter 2012).

Instead, it seems to me that Kierkegaard (through his pseudonyms) is partly emphasising the simple fact that we are born; that we are dependent beings. Even the victim, then, whilst clearly an exaggerated depiction of most of us, if seen as the paradigm ontological model of the self, serves as a very important corrective to the norm of the autonomous rational self of Kant. If the victim is altered to become a 'Finemanesque' vulnerable self, the corrective to the Kantian view is even stronger. Kierkegaard's picture, then, serves also as a more persuasive and sympathetic one than that of Spinoza, for whom, as we have seen, the self is largely determined by forces outside it.

The female characters described above are clearly embodied and emotional beings. To this extent, therefore, they offer a challenge to a humanism that would see the self as primarily a rational, invulnerable and autonomous thing. But the women are more than 'merely' natural beings; they are temporal beings, constituted partly by temporal flows that precede them and are outside them. They are dynamic and relational beings. Moreover, they are positioned as dependent and as in some sense powerless. Despite this, however – as noted above – the women of *Silhouettes* in particular offer a glimpse into the ultimate paradox that is the religious, for Kierkegaard, the paradox of the relation between a self and a moral ideal.

Specifically, I have argued in this chapter, that there is a crucial element of vulnerability, as set out in the various works of Martha Fineman, which is omitted from the frameworks of the various philosophers whose work I have considered here. It is frequently noted that Descartes and Kant offer pictures that deny or downplay embodiment and neediness. But it is not so often noted that Spinoza's work, too, downplays two elements that are significant in Fineman's work – vulnerability in general as the obverse of responsibility, but also the fact that vulnerable subjects are not the same thing as victims. They can be held responsible for their actions and they can influence and shape, given the right opportunities, the actions of others – both individuals and collective agents like the state.

Chapter 3

Vulnerability, Advanced Global Capitalism and Co-symptomatic Injustice: Locating the Vulnerable Subject

Anna Grear

Introduction

We live in an age marked by a certain palpability of material effects. We face threats in the form of climate change and related impending environmental and human crises; stark and deepening inequalities and destabilising mass human displacements on an unprecedented scale. In the light of such savage realities, it can be argued that the search for a greater degree of juridical responsiveness to the vulnerabilities inherent in bio- and socio-materiality is now an urgent ethical imperative. One of the most promising aspects of the growing scholarly interest in the concept of vulnerability concerns precisely the potential that the concept holds for much-needed deepening of ethico-juridical responsiveness to the complexity, affectability and vulnerability of the living order and of the multiple beings co-constituted by and within it. There is a need for law to face up to and embrace a certain non-negotiability of *ethical* demand emerging from the implications of living materiality itself, notwithstanding the fact that the precise implications of such ethical demand remain, in large part, undecided.

Against this background, this chapter offers reflections upon some of the epistemological, ethical and normative implications of vulnerability theory which become especially clear when the 'vulnerable subject' is explicitly refracted through the prism of bio-material embodiment and located within the materialities of advanced global capitalism – which – along with the climate crisis – now forms (I suggest) an indispensable backdrop for any adequate exploration both of human and environmental[1] vulnerability and of law's construction of subjectivity.

---

1   The term 'environment' is problematic, in so far as it indicates that which surrounds or, literally, spins around (*envirer* in the French) the 'subject': See A Phillipopoulos-Mihalopoulos (ed.), *Law and Ecology: New Environmental Foundations* (London: Routledge, 2011).

Vulnerability's Promise for an Ethico-Material Turn

The concept of vulnerability holds particular promise for an ethico-material turn. For a start, the concept has inherent links with a wide range of fundamentally material, context-sensitive concerns, a point underlined by the fact that 'vulnerability' is invoked in a range of fields which can all be *focally* characterised as concerning socio-material realities and issues. These fields range from the study of the vulnerability of human and natural systems to climate change, for example (where the concept and its instances draw from a range of expert domains embracing climate science, disaster management, health, social science, development studies, policy development and economics) (Brooks 2003, 2) to the study of the relationship between globalisation and forms of deepening human vulnerability (Kirby 2006). Vulnerability has increasingly been deployed in the fields of political and legal theory, as well as in the sociological theorisation of human rights – Turner, for example, has invoked 'embodied vulnerability' as an alternative foundation for human rights within a sociological account (Turner 2006), while, simultaneously, I have deployed the concept (slightly differently understood) as an alternative foundation for human rights within legal theory – most particularly international human rights theory (and for the specific purpose of a critique of corporate human rights and 'corporate legal humanity') (Grear 2006, 2007, 2010). Fineman, in the fields of legal and political theory, has argued that dependency (Fineman 2003) and (more recently) vulnerability (Fineman 2008) should be theorised as an alternative foundation for political and legal subjectivity. I have also recently attempted to deploy embodied vulnerability as part of a tentative critical and philosophical re-examination of the relationship between human beings and the environment (Grear 2011). Further examples abound, and vulnerability has, it is suggested, rich theoretical potential in a wide range of fields, contexts and arguments.

In order to clarify the meaning of the 'vulnerability thesis' for the purposes of the present argument, we can draw a distinction between it and 'vulnerability science'. Vulnerability science first emerged in the context of food security studies (Vincent 2004) and appears to concern itself with the analysis and systematisation of a broad range of social, material and contextual elements taken to populate the concept of vulnerability as a means of studying risks and related outcomes (and the related concepts of adaptation and resilience). By contrast, the 'vulnerability thesis' is overtly critical. The label refers to an approach (primarily located in the fields of political and legal theory) seeking directly to address the inadequacy and distortion produced by the dominant assumptions of the existing liberal legal and political order. The vulnerability thesis is perhaps best understood as being a *critical normative project* – in the sense that it combines a critique of the liberal order and its fallout (especially of 'a long and growing list of material and social inequalities' (Fineman 2008, 3) with an attempt to imagine an alternative foundation for the ethics of the legal and political order and for political and legal subjectivity, broadly understood. Importantly, as Fineman has emphasised, the vulnerability thesis explicitly rejects both the past and present deployment of the term 'vulnerability' to stigmatise certain 'populations': vulnerability is to be understood as being emphatically universal in scope – as an intrinsic, ineluctable characteristic (or given) of the human condition itself. It is also important to understand that the concept of vulnerability is deployed, moreover, as an avowedly heuristic device. It is invoked and explored precisely in order to open out new possibilities, fresh questions and invigorating avenues of critique (see Fineman 2008, 9) in the search for a more substantively just and equal social order.

Vulnerability's Backdrop: The 'Double-Excisions' of the Liberal Juridical Mythos

Central to the vulnerability thesis, as has just been noted, is an explicit critique of the shortcomings and injustices produced by certain operative closures of mainstream liberal and political theory. These shortcomings require closer examination, in order that the full promise of the vulnerability thesis might be more fully revealed.

Mainstream liberal closures, particularly in law, derive in large part from reliance upon philosophical assumptions – long contested in philosophy – but still nonetheless dominant in the cognitive architecture of liberal law and legal systems. In particular, the body-excising dualism of Descartes and the body-transcending rationalism of Kant combine to produce not only a disembodied subject but a related objectification of both the body and the world (Halewood 1996). Thus, as I have argued elsewhere, the disembodying closures of the liberal juridical order focally include a highly selective, complexly incomplete (and ultimately impossible) excision both of bodies and of socio-material context (Grear 2010). The same accusation has been levelled, moreover, at the Rawlsian liberal subject (Halewood 1996). Revealingly, Halewood has also unambiguously linked the disembodiment of the autonomous liberal subject to the body's objectified fungibility as a commodified, fragmented construct available for market exploitation (Halewood 1996, 1332–49). This, in turn, is directly related to the claim that 'liberal theory, as a result of its ethic of disembodiment, *cannot* yield substantive equality' (Halewood 1996, at 1335, emphasis added).

The excision of the body – and relatedly, of essential aspects of socio-economic context – tends to operate (and has done in socio-historical terms) in favour of certain highly particular interests – as will be argued below. These tendencies, moreover, seem to have converged with other impulses to produce an identifiable form of ideological hegemony which has in turn produced (and continues to reproduce) a dense and mutually reinforcing coupling between the imperatives of neoliberal capitalism and law in the contemporary globalised context reflecting, I suggest, a particularly pernicious extension of earlier couplings visible between the emergence of liberal capitalism and law in the nineteenth century (Norrie 2001; Federman 2003; Grear 2010, especially chs 3 and 4).

The complex double-excision of body and context is intrinsic, moreover, to the production of a mythic, 'even' juridical surface upon which law's equally mythic actors (autonomous, de-contextualised, (quasi-)disembodied (Grear 2010, 41–5) (pre-eminently, 'rational' contractors (Naffine 2003, 362)) glide upon a grid of linear, smooth, mutual and neutral interactions in order to operationalise a putatively unproblematic formal legal equality. This sense of orderly closure, of formal equality in a world of more or less coherent, seamless deontic relations, corresponds, of course, to the notional 'neutrality' of the liberal legal schema and to the broader structure of the liberal state as a whole, 'neutrality' being a central and defining normative characteristic of the entire liberal order (Fredman 1997).

In direct contrast to such excisions, the vulnerability thesis explicitly emphasises both embodiment and socio-materiality. The thesis renders analytically and ethically salient the very features so selectively and partially (in both implications of the term[2]) excised by law's Cartesian and Kantian- ontological assumptions and epistemic 'monolingualism' (Code 2006). Additionally, and centrally, the vulnerability thesis also directly attacks a range of further assumptions operative in the construction of the 'autonomous liberal subject' of politics and law, and is, in that sense, animated by concerns entirely consistent with those of a broad range of critical legal theorists and accounts addressing the ways in which the legal order performs its 'rationalising' function (Horwitz 1981, 1057) in the production of capitalistic privilege and disadvantage (Norrie 2001).[3]

Critical Accounts: Insights from the Genealogy of the Capitalist Liberal Subject

History, as has been noted, is the place where ideology breaks cover (Horwitz 1981, 1057). Insights drawn from critical socio-historical accounts of the development of the juridical subject suggest a particularly decisive set of developments converging in the eighteenth and nineteenth centuries to shape the foundations of modern liberal legal subjectivity in the service of capital. Such accounts point to a particular set of developments, emerging broadly from Enlightenment foundations, and resulting in the elevation of a particular form of disembodied rationalism within liberal law, the ascendancy of methodological individualism and the directly related production of the quintessentially rational, autonomous, juridical (male) individual of liberal legalism and capitalist economic theory (see Norrie 2001; Grant 2008).

The birth-frame of the liberal 'juridical individual' can also be related to the intimate nexus between the emergence and ascendancy of positivism within both

---

2 'Partially': meaning both 'without impartiality' and 'incompletely'.

3 The vulnerability thesis, however, moves beyond mere critique to embrace certain reconstructive ethical possibilities, those hinging on the implications, arguably, of an ethico-material turn – of which more, further below.

the sciences and law (De Sousa Santos 1995, 40) and to the triumph of rationalistic, programmatic control and the production of new forms of subjectivity. Revealingly, one account of such new subjectivities points directly to the startlingly simultaneous (possibly even paired) construction of the 'criminal' and the 'corporation' in 1886 (Federman 2003), a development reflecting the fact that these new legal subjectivities (along with what Hyde has called the production of 'ugly legal constructions of the body (Hyde 1997, 9)) were forged precisely in the service of the promotion and protection of capitalistic interests – the very same ideological programme linked to the elevation of positivism itself (De Sousa Santos 1995, 40).

These related constructions of capitalistic subjectivity and of bodily life, moreover, are in direct relationship with earlier, broader trends legible in the period concerning the emergence of a set of related, systematic forms of disciplinary control: Foucault, for example, has revealed the rationalistic (and 'expert') disciplinary control of the body in this period through the development of the prison system, hospitals, asylums, factories and the like (Foucault 1977) – developments arguably reflecting a common ideological template and expressed in a relentless and systematised control of bodily time and space, hour by hour. Such processes can be read, moreover, as producing bodies (both human and non-human animal bodies) as raw material for the emergent industrial capitalist order (Nibert 2002; Woodiwiss 2005), while liberal law and legal theory, in a corresponding reflex, muted the ethical significance of both embodiment and socio-materiality, suppressing the 'mundane fact that for law to function at all, it must first and foremost have a hold over bodies' (Sclater 2002, 1).

Such intensive control of bodily time and space represents an impulse still fully legible in various capitalist practices of bodily and spatial control. There is a red thread of continuity discernible between capitalism and law's disciplinary control of the body, the body's selective excision, 'legitimated' violence against embodied beings and the body's analogical reproduction in the privileged corporate form. It is, relatedly, no accident that liberal law has facilitated the systemic ideological advantages of corporate 'embodiment' (a form of idiosyncratic embodiment reflecting disembodied characteristics that no human body can ultimately hope to replicate or benefit from (Grear 2010)) to the marked detriment of human beings and communities all over the world (Baxi 2006). It is no coincidence, furthermore, that the liberal juridical individual's construction as hyper-rational, autonomous and quasi-disembodied (and its antecedents in Cartesian and Kantian ontology) has produced complex resistance to the full ethical and juridical implications of embodied vulnerability and that liberal capitalist law remains inhospitable, at a fundamental level, to the vulnerable complexity of the human embodied personality and her inextricable intimacy with her needs, locations and environments.

The complex and partial excision of bodies, and law's related controlling or excluding action, tends to fall, moreover, in revealingly patterned ways. It falls upon those whose human subjectivity has been rendered either partial or non-existent (at different stages of history) for the purposes of capitalistic 'progress' and for the preservation of the power of propertied elites – itself a familiar story accompanying

the journey of liberal rights discourse (Douzinas 2000; Ishay 2004). The tales of
the violence of law's engagements with those subjects whose embodied presence
is constructed as being somehow 'problematic' to 'progress' – those whose bodies
are 'in the way' – are legion. From the wholesale enclosure of land in the service of
industrial agriculture in England (Wood 1999, 67–94; Ricketts-Curtler 1920, 149);
to the dispossession of indigenous peoples under European colonialism; to the
corporate neocolonialisms in the developing world (Baxi 2006); to the continuing
global industrial predation of the environmental commons (Westra 2004); to the
highly predictable patterns of unevenly distributed patterns of advantage and
disadvantage within the developed world, a sense emerges in which all of these
were/have been or are still *juridically mediated* – (even if this mediation is not
simple or uncontested). Law, including the international legal order (and its human
rights regimes), stands marked by these familiar, oppressive patterns (Anghie et al.
2003; Kapur 2006; Marks 2003).

   In short, there is a compelling sense in which the excision of embodiment
and socio-materiality operates precisely (along patterned and discernible social
fault-lines) to regulate the body and simultaneously to excise the potentially
inconvenient normative implications of embodiment. In particular, these excisions
operate to suppress the *distributive implications* of (socially located) human bio-
material and socio-material vulnerability *as a foundation for juridical ethics.*

   Moreover, it is not too implausible, I suggest, to read the excisions enacted in
the production of the autonomous subject as being constituents of a structural form
of juridical 'blindness', operatively masking precisely the *juridical imposition* of
selective disadvantage, privation, violence and exclusion in the service of capitalistic
development both at home and overseas (Marks 2003). This selectiveness served
well the project of colonial imperialism, itself a phenomenon frequently linked to
the rise of the power (and legal subjectivity) of corporations such as the notorious
East India Company (Baxi 2006). Indeed, the very colonial 'progress' narratives
justifying the *rapere* (the 'taking') of the lands of indigenous civilisations called
upon central assumptions of (white, masculine) autonomy, rationality, mastery and
control so intimately linked to the design of the capitalist juridical mythos and
to Cartesian and Kantian ontology and epistemology (Tuhiwei Smith 1999; Jung
2002; Code 2006).

   Norrie, for example, exploring the genesis of nineteenth century industrial
capitalism's influence on the structure of English criminal law, provides a
revealing lens through which to appreciate the ideological dynamics at play in
the construction of the juridical individual (Norrie 2001). Norrie's account draws
attention to a high degree of ideological foreclosure operative in the links between
the protection of the property interests of the emergent capitalist elite and the
ideological production of the 'juridical individual' as a person-construct. As
Norrie puts it:

> In the place of real individuals belonging to particular social classes, possessing
> the infinite differences that constitute genuine individuality .. '[e]conomic man'

or 'juridical man' were abstractions from real people emphasising one side of human life – the ability to reason and calculate – at the expense of every social circumstance that actually brings individuals to reason and calculate in particular ways. (Norrie 2001, 23)

The excisions fundamental to the production of the liberal juridical mythos were, moreover, entirely consistent with the broader rationalising project of the actual historical context in which they occurred, and can be read as historically contingent productions accompanying the 'intellectual birth of liberal Western modernity' itself (Norrie 2001, at 31). The twin rise of legal positivism and of positivism in the epistemology of modern science were central elements of this process and, as noted above, precisely at the promotion of capitalistic development (De Sousa Santos 1995, 40). It appears from a range of scholarship that the industrialising capitalist emphasis upon large-scale systematisation, objectivism, rationalism and control is in direct alignment with the operative assumptions informing the construction of the paradigmatic liberal political and legal subject.

When we look more closely at this subject we can note that its highly capable, autonomous individualism is defined pre-eminently by a dense combination of pure rationality and will (see, e.g., Naffine 2003). This subject is a self-authorising construct – author, moreover, of the entire social order formed in a primordial contract with others entirely like him and authorising both rights and the state in the same mythic inaugural choice (Woodiwiss 2005). This subject stands at the centre of a world understood as a 'market place' (both of ideas and goods/artefacts), his relations conducted through the mechanism of contract (Douzinas 2000, 238), his social bond defined by 'consensual relations' of notional equality. Contract and the formally equal property-owning individual contractor thus provide the core sacral constructs upon which the liberal politico-juridical order was first promulgated and it was this rational autonomous individual which provided the substrate for the citizen (*as* the property owner) whose very citizenship arose directly from his contractual and proprietary relations (Short 1991, 34–5; Green 1998, 252).

There is a sense in which the 'social contract' provided the point of mythic origin for both state and citizen in the form of twinned mirror-constructs, laying, in the process, the justificatory foundation for the broad social organisation of responsibility within the liberal state. Unsurprisingly, within such a conceptual and ideological schema, dependency and vulnerability were (and still are) selectively stigmatised and positioned in opposition to the liberal autonomy and agency of the paradigmatic citizen and liberal legal actor. Dependency and vulnerability were also, perhaps inevitably, jointly and severally *privatised* – as Fineman has argued (Fineman 2003; 2008) in a way that disguises their social and institutional production.

It is important to emphasise that it is precisely the *masking* of the institutional and social nature of the construction of privilege, dependency and vulnerability that is at stake in the double-excision of bio-material embodiment and socio-material context. These are the operative preconditions for the formal equality of the liberal juridical mythos. As Halewood puts it,

> The liberal understanding of person, property and the physical body relies upon
> an important conceptual structure: the radical dichotomy between subject and
> object premised on the decontextualisation of the subject from the world of
> objects, including the body as an object rather than … *integral* to personhood. The
> separation of subjects from objects, by shearing all distinguishing embodiment
> or particularity, permits the formal equality of legal subjects. (Halewood 1996,
> 1340, emphasis original)

Liberal legal justice is thus constructed as being fundamentally abstract, general, universal and relatively blind to embodied and concrete particularities (Douzinas and Gearey 2005, at 127–8). This is even, perhaps, considered to be part of the great virtue of a liberal legal system. Yet, even if we should perhaps concede that some level of generality is important (necessary perhaps) for the achievement of predictable and relatively stable curial judgment, it is nonetheless problematic that the 'generality' of the liberal juridical scheme rests upon a foundational commitment to an *ultimately impossible* double-excision intimately related to well-rehearsed patterns of historical injustice and exclusion.

The disembodied 'self' produced in this conceptual scheme is a strangely mutilated and 'unencumbered' self (Douzinas 2000, 238). 'His' (for this is undoubtedly a masculine construct) greatest fear arises from a 'vulnerability' narrowly conceived of as a threat to his autonomy, and the nature of this construct's rationalism suggests that it is also strategically excised of temporality for, as Fineman has argued, the autonomous liberal subject is always, in paradigmatic terms, a human *adult* (male) standing in a highly selective relation to developmental time and processes – always paradigmatically fully formed and functional. In this sense, as Fineman has put it, the autonomous subject freeze-frames one singular stage of development – '*the least vulnerable*' (Fineman 2008, 12, emphasis added).[4]

Crucially, this complexly disembodied, decontextualised autonomous construct, with its formal contractual equivalence, is the ideal[5] figuration for a capitalist juridical order. Indeed, there is a sense in which this construct of the 'natural person' of law (the male, white, property-owning, natural 'man') is *hardly human at all*. Notwithstanding the fact that historically identifiable groups of humans constructed the autonomous legal subject in their own projected image and have disproportionately benefitted from its deployment, this construct, as I have argued elsewhere, is far more like the corporation than it is like the living human being (Grear 2010, especially chs 3 and 4). This is because the construct's particular combination of relative disembodiment and its seamless match with capitalist ideology combine to suggest the corporation, *not* the human being, as the 'ideal legal subject': The corporation as a 'person' (unlike the fleshy,

---

4   This fact alone suggests the potent critical tensions (approaching an oppositionality, arguably) between the vulnerable subject and the liberal subject.

5   In both the colloquial and the Weberian sense.

embodied vulnerable human being) suffers from no gap between itself and the disembodiment of the liberal legal perspective. It is also, as Neocleous has argued, the very personification of capital itself (Neocleous 2003).

Accordingly, the juridical mythos and the construct of the autonomous juridical individual radically fail to produce a genuinely even field of relations inhabited by equal actors. It produces, instead, a juridical field largely complicit in the genesis of capitalistic privilege.

Focusing on the Vulnerable Subject: Embodied and Embedded

In the light of the foregoing account of liberal law's double-excision in the construction of the autonomous juridical subject we can all the more readily appreciate vulnerability theory's particular promise for the much-needed ethico-material turn noted above. There are at least four points of promise in this regard. First, the vulnerable subject is both *fully embodied* and *ineluctably embedded* in lived actualities and material conditions. The vulnerability thesis makes both the embodied nature of its subject and the socio-materiality of its locations central theoretical concerns. It presents, in the process, an *ethical* case for placing, in Fineman's words, 'actual lived experience and the human condition … at the center of our political and theoretical endeavours' (Fineman 2008, 2). Secondly, the vulnerable subject is vulnerable in an enduring, universal sense (as an incident of human bio-materiality) *and equally* (and precisely *because* of its *embodied* (and therefore socially located) position) the vulnerability of the vulnerable subject is also radically particular and differentially experienced. There is a sense, therefore, in which the thesis traces the radical universal particularity of *corporeality itself* (Grear 2010, ch. 9) into its diverse structural locations and offers, in this process, an explicitly *post-identity conception* of the legal and political subject (Fineman 2008, 17). Thirdly, the political theory implied by the thesis and its ethic does not inherently privilege any one outcome of political deliberation informed by vulnerability-sensitive analyses or accounts: the thesis invites, if anything, a high degree of epistemic humility, because *subject-positionality* emerges as a central implication. Embodiment necessarily implies location/position within the social and 'environmental'.[6] This in turn informs embodied habitus and shapes subject-positionality. Furthermore, subject-positionality is arguably a key implication of the vulnerability thesis's critique of liberalism's assumption/imposition of the 'neutral' viewpoint, or the view from 'nowhere'. Fourthly, as I have argued elsewhere, the embodiment from which our vulnerability arises also unites us, in an important sense, with the *vulnerability of the living order itself* (Grear 2011) – surely, a central theoretical insight required for new ways of 'doing humanity' together within a living order in crisis (Grear 2011).

---

6   See n. 1 above.

This last insight points to the *breadth* of vulnerability's theoretical potency for law's much needed ethical and juridical responsiveness to materialities. Vulnerability reflects or *re*-presents to us a fundamental, trans-species ontic commonality – a form of shared quintessential *affectability* as a condition or quality of creaturely existence itself. We live in a 'condition of non-intentional, heteronomous and more or less *vulnerable* openness to the surrounding world' (Vasterling 2003, at 214). Our very corporeality means that we are porous – interrelationally and radically open to the world. Our bodies, which, as Merleau-Ponty has insisted, are a living, sensory circuit with the world (Merleau-Ponty 1962; Adams 2007) form the dynamic, living bond through which we co-relate with and in the world, not as isolated Cartesian *cogito*s, but *inter-corporeally*. The subject/object split, so foundational to the Cartesian/Kantian foundations of the liberal autonomous subject and so fundamental to its production of alienation, is challenged by a radical intimacy of affect and effect – by a dynamic, open inter-coupling in which vulnerability (as a key incident of embodiment) forms a core element of our inter-permeation with each other and the world.

Vulnerability is then, as universal as human corporeality itself, yet remains (like human corporeality) simultaneously and radically *particular* and fully responsive to its social, environmental and structural locations and mediations. As an intermediate matter it is possible to conclude that the vulnerability thesis has philosophical implications entirely consistent with the necessary ethico-material turn in legal theory – implications with relevance for a range of areas of contemporary and future concern embracing, for example, climate justice; inter-species ethics and so forth, but, just as importantly, for an entire range of intra-species concerns related to distributive justice and ultimately to real and deeply uneven distributions of life and death in the global age.

Underscoring Ethico-material Urgency: The Vulnerability Critique in a Globalised Context

The vulnerability thesis, as Fineman has argued, addresses an ethical summons to the state [and its law], which should become, in the light of the imperatives facing it, 'both more responsive to and responsible for the vulnerable subject' (Fineman 2008, at 2). In this regard, Fineman's account of the vulnerability thesis can be read as setting up a dual or paired reformulation of the politico-legal subject and the state – a mirror move to the twinned emergence of the autonomous political and juridical subject and the liberal state – and exactly the kind of reformulation considered by Fineman to be fundamental to the 'reimagining that is essential if we are to attain a more equal society than currently exists in the United States' (Fineman 2008, at 2). Fineman's account is also an explicit response, not only to the human vulnerable subject as such, but also to the vulnerability of the (simultaneously vulnerability-producing) multiple institutions shaping contemporary society (Fineman 2008, 1–2). Fineman's version of the vulnerability thesis, accordingly, turns our attention directly to the *socio-structural implications* of a vulnerability account.

While Fineman's account of the vulnerability thesis emerges from her long-time critical engagement with the shortcomings of US equality law and discourse, her approach is closely compatible with a range of contemporary critical work engaging with the structural inequalities of advanced corporate capitalism in the context of neoliberal globalisation. The characteristics of the neoliberal global order have profound continuities with the discrepant power relations, ideological closures and constructs of formal equality forming the core target of Fineman's vulnerability-critique of the US approach to state–society relations, notwithstanding some important differences (such as the relative absence within the US of international human rights discursivity). A particularly important linkage between Fineman's specifically US-centric concerns and a wider critique of globalisation, for present purposes, emerges in the virtually hegemonic social dominance of 'US-style' corporations and multinationals. So entrenched, in fact, is a virtually monolithic corporate domination operative at municipal, trans- and international levels that it is meaningful to speak in terms of a wholesale 'corporatisation' and 'commodification of the social spheres' (Grear 2006, 190). In fact, at the globalised level, this reality becomes almost suffocating in its implications: the one feature of globalisation upon which its theorists agree, 'regardless of their disciplinary, analytic or ideological inclinations [is the fact that] corporate global rule is already here' (Shamir 2005, 92), and these corporations are, by and large, US-style transnational corporations.

Additionally, Fineman's concerns with the failures of traditional US equality discourse find a haunting analogue in the observable trajectories of the unequal imposition of peril and privation in the globalised context. The poorest peoples and nations of the earth are forced disproportionately to bear the deepening social costs of capitalism while the selective hollowing out of nation-state sovereignty forms a complexly constituted analogue to the US state non-interventionism in relation to socio-economic disadvantage. The lack of global state-political intervention to constrain the excesses of the market mark the more or less global demise of the *'redistributive'* state (Baxi 2006, 248) while the overwhelming majority of states (as an extensive body of research and scholarship reveals) are now either in hot in pursuit of neoliberal priorities (as the US is) or (as is the case for many states in the Global South) rendered forcibly captive to the imperatives of an ascendant neoliberal capitalism through the conditionalities imposed by international financial institutions, themselves deeply influenced by global corporate interests (Baxi 2006; Smith 2011). Consistent with this situation, in both the US and in the broader globalised arena, we also see a high degree of neoliberal state responsiveness to anxieties concerning the future of global corporate capitalism itself (to a perceived vulnerability, it should be noted, that results entirely from the predatory behaviour of key capitalist actors and institutions and their relative immunity from control and accountability).

A vulnerability analysis, placed in the globalised context, draws our attention directly to the high human and environmental cost of such highly selective forms of state responsiveness. Kirby, for example, has meticulously traced the dense causal networks between neoliberal globalisation and escalating patterns of deepening human vulnerability on a whole set of measures, while my own work draws attention to the dense, patterned linkages between Nibert's 'entanglements of oppression' (the oppression of women and other non-dominant humans, animals and the environment under conditions of corporate industrial capitalism) (Nibert 2002) and the exclusory implications and effects of the *constructus* of the autonomous liberal legal subject and its role in the corporate subversion of international human rights discourse (Grear 2011). Fineman's call for the responsive state, when placed within the neoliberal globalised context, implies that states need now to become fully responsive, not to the current imperatives of voracious and apparently illimitable forms of consumer and corporate capitalism, but to the implications of multiple forms of vulnerability located within the substantive, material conditions of globalisation. However, as will be argued below, the implications of such a call are not straightforward.

Unevenness, Tilt and the Co-symptomatic Nature of Global Injustice

The trope of the vulnerable legal and political subject forms a key part of the necessary juridical re-imagination of the role of materiality required by current exigencies. However, this subject's situatedness is also inescapably important. It is fundamental, if Fineman's vulnerable subject is to perform its potentially transformative role as a heuristic mechanism in a political and juridical re-engagement with questions of substantive justice, that we render fully visible the locations, spaces and positions in which the vulnerable subject must now do its work. It is ethically and theoretically important to insist upon the fact that the vulnerable subject inhabits a world very far removed from the putative evenness of the liberal juridical mythos.

Fineman's vulnerability thesis quite naturally draws our attention to the material *unevenness* of the social world in that socio-economic disparity forms a core concern of her work. Unevenness – as a general theoretical matter – is, moreover, a subtending feature of the living order itself, woven into (as it were) the imbalances, ruptures and inequalities of the social. The world, even as a geophysical matter, is uneven. In fact, nothing in the lived reality of the materiality of life looks remotely like the putatively 'even' surface of the liberal juridical mythos: beings are born or produced with inherently and naturally differential levels of capacity, they are differentially located in differing environments which are differentially hospitable or inhospitable to life in variant degrees and ways. Some geophysical locations, for example, force itinerant motion and/or exposure to ravaging elements (such as to profound heat or cold), causing, in some cases, the reduction of life patterns to contingent strategies of bare survival. This subtending unevenness is a significant feature of reality – even 'before' we add to it the violently tilted structural production of injustice.

Far from negotiating contractual relations across an 'even' plane of individualised formal juridical equivalence, the vulnerable subject is ineluctably embedded within the messy, contextual, concrete, fleshy imperatives, potentialities and limitations of a fully embodied, particular and collective life – a life lived fully open to the draughts, predations and complexities, moreover, of a distinctly *uneven globalised world* (Radhakrishnan 2003): the actual conditions within which the vulnerable subject exists in the globalised world order are characterised by complex and precipitous gradients of tilt produced by Gordian ideological closures in favour of the interests and priorities of global corporate capital. The materialities of the globalised world order are *symptomatically* (Radhakrishnan 2003) marked by the production of savage and spiralling levels of distributive inequality, forms of violent injustice (such as climate injustice and environmental racism (Westra and Lawson 2001) and anthropogenic climate change driven by a seemingly pathological commitment to industrialism and consumerism. In fact, the neoliberal capitalist priorities and imperatives driving globalisation continue to produce widening disparities on a scale now urgently requiring us, as an ethical matter, to embrace the *theoretical centrality of unevenness* (Radhakrishnan 2003) or, perhaps, more explicitly, the theoretical centrality of a *tilted ideology which systematically and* adaptively *privileges corporate capitalist power*.

This, moreover, implicates the 'law and politics of disembodiment/embodiment' (Baxi, in Grear 2010, at xvi) – not least in the form of the immense juridical (and material) advantages accruing to the capitalist corporation through the mechanism of legal personification and the liability shield constituted by the corporate veil. (For more on the complexity of the problems presented by this, see Dine 2012.)

It is possible to read the corporate form as being a complex analogue to the Hobbesian state, for the corporation is an artificial body 'created by contract' in which the '"corporeal interchangeability" [of its members] divests it of the vulnerability that accompanies a corporeally specific body ... [producing a] transmogrification of that corporeality specific vulnerability into a "common Power"' (Whitney 2011, at 557, citing Gatens 1996, at 26 and 161). The 'common power' generated in the case of the capitalist corporation is disembodied in ways rendering it a notoriously complex target for the imposition of legal accountability – an accountability (revealingly) most difficult of all to obtain for corporation-enacted harms to human beings, non-human animals, living systems and the environment (Simons 2012).

It has already been noted that the juridical imaginary of liberal capitalism thoroughly inclines its field of engagement in favour of a relatively disembodied, decontexualised person – the autonomous juridical subject. This subject, as noted above, is defined by its radical autonomy, its hyper-rationality and self-constituting will. It exists in the matrix of contract, is intimately co-imbricated with the liberal conception of private property and 'fits' the corporation far better than it fits the messy socio-corporeality of the living human being. The result is that within the putatively 'even' juridical mythos, the human being is rendered infinitely *more fictitious'* than the corporation (Douzinas and Gearey 2005). Accordingly, the vulnerable human subject is systemically (and unevenly) disadvantaged by the *gap* between the juridical mythos and the uneven living real. This effect, moreover, is amplified in the context of the globalised neoliberal order, for this is an order in which the transnational corporate form deploys protean modes of mutation (simply unavailable to corporeally specific human beings) in order to evade liability even when states *do* attempt to hold corporations to account (Dine 2012) rather than acting (as they predominantly do) as midwives to the neoliberal global order and its priorities (Gill 1995, 2002). While the globalised world remains perilously full of policed borders for vulnerable embodied beings pressed up against them by climate change, violence, socio-economic privation and other urgent exigencies, the globalised world remains, by contrast, fundamentally borderless for capital (Baxi 2006).

The power of global capital to evade the limitations associated with corporeally specific embodiment in relation to the imposition of liability is undergirded, moreover, by capitalism's uncanny ability continuously, adaptively and reflexively to adopt the guise and languages of its putative critiques and counter-values. Even the realisation of an order of international human rights for embodied vulnerable human beings, for example, has effectively become dependent upon the prior recognition of an order of rights for global capital (Baxi 2002, 2006). Baxi, in making this argument, suggests that any serious sociological reading of international human rights law now forces the conclusion that international human rights have been 'critically appropriated by global capital' (Baxi 2002, 147). This bleak assessment reflects the way in which sustainable development and (its intended critique) sustainability discourse (even within progressive multi-level governance settings) risks incremental capture by the ideological and procedural dominance of corporate actors – while the language of 'eco-system services' signals the depressing installation of essentially marketised-anthropocentrist values within putatively 'green', 'progressive' agendas. The persistence of global capital in adopting the mantle of its counter-values and, in the process, semantically blunting their critical potency, when placed alongside the deepening inequalities marking the materiality of the uneven globalised world order, richly suggests the heuristic utility of placing the vulnerable subject within a framework of analysis paying *explicit* and *sustained theoretical attention* to the precipitous degree of imbalance now characterising twenty-first-century globalisation.

The production of the increasingly asymmetric socio-material and juridical relations of globalisation can even, as Radhakrishnan argues, be understood as 'co-symptomatic'. Indeed, Radhakrishnan argues that

> it is only on the basis of a theoretical ethic [based on the 'symptomatic *immanetization* of unevenness' (Radhakrishnan 2003, at vi)] that a young entrepreneurial billionaire can be persuaded to feel, perceive and understand his or her reality as an inhabitant symptom of global unevenness – as much of

a symptom as the abject and voiceless poverty of a homeless being anywhere in the world. In other words, within the etiology as well as the pathology of the disease [of capitalism], both the billionaire with a plutocratic lifestyle and the instant-to-instant contingency of the homeless person are *co-symptomatic*. (Radhakrishnan 2003, at vii)

It is possible to argue that co-symptomatic injustice could be read as being an inherent implication of the vulnerability thesis in so far as the thesis invokes relationality. However, there are nuances in the concept of the co-symptomatic that are not rendered apparent by the concept and terminology of the relational as it is normally deployed. While the concept of relationality captures a wide range of modes of interconnection, the idea of the co-symptomatic highlights the *pathological* (Radhakrishnan 2003) forms of interaction characterising advanced corporate capitalism. The co-symptomatic, in this context, captures the kinds of dysfunction, in other words, not often co-thought with relationality in its everyday sense. The notion of the co-symptomatic highlights the perverse dynamics and capitalist etiology of the radical and *immanent* unevenness now affecting populations of embodied vulnerable bodies acted upon by impersonal, anonymous communicative systems too complex to control (Teubner 2006) in a globalised order where, as Beck argues, the economic power of global business has become a form of 'political meta-power' (Beck 2005/6, 117). Even the concept of 'agency' becomes, in this context, highly complex and contingent – the political meta-power of capital means that an insidious politics of side effect operates as a form of '*domination by nobody*' (Beck 2005/6, at 117, emphasis original).

This situation poses genuinely complex challenges for the prospect of the vulnerability-responsive state and its potential to transform life in the twenty first century. The concept of the 'co-symptomatic', and its implications of an etiology and a pathology points up global capitalism as form of sickness (Radhakrishnan 2003) – as *process* – manifesting in flows and interactions far too elusive to track and favouring transnational conglomerations of corporate power mutable enough to frustrate state attempts to control them (Dine 2012). Globalisation presents a heterogeneous tumult of processes amounting to a (literally) fatal hegemony. Indeed, Beck has argued that under the conditions of neoliberal globalisation, the very nature of power itself has changed (Beck 2005/6). This reality renders accountability and redress highly elusive. In such a landscape, the state is just one element in an extensive system of capitalist interactions. The theoretical freedom of the state from market and profit controls imagined by Fineman becomes difficult, accordingly, to make meaningful in the globalised context. Indeed, the decline in nation state power urgently necessitates a reconceptualisation of the state itself (Beck 2005/6). There are now genuine doubts attending the very idea of the state's ability to be adequately responsive to the violent unevenness characterising the ethico-material urgencies of our age. States, it seems, are complexly captive to (even as they are also constituted as midwives of) the overarching context of neoliberal imperatives. The undeniable complexities effecting the mutation of the state under the conditions of advanced globalisation, seen through the lens of co-symptomatic injustice, suggest the need for fuller theorisation concerning the precise meaning of (and possibilities for) Fineman's 'responsive' state at the global level.

Radhakrishnan's overt deployment of 'unevenness' as a semantic principle is designed to reflect what I have implicated above as being a pre-loaded, part-calculated (agency is an extremely complex theme as already noted), multi-sectoral, systemic, evolutive, dynamic and colonising form of global asymmetry amounting to a process of global *predation*. Combining the theoretical immanentisation of unevenness with the notion of the co-symptomatic in the context of globalisation is a powerful way to emphasise the global *production* of intrinsically related vulnerabilities along highly *patterned* lines. The *patterned and predictable* nature of the co-symptomatic production of power and deprivation – and the vast discrepancies, for example, between Global North and Global South – point suggestively back to the linkages between the neoliberal order's self-presentation as a progressive (colonial) project and to the long historical arc of capitalistic 'progress' narratives (Baxi 2006) and the practices of the mediation of life and death in which the *notional evenness* of the juridical mythos has played such a central, rationalising role. In this sense, the notion of the co-symptomatic brings a sharply political heuristic into explicit contact with the vulnerability thesis, nuancing its implications and locating the vulnerable subject in an unmistakeably twenty-first-century life-world: It is in a complex field of co-symptomatic, subtending and evolving asymmetries that individual embodied human beings are forced into mythic legal equivalence with the corporate personification of capital (no matter how large, dispersed or powerful corporations may in reality be). Relatedly, the construct of the person, whether corporate or human, bears little relation to the lived, corporeal realities of concrete lives. The gap between law's subjects and living beings gives good reason to endorse Fineman's central call for the replacement of the autonomous liberal actor by the vulnerable subject – but at the global level it becomes especially clear how important it is to keep in mind the fact that the *patterned and predictable* asymmetry of privilege and disadvantage produced by autonomous legal subjectivity is complexly co-constitutive with predatory neoliberal globalisation. We must draw *explicit* attention to the *exact* correspondences between the entangled oppressions of marginalised humans, animals and the 'environment' marking the history of corporate industrial capital (to refer, again, to Nibert's rich sociological work) and the co-symptomatic forms of injustice marking precisely the historical contours of the privileged autonomous legal subject (and that which it excludes, particularly as it was shaped in the inauguration of the age of industrial capitalism). By deploying a notion of co-symptomatic injustice in order to nuance the heuristic value of reflection on vulnerability theory for the globalised context, theory would follow (to appropriate the words of Radhakrishnan) 'a deeply ethical impulse' (Radhakrishnan 2003, at vi).

Some Interim Implications

What then, might some implications of this 'deeply ethical impulse' be? It is suggested that, minimally, there are three theoretical gains. The first relates to the way in which an additional critical dimension is added to the interrelationality intrinsic to the corporeality of the embodied vulnerable subject by drawing our attention to meta-themes attending the analysis of power and the politics of disembodiment in the global age. The second gain builds upon the implications of the argument offered here to suggest the need for modes of particular *ethical* sensitivity to those most oppressively affected by the co-symptomatic global production of power and disadvantage. Thirdly, we are pointed towards a particular need for *epistemic* sensitivity towards the most co-symptomatically disadvantaged subjects in our communities of knowing and acting.

Turning to the first theoretical gain, it is an intrinsic implication of vulnerability theory that the embodied subject is always and everywhere an inherently interrelational subject (with the potential not only for suffering and pain but also for profound forms of flourishing and *co-flourishing* (Grear 2010, ch. 6). Embodied beings necessarily emerge into a world already marked by an 'other' from whom they have derived their existence – usually, in the case of human beings and many non-human animals – in a literal gestational dependency of bodily enfoldment. In this sense, for embodied beings, perhaps especially for human beings in their ethical relations, the other is always 'prior' in the sense of 'there first' as point of origin and reference. We are always, therefore, inherently social. Moreover, science reveals to us the fact that we are interrelational 'all the way down': the biomaterial unfolding of embodied life takes place as an inherently interrelational being-in-process constituted by multiple cellular, molecular inter-permeations within and through the human body itself. Haraway points out that 'human genomes can be found in only about 10 per cent of all the cells that occupy the mundane space I call my body; the other 90 per cent of the cells are filled with the genomes of bacteria, fungi, protists and such, some of which play a symphony necessary to my being alive at all ... to be one is always to *become with* many' (Haraway 2008, at 3–4). These 'world-making entanglements' and the 'material-semiotic nodes or knots in which diverse bodies and meanings coshape one another' (Haraway 2008, at 4) suggest that a radical interrelationality both inaugurates and constitutes our existence in a multitude of rich ways, at 'micro' and 'macro' levels.

It is also worth emphasising that we, as embodied subjects, inevitably exhibit mutability throughout unfolding life stages, reflected in shifting levels of interrelational dependency as the trajectory of embodied life unfolds in its patterns of gestation, birth, growth, health and illness, decline and death (Fineman 2008). This has the important implication that we are *never* an *ens completens* even as a fully formed adult. Our interdependency (even when experienced as radical dependency) is therefore an inherent implication of our corporeality itself. We are *carnally* inter-formed, and this is a living socio-material reality or given of our existence that would remain true even if we were to isolate ourselves from other human beings: our bodies always remain ontologically open, porous, living circuits of interrelationality (Kirkman 2007).

When this focus upon the interrelationality implicated by the vulnerability thesis is explicitly extended to embrace the co-symptomatic, it gains a fresh and critical political potential. Both the inescapability of interrelationality and the nature of co-symptomaticity in distinctive, nuanced ways, demand a fuller account of their implications for ethics, distributive responsibility and the meaning of political co-location. This leads us to the second theoretical gain. Globalisation, if anything, has deepened the necessity of adverting to the radically asymmetric realities of globalised interdependencies. Minimally, the notion of co-symptomatic injustice suggests the need for a far fuller and more inclusive account of responsibility – and specifically, for a more substantive and radical account of transnational corporate responsibility combined with a special ethical responsiveness to the most excluded, impoverished human beings and communities. This second gain also arguably moves beyond the concept of the responsive state to place particular responsibility upon all those co-symptomatically advantaged by the globalised context – including privileged individuals, as Radhakrishnan's analysis implies. In particular, it also invokes the responsibility of international institutions and quasi-state private actors to attempt to ameliorate the destructive fallouts of neoliberal capitalist imperatives (and to strive to respond to those most disadvantaged by the corporation's gain, no matter how complicated this might in reality be).

Thirdly, this in turn mandates the need for a particularly responsive willingness to hear from and respond to the most disadvantaged communities and individuals of all. In practical terms, this would imply a renewal or transformation of participative structures in multi-level governance fora and the related transformation of advocacy into an epistemically responsible practice explicitly open to a diverse ecology of knowledges (Code 2006). The need for epistemic openness may also enrich existing practices and point towards the aperture of hope presented by social movement activisms and civil society movements resisting, or attempting to resist, the predations of global capitalism. Such practices and movements might be expected to enhance, at least partially and contingently, the state's ability to be responsive to vulnerability. This third gain invokes, in a sense, a particular kind of political sensitivity to the epistemological implications of embodiment, inter-relationality and the co-symptomatic nuance of global injustice.

Our embodiment means, as Merleau-Ponty has argued, that we are always necessarily corporeally 'positioned', and that our perception is shaped (or deformed) by embodied limitation. Thus, unlike the disembodied autonomous subject whose ocular-centric epistemology produces a monocultural 'view from nowhere', the embodied subject is always positioned and has an incomplete view. Embodied perception readily implies a notion of epistemic limitation, and hints at the need for epistemic humility – for an open acknowledgment in both theoretical and practical terms of the vulnerability of perspective arising from the limitations (both real and symbolic) of the body itself as a field of perception. Our corporeal interrelationality richly suggests, therefore, the need for forms of radical epistemological openness to the insights of others. The theme of co-symptomatic injustice takes this further, though. It underlines the need for epistemic responsibility towards those *most disadvantaged* by capitalism's structuration of power – and it places particular responsibility for 'hearing' and 'responding' upon those most *advantaged* by it. It calls for a radical commutative commitment to embracing insights and claims emerging from a more open and inclusive ecology of ways of knowing (Code 2006) rooted explicitly in the constructed forms of 'otherness' accompanying the production of the capitalist order. This, in turn, suggests new forms of organising and acting with and through particular communities of concern and people's movements representing all those (themselves and/or others) most affected by the co-symptomatic fall out of the exercise of capitalistic privilege in an age of hyper-profit gained at the expense of vulnerable living materiality in all its forms.

Concluding Thoughts

Fineman argues that the concept of the vulnerable subject, combined with a conception of the state as bearing particular responsibility for the mediation of the relationship between the vulnerable subject and 'asset-conferring' social institutions, provides a potent way of arguing for the re-distribution of important sources of resilience in the face of our universal and radically particular human vulnerability (Fineman 2008). Despite Fineman's focus upon the United States, it is clear that the vulnerability thesis offers a theoretically informed critical space for a thoroughgoing interrogation of the power-distributions operationalised by neoliberal globalisation. One normative implication of such an approach is that the state (and politics) should attempt to re-assume some kind of resistive role in challenging the stranglehold of capitalist economic hegemony at both national and international levels. At both these levels, however, the concept of the state itself needs to evolve to take on board the complex contingencies and realities outlined by scholars of globalisation. Ultimately, it seems correct to conclude, with Coyle (this volume) that the most hopeful means of resistance lies in the positive place of 'intermediate communities' giving life to 'specific networks of solidarity'. Such networks may also include small businesses (Kuo and Means, this volume) – but the fundamental point is that these are *situated* networks responsive to lived realities. They implicitly express a critical politics of embodiment against the hegemonic, anonymous forces of globalisation and forms of *domination by nobody*. In fact, Silva's account of account of the social movement activism in Latin America that supported a shift towards a de-commodification of labour and land, empowering the state to be more interventionist in its attempts to reform neoliberalism, suggest that the decline of the redistributive state may not be entirely irreversible when bolstered by people's movement activisms, intermediate communities and networks of solidarity (see Kirby 2011 for an illuminating discussion of this). The central role of the vulnerable subject in this kind of ground-level energising of political resistance to economic hegemony is one of the most hopeful conduits, arguably, for the kind of renewed accountability required in the face of co-symptomatic global injustice – even if such possible reversals remain radically open to reversal in turn and are replete with challenges.

When the idea of the co-symptomatic is added to Fineman's account, it implies a central state duty directly to challenge the power disparities of neoliberal globalisation, but it also necessarily implies the related need to create the structures of accountability through which to make global corporate power responsive and responsible, moving it beyond the predatory instrumentalism currently characterising its 'relationship' with the vulnerable living order. This minimally implies the state-funded provision of participation and advocacy mechanisms fully responsive to the voices and experiences of the marginalised and socio-economically disadvantaged (especially those disproportionality forced to bear the *privatised burdens* (Fineman 2008) of the structurally produced imbalances so evident in globalised co-symptomatic injustice) and – crucially – free from the usual corporate financial dominance over 'participatory' processes. There is some hope, perhaps, that by this means and others vulnerability can play a central catalysing role in the production of political strategies for such an attempted re-formation of state priorities. Vulnerability is a key element, then, of a potentially transformative embodied politics – for, as Kirby argues, Silva's 'persuasive reading of the reactions to neoliberal globalisation in Latin America has the benefit of highlighting vulnerability as the central impact on the lives and livelihoods of the majority and as therefore *motivating reactions to globalisation*' (Kirby 2011, at 101, emphasis added). Vulnerability is *body-lived* in a way that the politics of disembodiment can never respond to other than by *capitalising upon it* (literally).

Finally, however, it seems important to concede the inevitability that the concept of vulnerability will itself remain as open as any other concept to a pernicious range of deployments, including the adaptive semantic strategies of corporate capital in its responsibility-evading mutations. The notion of co-symptomatic injustice explicitly points us precisely to the need for constant critical responsiveness to the pathology of neoliberal capitalism as a *process* – demanding, in response, an on-going, adaptive, critical awareness of shifting relativities and relationalities of position, power, responsibility and relative vulnerability. Thus, while multinational corporations can rightly claim to be imbued with a form of vulnerability, their vulnerability, when placed in a *co-symptomatic* nexus with the deepening of human corporeal vulnerability and the vulnerability of animals and living systems, suggests a reflexive aperture through which, at least, we might build some adaptive forms of critical resistance to the reduction of vulnerability itself to mere semantic weaponry in the pursuit of 'business as usual' in a radically uneven globalised world order.

Chapter 4
Vulnerability and the Liberal Order

Sean Coyle

Writing in 1991, after the spectacular collapse of communism in the former Soviet republics, Pope John Paul II asked whether capitalism is the victorious social system, the path to true economic and civil progress. His answer was cautious and complex. Freedom and promotion of human creativity in the economic sector is to be welcomed and affirmed, but that same economic freedom will come to be despised if it is not 'circumscribed within a strong juridical framework which places it at the service of human freedom in its totality, and which sees it as a particular aspect of that freedom, the core of which is ethical and religious' (*Centesimus annus* 1991, s. 42). A similar note of caution about the ultimate direction of capitalism is sounded by the English political philosopher John Gray. The market society has incalculable advantages over earlier, feudal and socialistic forms of social ordering, but subverts these advantages at the moment that its central institutions become free-floating and autonomous (as perhaps logically they must), detached from the fabric of the communities which they originally served (Gray 1995, 89–121; see also Gray 1995, chs 2 and 3). How is one to respond to this tendency in capitalism? By deepening one's commitment to its noble aspects, or by distancing oneself from too enthusiastic an embrace of capitalist ambitions? *Centesimus annus* shies away from offering a general theory of society:

> The Church has no models to present; models that are real and truly effective can only arise within the framework of different historical situations, through the efforts of all those who responsibly confront concrete problems in all their social, economic, political and cultural aspects, as these interact with one another. (*Centesimus annus*, s. 43)

The Church's hesitancy over capitalism provides a useful context in which to consider the problem of vulnerability. 'Universal' and 'constant' (Fineman 2008, 1) though it may be, it is necessary to place vulnerability in context. Liberal political order is associated with a situation in which the human being, in becoming an 'individual', confronts a new set of vulnerabilities. Stemming from a free market, it is possible to interpret these vulnerabilities in different ways according to one's underlying philosophy of the market. Classics of liberalism and capitalism indeed lauded the new strengths supposedly created by the market. The absence of economic barriers leaves man free to trade and to accumulate, but it also opens the door to exciting social freedoms: the ability to choose one's own profession, and to determine one's own priorities. Individuals, but also land and labour, are liberated from the social structures in which they were previously embedded, free to find new meanings. No longer in the hands of an oligarchy, man's destiny lies increasingly in his own hands.

But the same processes of liberalization also invoke feelings of vulnerability and dispossession. The individual in becoming free of social structures also becomes a commodity. Those who are less skilful, who have less to offer, face the prospect of unemployment. The same market forces that distribute resources and labour to the most productive are also responsible for creating high rents and mortgages, wage-slavery and joblessness. Markets create not only wealth but also poverty: new obstacles to social mobility. Those who suffer most from the ruthless operation of market forces feel that their fate is governed by unseen forces: their destiny lies not in their own hands but truly in 'invisible hands' that remain staunchly indifferent to their needs.

Except in those few instances where communist ideas successfully established themselves, arguments between capitalists and socialists have taken the liberal political order as their battleground. This did not happen by accident. Capitalism is properly defined not against socialism but against traditional societies in which production and consumption, in being governed by traditional structures of religion, social custom and ritual, are essentially unchanging. Traditional orders of society (such as feudalism) were premised upon the classical assumption that good government represents harmony, so that the excellent society is a harmonious one. The aspiration of harmony demanded a highly complex system of social and political rules which limited not only social mobility (a threatening and execrable idea) but also the conditions in which products are exchanged. In the course of the eighteenth century, a new framework of thought appeared. Adam Smith's work points the way to this new understanding: good government recognizes the permanency of conflict and competition, and seeks to harness its forces for the purposes of creativity. The worst instincts of man cannot be excluded by the 'correct' form of government, but must be put to work for the good of all society. Left to themselves, man's needs to accumulate and acquire wealth lead only to destruction. Resources and labour are stripped from the hands of the less skilful and placed in those of the most productive. Efficiency is indeed ruthless in what it destroys. Capitalists and proto-capitalists wish instead to place human greed within a creative framework: the open market. This 'invisible hand' will succeed in redistributing wealth to areas of need in a way that has little to do with what each person actually intends.[1]

Smith's own works illustrate the tendency of capitalist ideas to bring about a broader social transformation. In his earlier text of 1759, *The Theory of Moral Sentiments*, the invisible hand is first presented as a functional working of the structures and political assumptions of the class system. Vanity, which sets

---

1 Smith 1776, IV.2: '… he intends only his own gain, and he is in this, as in many other cases, led by an invisible hand to promote an end which was no part of his intention.'

in motion the imagination of the wealthy classes, both animates and feeds the economic system: in 'expand[ing] itself to everything around', the imagination of the rich shall prompt them 'to cultivate the ground, to build houses, to found cities and commonwealths, and to invent and improve all the sciences and arts, which ennoble and embellish human life ...' (Smith 1982, IV.1). By 1776, the fingers of the invisible hand have grown longer: tied no longer to the actions only of the rich, the invisible hand is the product of the behaviour of 'every individual', whose pursuit of gain causes them '"necessarily"' to labour in a way that redounds to the benefit of society (Smith 2003, IV.2). Modes of exchange that were traditionally embedded within social structures from which they derived their meaning (such as the feudal exchange of land for service) are now 'open'. The removal of barriers to trade (economic liberalization) brings with it social liberalization. Conservative proponents of the free market like to point to these processes as examples of capitalism as a creative force, but in fact they function equally as representations of the market's tendency to produce social *destruction*: the collapse of social organization and the system of meanings that the 'market' was originally meant to serve. Once the process of economic liberalization has begun, it is very difficult to prevent its spread to all areas of life. Kinds of human behaviour that are not intended to be profit-maximizing become engulfed by the market: the activities of universities provide one example of this.

In the eyes of its defenders, the capitalist economy and a liberal social order are necessary given the basic orientation of the human condition. Socialists try to deny the necessity of greed as a basic instinct, but their constructions, which are intended to eliminate its operation, produce misery and poverty on a scale far greater than anything the free market has delivered. Conservatives are quick to seize upon these facts in order to justify their vision of a liberal society oriented toward free enterprise. But their own position is not less open to problems. Capitalism does not eliminate poverty, but tries to argue that the deepening division between rich and poor, haves and have-nots, is nevertheless accompanied by a steady enrichment of the vast majority of society, including the predicament of its poorest sectors. Inequalities between rich and poor are not justified, but they are inevitable consequences of a necessary system.

One century before the appearance of *Centesimus annus*, the Church confidently proclaimed solutions to the predicament of the neglected classes. The encyclical *Rerum novarum* called for a fundamental Christian critique of the market (*Rerum novarum* 1891, s. 16). Socialism is to be resisted. The market and private property can be harnessed for the common good. Capitalist institutions can be made just, built upon a foundation of Christian justice. Solutions must come from the Church and from Christians specifically (ss. 16, 27, 55). By 1991, the Church sounds more cautious.

With the collapse of communism in the East, the predicament of the poor across the world has deepened. Evils have proliferated, creating new struggles for justice. Each age of the world will bring 'new things' that must be confronted (*Centesimus annus*, s. 61). Poverty threatens to assume massive proportions, while 'tragic crises loom on the horizon' (s. 57). Christians and non-Christians alike must bear responsibility for creating just arrangements (s. 60). There are no theories, but only actions; no answers, only deeds.

In the light of the failure of conservative and socialist perspectives on the market to address the plight of the vulnerable classes, what if anything can be learned from their philosophies? The proliferation of centrist positions on both the left and the right testifies to the inadequacy of both positions to confront the realities of vulnerability in the liberal order. I intend to ignore this central ground, home to 'capitalists with a conscience' and free-market socialism, except in so far as demanded by the context of liberal political order. I will consider what might be taken from these rival positions, and in the light of this I will offer some thoughts on Martha Fineman's analysis of vulnerability and her call for a more 'responsive' state. Above all, I would like to impart some sense of the Church's insight that doctrinal possibilities can confer a fatally misleading sense of what is achievable in practice, and consider where this leaves us.

Conservatism

Conservatives connect vulnerability with freedom. Full of ideas of personal liberty, they insist that, as the state increases its organization of the welfare of the private sphere, people will become less resilient. Individuals must learn to stand on their own two feet if society is not to produce a class of dependent people. They have a point. Individuals will become masters of their situation only if they are allowed to create their own arrangements. Human freedom is a more effective solver of problems than the government's legislative schemes. But the same conservative philosophies also increase vulnerability, leading many to curse the inhumanity of a faceless system (the market) which fails to respond to their needs.

Socialists rightly criticize conservatives for their failure to understand vulnerability. Many of the things that make people vulnerable (economic poverty, health, treatment of minority groups) do not abate in the face of increased opportunity. A social philosophy which leaves people to sink or swim will not render vulnerable individuals more resilient in the face of their vulnerabilities, nor force them to become resilient enough to overcome them. Conservatives will always fail to tackle vulnerability because the premise of their position is founded upon an appeal to the prosperity that market institutions deliver (Gray 1993a, 67). Considerations of justice can only intrude to modify free market forces that are already in operation: trespassing upon the freedom of the market by imposing order upon it. A certain reluctance (if not hostility) toward attempts to *structure* resilience, redressing the balance between haves and have-nots, remains a deep-seated feature of conservative thinking. Pointing to the ruin created by socialist central planning in communist regimes, toward the waste and crushing poverty associated with such systems, conservatives attempt to occupy the high ground. They argue that it is an illusion to think that there are real alternatives to the capitalist system. There are no superior social systems. The proper context in which considerations of justice operate is the free-market society. The collapse of many communist systems in the East reveals the inevitability of failure in attempting to pull out the market at the roots, by replacing it with systematic organizational ideas. Justice cannot *precede* the market!

Convinced of the necessity of the market, conservatives in developed countries will always favour growth over equality. They rightly accuse socialist regimes of achieving (measures of) social and economic equality only at the most appalling levels of poverty and unfreedom. At the same time, conservatives are wrong to equate prosperity with moral progress. They argue that societies make moral progress only when they can afford to do so: the abolition of slavery in the West depended on the affluence of the classes who could afford to dispense with them. Material security is necessary in allowing human beings the luxury to have ideas about their situation. Their predicament is not necessary (all that they can afford), but amenable to change. But, in another sense, markets have been accused of bringing about moral degradation. Market societies respond only to those needs that are 'solvent' (Centesimus annus, s. 34). Where even basic needs are divested of purchasing power, they are condemned to remain unfulfilled. Free economies respond only to 'marketable' needs: pornographic and many other forms of exploitation are permitted to flourish in response to moneyed demands, whereas deeper needs (such as dignity and resilience) find it difficult to be recognized. There is no doubt that markets, in promoting consumption, generate 'false' needs at the expense of 'real' needs. Are socialists right to argue that conservatives fail to take vulnerability seriously?

In one sense, conservatives do not seek to structure resilience, for the very reason that they make little attempt to 'structure' vulnerability. Allowing market forces to take their course, vulnerabilities are left to lie where they fall. The majority of vulnerabilities (those created or exacerbated by poverty) are not distributed according to specific plans, but by the operation of the 'invisible hand', which in distributing the benefits of the market also distributes harm: low wages, job insecurity, unemployment, high rents, and unaffordable commodities, and thus also health- and welfare-related vulnerabilities. For a whole range of reasons (among them the perceived inability of the state to be responsive in the face of an ever-changing situation), the first and most prolific line of defence against such vulnerabilities is the transactional behaviour of those most deeply affected, who will contract and bargain their way to a better situation.

In another sense, conservatives cannot avoid structuring resilience. The market itself is a mechanism for distribution and, in this sense, 'structures' society. The very freedom of the market is the removal of restrictions on trade stemming from social structures within which exchanges of products previously operated. The decision about what is to be left to market forces, and what is to remain or be placed within the determination of social considerations, is nothing other than a question of 'structuring'. A free market is not that which remains once all regulation and control has been withdrawn. Markets are not fully spontaneous but require constant direction. Without this direction the market would extinguish itself either through dissolution or by pursuing its other tendency into monopoly. Modern markets constantly threaten to unravel as the result of a thousand complications that are internal to their own operation. In the absence of all intervention, the market would be indistinguishable from chaos. Markets cannot function without a stable system of contract law for the enforcement of bargains, and a system of property law for the recognition of claims. The image of the market as having gained 'independence' from the social structures in which it was embedded is an illusion. Markets always presuppose a larger social context into which they fit: the question is to what extent the social structures have ceased to be serviced by the market, but exist largely or solely in order to sustain the market's operations. (One sees this for example in arguments about the classification of the law of contracts as a branch of commercial law vs. its traditional association with a law of obligations.)

Overwhelmingly dominated by economic considerations, conservatives find it hard to think of vulnerability as a moral issue. Frequently, they conceive of vulnerability in the only terms the market understands: basic needs. Aware of poverty, conservatives argue that the economy needs a safety net: schemes and programmes for the least well-off. Two assumptions underpin this understanding. The first is that vulnerabilities are capable of being addressed in so far as basic needs are capable of being met through the resources of the state. The second is that vulnerabilities can be overcome (erased) if individuals can be placed in a position in which they are capable of meeting their own needs. Conservatives wish above all to make individuals responsible for their own vulnerabilities. Reliance on state benefits is therefore stigmatized as a failure, or in many cases a refusal, to exercise one's talents in a reasonable way.

Conservatives understand vulnerability in terms of what a person *needs*. As much as their vision is limited by the horizons of the market, conservatives fail to appreciate that vulnerability is a question not simply of need but also of an individual's total situation. People need society as well as economy if they are to achieve their aims. People are not in the main (or without great loss) 'self-sufficient' but require the society of others for their completion: the human being is not an *ens completum*. When in the presence of strong family, friendly and neighbourly ties, the individual is less vulnerable, more supported. It is well known that market forces erode these ties. As market imperatives come to dominate political policy, the well-being of the community is progressively divorced from measures of its structural strength and integrity, the wisdom and fittingness of its customs, and comes to be associated with a different measure: economic growth. The privatization of wealth brings with it the privatization of family life, the huge expansion of the 'private realm'. Individuals are more private, but their vulnerabilities and insecurities also become largely private matters, 'public' only to the extent that state-organized welfare mechanisms provide relief from them. Under sustained capitalist conditions, 'communities' are no longer sufficiently organized to respond to the issues that affect them. Crime is more shocking not because it is more widespread but because it is individuals who must deal with its effects. Inequalities of wealth are less pronounced but more difficult to bear for those who depend upon the state for their income. The community is no longer concerned with the plight of the poor, but has replaced this feeling with another one, fear – suspicion of an underclass that might reasonably be supposed to covet or resent the blessings of the middle classes. Driven by the market, aware of the prosperity it has brought, communities eventually absorb capitalist assumptions into their modes of thinking. They end up asking why those on benefits, or those who turn to crime, cannot simply use the market and their own initiative to better their situation, gathering wealth for themselves. The underclass is largely responsible for its own vulnerabilities!

Critics of conservatism (or specifically neoconservative capitalism) appeal to such considerations in an effort to demonstrate that the advance of the market does not ensure moral progress, but brings about moral and social disintegration. Markets privatize vulnerability just as effectively as they privatize wealth. The loosening of neighbourly bonds frees the individual, but also robs him of the very thing that makes him resilient in the face of his vulnerabilities.

Socialism

Aware that freedom alone is not sufficient to enable people to overcome their vulnerabilities, socialists prefer to connect vulnerability with a different idea: *justice*. Following their instinct for greater organization, they demand that help must be available to those who are powerless to take charge of their situation. While this may be difficult to argue with, there is, however, no doubt that this creates new focuses for dependence. Conservatives are right to be suspicious of systems that produce complacency or dependence upon state benefits. Alleviating the effects of certain forms of vulnerability, socialists have encouraged people to become vulnerable in other ways, reliant on systems of support over which they have no meaningful control.

One dynamic of the socialist understanding of justice is often overlooked. In equating vulnerability with welfare need, socialists have in effect sided with conservatives in arguing that the market will finally provide the required solutions. The market is not to be abolished, but re-ordered. Its existence is not to be called into question, but it requires more structure, more direction. Their concern is not to question the market's priorities, but to ensure their wider distribution. Free-market capitalism is to be replaced by state capitalism. Those in poverty do not want a different way of life from that of the middle classes, but wish to emulate them, accessing and enjoying the same goods. They no longer wish to annihilate the middle classes but aspire to join their ranks. The underlying values of society and of the market itself are not denied but reinforced: society is not appointed to a public, collective good, but to the protection of private lives and private property (Perreau-Saussine 2007, 11). Socialism will always play second fiddle to conservatism in liberal societies for the reason that it will always be predominantly the ideology of an underclass which does not want to challenge the priorities of the middle classes, but wishes instead to share in their wealth.

The instinct of socialists that the most acute vulnerabilities stem from, or are exacerbated by, poverty is essentially correct. However, they are wrong to regard poverty as largely a monetary phenomenon. Vulnerability cannot be cured through redistribution alone. Understood less in monetary terms but 'situational' ones, the vulnerability of the poor is a product of phenomena such as the breakdown of families and of good relations among neighbours. As social traditions are eroded by the market, more is lost than merely an instinct of responsibility and fellow-feeling. Skills and trades cease to be practised or communicated, leading to lack of mobility and increased dependence. The idea of 'social needs' becomes lost or subsumed under the idea of 'wealth'. Whereas conservatives place responsibility upon the poor themselves for their situation, socialists invest responsibility in an altogether abstract and faceless entity: the community 'as a whole'. Taxation and welfare schemes become a surrogate form of social responsibility in a system in which no one bears responsibility.

Socialist-minded liberals also resemble conservatives in associating vulnerability with a key liberal phenomenon: mobility. Socialists and conservatives approach this idea from different ends, but their assumptions are otherwise remarkably similar. Where individuals are vulnerable it is because they lack the power to alter their situation, to change things for the better. They must be moved out of the path of the considerations which make them vulnerable. Whereas conservatives seek to increase social mobility through the very absence of organization, socialists understand that unstructuredness can itself result in lack of mobility. The achievement of large-scale social mobility requires organization. For conservatives, nothing matters more than the elimination of structures which inhibit freedom. The defeat of this last enemy will allow men to escape all others: surely no one who is the author of his own situation can be afflicted by vulnerabilities? More aware of the enormous range of human vulnerabilities, socialists prefer to put the power of the state behind the effort to mitigate them. It is not individual freedom but distribution that will triumph. The poor are to be lifted out of the path of vulnerability through the wealth of the rich.

Despite these similarities, socialists take a more political view of vulnerability than do conservatives. One might say that in placing responsibility largely in each individual's own hands, conservatives have significantly de-politicized vulnerability. Vulnerability is a political issue only in so far as one must call into question the justification for drawing the public–private division in this way. For the socialist, vulnerabilities are directly, rather than indirectly, politicized. They are part of an ideology to be placed at the heart of politics. Overwhelmingly, socialists wish to *structure* resilience. Equality is the primary consideration: if vulnerabilities cannot be eliminated, they can at least be diluted by being more evenly distributed. Resilience is to be built into the very structure of society. Many forms of vulnerability are therefore theorized as variants of a single form:

'vulnerabilities of scale'. Socialists are less concerned with cardinal measures of vulnerability than with ordinal measures.

Taking a scalar approach to resilience, socialists (like conservatives) blind themselves unnecessarily to aspects of vulnerability that are situational rather than need-based. It is not only lack of money that causes people to become stuck in disadvantageous situations or downward spirals. As the market redefines the needs of the more affluent classes, the demand for certain skills drops, causing problems for those who lack skill-mobility. Family breakdown and instability cause people to become more reliant on their own meagre resources, resulting in lack of opportunity. The ubiquity of the middle-class lifestyle, the inescapable power of advertising, reduce the ability of society to distinguish between 'real' and 'imagined' needs. The result is a market in debt, with the burden falling heaviest upon the least well-off, further reducing their room for manoeuvre. Socialists (at least liberal socialists) do nothing to address these factors, being essentially uninterested in challenging the picture of man as a creature in pursuit of the fulfilment of his desires. What they wish to do is combine this image with a mode of organization that will limit each person's pursuit of his private goals in the name of equality for all. They no longer investigate the causes of social breakdown because they regard it as synonymous with the 'liberal freedom' that they wish to secure for all. They wish only to place man's acquisitive instincts, and his private enterprise, within the scope of a superior organization. The original socialist dream has propagated beyond the confines of 'true' socialism to become the desire of many liberals: the just society, based not upon the just instincts of its citizens (who may pay taxes very reluctantly) but upon the very foundations of the liberal order, the 'basic structure of society' in Rawls's terminology (Rawls 1991, ch. 1).

One could say that Rawls's theory itself resembles a socialism that has given up the class struggle. Informed by powerful instincts of equality, concerned to provide for the least well-off in society, its primary aim is to argue for a fair distribution of 'primary social goods', among which feature prominently: liberty, opportunity, income and wealth. Intended to be unbiased between possible conceptions of the good life, it has nevertheless been suggested that Rawls's theory inherently gives preference to acquisitive or individualistic lifestyles: each of the 'primary' goods is a central constituent of a lifestyle founded upon the accumulation of 'goods' and profit, even if they do not erect barriers to other priorities. Can one say that money and liberty also offer assistance to other forms of life (such as the founding of a spiritual community), even if they are not central to them, and are in this sense 'neutral'? (Simmonds 2008, 67–8). That is perhaps the case, but the centrality of liberty, opportunity and ideals of wealth accumulation actively oppose the rebuilding of a more integrated, close-knit society. The just society will not fetter a man with too many responsibilities: only taxation. The individual will not 'know his place', but create his own. The liberality of Rawls's theory equates to a more honest socialism for socialists who have limited their critiques of capitalism to calls for a wider distribution of the benefits of growth. They fail to address, and even compound, the defining characteristic of the modern citizen: alienation.

It is by being alienated from his fellowmen, more than by being poor, that the individual becomes most vulnerable. Valuable, indeed essential, in so many other ways, it is the market itself that is responsible for this dislocation. This situation will continue so long as market priorities are allowed to become independent of and unfettered by the communities they previously served. The market must be put back into the service of the community to a much greater extent; society must be more cohesive, if people are to become truly capable of facing their vulnerabilities.

The Responsive State

Conservatives and socialists see vulnerability in all too structural terms. Neither sees vulnerability as a natural phenomenon but as something created by the wrong sort of structure. The right structure – or absence of structure – will overcome it. Socialists insist that vulnerability is 'done to us' by the vast and unfeeling middle classes. What better way to deal with it than to limit the wealth and freedom of those classes, thus also broadening them out significantly? Conservatives think of vulnerability as something individuals do to themselves, by failing to exert their talents on the open market. They must use more genius or cunning in finding an acceptable price for their abilities, or pay the price of unemployment.

In adverting to these structural characteristics of resilience, both conservatives and socialists come close to believing that vulnerability has a political solution, through which it can be eliminated. Although it is true that the state's organizational power can affect or limit certain forms of vulnerability (health or environmental conditions for example), it is necessary to maintain sight of the fact that vulnerability is fundamentally an *embodied* experience and not exclusively a structural one. Recipes for the transformation of society into a just political order have not fulfilled their promise. The image offered of the liberal polity by Rawls, and others, is but an idealized distortion of actual conditions, masking the fact that divisions between rich and poor have become more entrenched (Geuss 2005, ch. 2). The dream of socialism itself terminates in the nightmare realities of communism. Within liberal societies, socialist parties will never fulfil their promises because they rely upon middle classes that will never vote taxation upon themselves in the levels required for the realization of the socialist's dreams. At the same time, the dreams of conservatives have been no less unsatisfying. Freed from traditional social customs, individuals did not rise up and claim for themselves the prizes offered by the market. The worst-off did not escape their poverty. The market's invisible hands turned out to be far more powerful and far more capricious in their effect than the hands of either individuals or the government.

It is in this context that Fineman's analysis must be situated. Resisting the conservative tendency to demand the state's withdrawal from the 'private' and 'economic' spheres, she insists upon a more 'responsive' state. But despondent about the limitations of socialist government, its tendency to authoritarianism and stifling bureaucracy, she wishes to advance a more subtle and nuanced, less monolithic, understanding of the state: one based above all on *law* (Fineman 2008, 5–6). The ideologies of the market encourage one to think of institutions such as the family and the corporation, as private entities, handled through private ordering. But one must not forget that such institutions are 'constructed and evolving' and that '[b]oth intimate and economic entities are creatures of the state, in the sense that they are brought into legal existence by the mechanisms of the state' (6). Law determines the boundaries within which such entities are both recognized and entitled to act in society; forms of private ordering are themselves dependent upon contracts that are constituted and controlled by the laws of the state (7). As such, one must recognize that the state is manifested not only in the classical organs of government, but 'through complex institutional arrangements' that are not altogether outside the scope of public authority (6). In themselves potentially unstable, susceptible to corruption and market fluctuations, and prey to a thousand affecting forces, such institutions also exhibit vulnerability, making reliance upon them particularly frightening (13).

In the light of these concerns, and concerns over costs, Western societies have witnessed the progressive withdrawal of the state's responsibility for the functioning of public institutions. Increasingly, the management of public provision in the fields of education, healthcare, energy and other sectors, and essential aspects of social services (such as refuse collection) are carried out by private corporations. Competitive tenders reduce costs for the state, which can no longer afford to supply essential goods and services. Fineman worries that corporate concerns will be less willing to pay attention to the concerns of the vulnerable, responsive first and foremost to the expectations of their own shareholders. Regimes created and administered by private concerns are not of a kind to maximize opportunities for individuals to develop the range of assets and skills they require to become resilient in the face of their vulnerabilities (Fineman 2008, 20). Corporate interests will dominate over the needs of the individual. As private enterprises swallow up the roles traditionally performed by the state, the fate of the individual indeed lies increasingly in 'invisible hands' that he is fundamentally unable to identify, and against which he has no real recourse.

How should one respond to this situation? Fineman is right to suggest that the state's control and its structuring of corporate interests need to become more visible. One will see that the fingers of the state have not truly withdrawn, but have become inactive. Fineman wants to see the state become more active: ensuring to the extent possible that public goods are distributed according to values that are truly social rather than merely corporate (Fineman 2008, 8). In this, she echoes the sentiments of *Rerum novarum* and *Centesimus annus*, wishing to 'make sure that the laws and institutions, the general character and administration of the commonwealth, shall be such as … to realize public well-being and private prosperity' (*Rerum novarum*, s. 32). Both *Rerum novarum* and *Centesimus annus* envisage a far more responsive role for the state in ensuring the distribution of the market's benefits to all in society (see, e.g., *Rerum novarum*, ss. 47–8; *Centesimus annus*, ss. 33–42). The state cannot be excluded from the domain of private contract: under no circumstances must it permit 'unbridled capitalism' to press forward unhindered (*Centesimus annus*, ss. 7–8). The state 'has the duty of watching over the common good and of ensuring that every sector of social life, not excluding the economic one, contributes to achieving that good…' (s. 11).

Can one share in this hope, the hope that the state may find ways to escape the boundaries of the market and establish a more thorough and sensitive regime of equality (Fineman 2008, 20, 23)? Fineman suggests that the state has something distinctive to contribute because it is 'theoretically freed from the market and profit constraints placed on individual industries and businesses' and is thus in a 'superior position [to implement] public values' (8). Can one any longer rely on this independence, even at the theoretical level? Privatization is one option open to governments that can no longer realistically afford to supply public goods and services on the traditional model. It is axiomatic that private providers in areas such as transport, the criminal justice system and infrastructure industries will only enter such markets if they remain free to turn significant profits. Reliant upon the cooperation of large corporations in complex ways, the boundaries within which governments can regulate such industries are not as wide as might be desired. Modern governments more than ever find themselves tied to the success of the economy, including its largest corporations. One can see why certain economists and lawyers assert that 'vulnerability analysis' is no more than a restatement of human rights ideas: given the constraints within which governments operate, significant restrictions upon competition must come primarily from the international rather than the domestic level if the nation is not to lose business, become less competitive, more reliant upon imports and foreign investment, and generally less affluent. Operating ever more in a globalized context, the assumptions of turbo-capitalism are increasingly incapable of being reversed 'unilaterally'.

Structuring Resilience

Vulnerability and resilience are probably best understood when they are detached from politics and placed in a context that is neglected by both left and right versions of liberal politics: civil society. Partha Dasgupta recalled the tendency of Marxism to operate as an elite theory, predominantly employed by intellectuals whose promises turn out to be 'words, words and words, and got lost along the way …' (as cited in Skinner 2002, 5). The impact of Marxism upon the value systems of the poor in Asia and elsewhere has been very limited; there is 'little evidence that the poor householders in rural Asia or Africa are interested in much more than tilling the soil, raising a family and relating to neighbours. These are the central concerns of anyone wishing to live, not merely that of the peasant' (ibid.). But, elsewhere, in societies where communist totalitarianism took hold, civil society was ruthlessly dismantled: the only organization compatible with the 'national security' state is the organization of the state itself. All institutions, from the family to the corporation, must be placed under state control, becoming instruments of 'policy' (Gray 1993b). But the conditions of market capitalism have not been kinder to communities, diminishing their cohesiveness. Successive governments in the West have progressively eliminated those intermediate institutions, especially trades unions, which in modifying or limiting the 'free' operation of market priorities are guilty of 'restrictive practices' (Boyle 1998, 19). Today, the individual 'is often suffocated between two poles represented by the State and the marketplace' (*Centesimus annus*, s. 49).

The predicament of the vulnerable in liberal societies needs to be understood above all by reference to the progressive erosion of civil society. It is not as individuals that vulnerable persons become resilient. Typically, vulnerable persons do not have the internal resources necessary to face or overcome their vulnerabilities. The individualistic aspect of liberal politics, which theorizes the liberal subject as an *ens completum*, limits its horizons to the endless manipulation of the individual's situation. Liberals tend to conceive the relationship between individuals and society in terms of one idea: mobility. Vulnerabilities of both choice and scale are confronted by moving individuals out of their path. Instead, liberals should learn to accept that persons are completed by society. Human beings are indeed social animals. Their resources for dealing with problems of living are not exhausted by their own strength, but possess a social dimension. Liberal politics operates to suppress this dimension, but wiser minds (Aristotle and Saint Augustine for example) perceived that it is the proper role of politics to foster and exalt civil society. The power of vulnerabilities over the vulnerable is finally diminished not by right order alone, but where men learn to be good neighbours.

The encyclical *Rerum novarum* leaves no doubt as to the essential characteristic that is required: *justice*. Economic and civil freedom must be allowed to exist, but under unbridled market prerogatives the essence of this freedom can become 'self-love carried to the point of contempt for God and neighbour' (*Rerum novarum*, s. 17). Individuals must absolutely learn to accept that their self-interests are limited by demands of justice. Where there is no faith in the inclination of individuals to grant justice, an enlargement of the state's interventionist policies is likely to operate to the detriment of both civil and economic freedom. Men will grant only what they are obliged by law to grant; socialist societies are in this sense just as unfeeling as those driven by private enterprise. Civil society manifests justice at the level of deeds which are conditioned not by principles but by love of neighbour, a respect for the dignity of other persons. Self-love must itself be conditioned by love of others. Such love is not of course ecstatic and spontaneous, but requires order: 'recourse ... to societies or boards' such as trades unions and workers' guilds, mutual associations and fraternal societies, and various institutions for welfare and charity (*Rerum novarum*, s. 45). At the close of the nineteenth century, Pope Leo XIII called for such institutions to be run by and according to the principles of men of Christian piety (*Rerum novarum*, s. 53). As the twenty-first century came into view, his successor widened this call: 'intermediate communities' which 'give life to specific networks of solidarity' constitute 'real communities of persons and strengthen the social fabric, preventing society from becoming an anonymous and impersonal mass' (*Centesimus annus*, s. 49). The strengthening of civil society is the work not only of Catholics but of all men, as a shared responsibility (s. 51). In 1991 there was 'a reasonable hope that the many people who profess no religion will also contribute to providing the social question with the necessary ethical foundation' (s. 60).

Popes Leo XIII and John Paul II called for a kind of 'guild capitalism' to replace the turbo-capitalism of modern times, and to dismiss the spectre of Marxist promises to transform society, which 'create utter confusion in the community' (*Rerum novarum*, s. 4). They demand a moderate social and economic freedom, accompanied by moderate levels of state intervention. The state should use its powers only to support the institutions of civil society, to provide them with adequate resources and to ensure their fair operation, sometimes protecting them from the market. But governments should never lose sight of the fact that 'needs are best understood and satisfied by people who are closest to them and who act as neighbours to those in need' (*Centesimus annus*, s. 48). They must not surround protective institutions in red tape and bureaucracy. Above all else, it is the responsibility of civil society to extend its benefits to all men, not simply to a specific class: 'We are not dealing here with man in the "abstract", but with real, "concrete", "historical" man. We are dealing with each individual ...' (s. 53). Like Fineman, the Church calls for a 'responsive' state in conjunction with civil freedom, but the state must respond in the right way. Too excessive a mode of political interference will erode civil society, which requires the freedom to organize itself toward the common good. But neither must the state withdraw too much, leaving fundamental issues of the common good to the realm of private initiative or at the mercy of corporate interests. The needs of justice cannot be met without the state's involvement, but are not capable of systematic integration into society unless the community itself becomes more integrated, more responsive to the needs of others.[2]

What can be drawn from this? The market-driven society famously leads to social fragmentation and disintegration. As jobs and even families become less secure, less permanent, individuals increasingly face their vulnerabilities alone. The rejuvenation of civil society is absolutely necessary. The idea of civil society is the community's own organic structures of responsibility and mutual assistance ('fellow feeling'). Men must rebuild social ties, a sense of civic responsibility or pride in one's community. Above all, justice must come before excessive self-interest. Unfortunately, the free market works against such instincts. Men are fundamentally placed in competition with one another. Declining advantages that are illegitimate or exploitative will not prevent others from pursuing them

---

2   One might contemplate also the striking similarity between Fineman's desire for a wide-ranging reconceptualization of current social arrangements (Fineman 2008, 21 n. 53) and the Church's recognition that genuine relief for the poor and the vulnerable 'may mean making important changes in established lifestyles' (*Centesimus annus*, s. 52).

instead. In so far as people's livelihoods depend on the market, many are literally powerless to avoid such options.[3] In a world in which the market has significantly diminished organic notions of civic responsibility, it falls to the state to regulate interpersonal relationships in a more formal way.

I have suggested that the power of the state to mitigate the effects of the market is much more limited than we would like to admit. Increasingly, it is the demands of the economy that control government rather than vice versa. To some extent trapped by the realities of a globalized economy and the limitations of the ballot box, it lies outside the power of state and citizens to instigate social change on a large scale. One is thrown back on the informal resources of civil society, asking what it is possible to achieve. The Church is correct when it places its faith in 'all people of good will' to do what they can to change things.

But there will always be a considerable disparity between the possibilities that are open to the civil order, and what it actually achieves. It is unrealistic to think that citizens of the liberal order would be willing to give up their privacy and independence in order to feel less vulnerable. Attempts to foster resilience within communities will therefore always be severely limited. But liberals on the left and the right have compounded this problem through their disinterest in a civil order that they have given up trying to direct, devoting their energies instead entirely to the structure of the political order of society. Socialists and conservatives must refocus their attention. They must cease to fight vulnerability through the class struggle or the market. A politics that aims to establish a genuine resilience in its citizens must turn its gaze toward civil society. Its watchword should be neither regulation (as with socialism) nor freedom (as with conservatives), but enablement. Resilience is created and fostered at the level of communities that have taken justice into their hearts.

---

3   Indeed, those whose livelihoods are most vulnerable are least able to adopt an 'ethical' approach to advantages.

Chapter 5
More than Utopia

Morgan Cloud

Utopia and Religion[1]

It is possible to classify Martha Fineman's vulnerability theory[2] as provocative social criticism, but nothing more. To do so underestimates its significance. Fineman's vulnerability theory provides the theoretical justification for transforming social values to enable us to reshape public institutional forms and behaviors (see Fineman 2004, 277). In this chapter I explore this more ambitious quality of Fineman's vulnerability theory by discussing it in the context of the ancient tradition of utopian literature. The best utopian literature invariably offers biting criticism of the authors' societies, but it does more. The most significant utopian writers challenge the legitimacy of their societies' fundamental values. They imagine worlds different from their own, better worlds organized around values that transform the behavior of institutions and individuals. Anyone familiar with Fineman's vulnerability theory will recognize that this could also be a précis of her work.

To explore the relationship between the tradition of utopian literature and Fineman's vulnerability theory, I begin with Thomas More's *Utopia*, one of that genre's most influential books, and one that offers provocative comparisons to Fineman's work. For half a millennium, *Utopia* has been studied and embraced by radicals and reactionaries, atheists and religious zealots, philosophers and fools. The book has received sustained interest in part because More was a subtle but superb stylist; in part because of its biting critique of English society and institutions; in part because of its fantastic yet fascinating portrayal of a country providing a better life for its people than existed in any known society. It is More's vision of an "imagined place or state of things in which everything is perfect" (*New Oxford American Dictionary* 2005) that has had an "enormous influence … on men's minds … not only on socialist Utopians of the nineteenth century … but on men of its own time, that is, the sixteenth century." By the middle of the twentieth century, *Utopia* was adopted by thinkers from across the spectra of social and political theory:

---

1   I am indebted to Christina Sladoje for her outstanding research assistance and to Steve Tipton and Paul Zwier for their wealth of knowledge and helpful insights.

2   This chapter refers to Fineman's ideas as "vulnerability theory" for stylistic reasons only. Many other theories of vulnerability, applied to myriad topics, abound in the world. They are excluded from my use of the phrase in this chapter.

> Many claimed it: Catholics and Protestants, medievalists and moderns, socialists and communists; and a well-known historian has recently turned it over to the Nazis. Methods of legitimating claims vary widely, although most are necessarily based upon ideological interpretation of More's book. Over the past generation, however, in all of the welter of claim and counter-claim, one single interpretation has emerged to dominate the field ... "the Roman Catholic" interpretation of Utopia. (Elliott 1992, 181)

The Roman Catholic interpretation is useful and unavoidable. In *Utopia*, More rejected the dominant social, political, and economic theories of early sixteenth-century England and instead imagined an ideal society based upon universal religious truths. More's interpretation of Christian theology was the source of these universals, which he asserted were consonant with right reason, true pleasure, and justice—as realized in his Utopian society. When outsiders finally brought Christianity to their remote island, many Utopians embraced it as a religion that embodied the values that already guided life in their pre-Christian society (More 1992, 73). We learn this from More's storyteller, the explorer who brought Christianity to the island.

The storyteller was a man named Raphael Hythloday, a fictional crew member on most of Amerigo Vespucci's voyages to the New World. During his final voyage, Hythloday decided not to return to Europe with Vespucci, instead remaining in foreign lands to continue his travels of discovery, which eventually took him to Utopia, an ancient island country so isolated that it had been unknown in Europe throughout history (More 1992, 33). Hythloday recounts the story of his travels in dialogues with characters, some of whom were named after real Englishmen. The primary dialogist is named More. Hythloday's description of Utopia surprises, perhaps even shocks, More and the others. The Utopian economic system caused the greatest consternation.

Utopia was a communist paradise, and its economic structure was an essential element in making Utopia the best of all possible worlds. Private property and money both were abolished. No classes distinguished by wealth—or the lack of it—existed. Eliminating idle upper classes who lived unproductive lives meant that Utopians produced more food and other necessaries of life than they needed to survive. Universal social, economic, and productive equality generated a surfeit of goods shared by everyone. In such an economy of surplus and sharing, money was unnecessary.

Communism was central to the success of Utopia. Hythloday argued with a skeptical More that life in Utopia—when compared to other countries—teaches that

> as long as you have private property, and as long as cash money is the measure of all things, it is really not possible for a nation to be governed justly or happily. For justice cannot exist where all the best things in life are held by the worst

citizens; nor can anyone be happy where property is limited to a few, since those few are always uneasy and the many are utterly wretched.

[...]

Thus I am wholly convinced that unless private property is entirely done away with, there can be no fair or just distribution of goods, nor can mankind be happily governed. As long as private property remains, by far the largest and best part of mankind will be oppressed by a heavy and inescapable burden of cares and anxieties. (More 1992, 28)

Like Fineman today, More imagined a society that was better because its institutions ensured a more equal distribution of assets that ameliorated the burdens and anxieties suffered by everyone, particularly the disadvantaged members of society. But Utopia's economic theories were not the sole reason it was perfect; so were its foundational values. Its communist economic model conformed both with natural justice and the divine justice preached by Jesus Christ. When they learned about Christ and his teachings, many Utopians embraced Christianity because "Christ had encouraged his disciples to practice community of goods, and that among the truest groups of Christians, the practice still prevails" (More 1992, 73). The principles upon which Utopia was based mirrored the true religion of Christ and not the corrupted Christianity practiced in Europe.[3]

The 500 years since More wrote *Utopia* have witnessed repeated failures of communist societies in Europe and the Americas. Many have been small, agrarian communities. Some have been nation states. This history is one obvious source of the commonly held idea that utopian schemes for social improvement like More's are "impossibly ideal, visionary, idealistic" (*Shorter Oxford English Dictionary* 2007) and doomed to fail in the real world.

More's mythical Utopia was not so fragile. It was the most stable of societies, thriving for millennia after King Utopus founded it. Utopia survived in part because its social institutions aggressively regulated and channeled citizens' actions until they conformed in every detail with the values of social equality, justice, and personal responsibility. Unlike most actual communal utopian experiments, fictional Utopia thrived because of the remarkable virtues of its people, virtues that were inculcated, enhanced, and reinforced by Utopia's social institutions.

First among their virtues was work. Utopians were superb and disciplined workers. One occupation was mandatory for all—farming—although some people labored in the fields for only a small portion of their working lives (More 1992, 32). In addition to farming, everyone learned a trade "such as wool-working, linen-making, masonry, metal-work, or carpentry" (37). The Utopians' work

---

3   More 1992, at 27 ("But preachers, like the crafty fellows they are, have found that men would rather not change their lives to conform to Christ's rule, and so ... they have accommodated his teachings to the way men live, as if it were a leaden yardstick ...").

ethic—enforced by official pressure when necessary—meant that "no one sits around in idleness and … everyone works hard at his trade" (ibid.). As a result, Utopians actually worked fewer hours per day than did residents of England and Europe. Because everyone labored diligently at productive labor,

> no one has to exhaust himself with endless toil from early morning to late at night, as if he were a beast of burden. Such wretchedness, really worse than slavery, is the common lot of workmen in all countries except Utopia. Of the day's twenty-four hours, the Utopians devote only six to work. (ibid.)

Utopians had free time each day to devote to activities other than work, but even in recreation they were disciplined and productive. Each person could decide what to do during the specific hours prescribed by the society for recreation, as long as "he does not waste them in roistering or sloth, but uses them busily in some occupation that pleases him. Generally these periods are devoted to intellectual activity." Yes, when they were not laboring in the fields, Utopians preferred to improve their minds or increase their skills rather than waste time on frivolous forms of recreation. For example, Utopians had "established the custom of arising before dawn to attend lectures" (ibid.). In the evenings, they devoted precisely one hour to recreation, typically devoted to some productive activity like gardening in good weather, or to playing music or other uplifting activity in bad (ibid.).

Utopians did not waste time with recreational vices common throughout history. "[T]here is no chance to loaf or kill time …; no taverns, or alehouses, or brothels; no chances for corruption … . Because they live in the full view of all, they are bound to be either working at their usual trades, or enjoying their leisure" (ibid., 45). Not surprisingly, socially unproductive games like "gambling with dice" were not permitted (ibid., 38).

Some critics have argued that More intended *Utopia* to be a satire (Ackroyd 1998, 174–6) and the historical record suggests that More and his humanist friends may have engaged in a tongue-in-cheek "conspiracy" to fool credulous readers into believing that Hythloday's stories were true (Adams in More 1992, 108–33). Regardless of More's actual intentions, his portrayal of Utopians lends itself to parody. Although Utopia was an authoritarian state, it was inhabited over the millennia by the most virtuous, sober, well-behaved people in history—real or imagined.

Their lives were ordered and regulated and endlessly productive. Like Mary Poppins, they were "practically perfect in every way." Imagining what living in Utopia would actually be like, I am reminded of Mark Twain's description of the biblical heaven: "[T]he human being's heaven has been thought out and constructed upon an absolute definite plan; and that this plan is, that it shall contain, in labored detail, each and every imaginable thing that is repulsive to a man, and not a single thing he likes!" (Twain 1909).

More's caricature of an ideal citizenry is one source of the idea that utopias are idealistic and unrealistic fantasies.[4] More's communist Utopia thrived where others failed because its people exhibited virtues rare even among individuals in the actual world, and even more rarely exhibited by a country's entire population. It is not that people lack the capacity to live selflessly and for the collective good. Many individuals exhibit those qualities, at least for portions of their lives. But to claim that the population of a country can live according to those values day after day, life after life, century after century, asks us to ignore what we know of the actual world. From this perspective, it is easy to understand how some might view More's portrayal of Utopians as an elaborate spoof.[5]

But I think another interpretation is more consistent with the book's contents, and with what we know of More himself. *Utopia* presents More's attempt to imagine a society in which the values he prizes most are embodied in its institutions and its people's behaviors. More's imaginative recreation of the world revealed the society in which he would have lived had he possessed the godlike power to create it.

Some of the clues are obvious. More the author concludes the book by having the narrator More summarize his responses to Hythloday's account of Utopia:

> [T]hough he was a man of unquestioned learning, and highly experienced in the ways of the world, I cannot agree with everything he said. Yet I confess there are many things in the Commonwealth of Utopia that I wish our own country would imitate—though I don't really expect it will. (More 1992, 85)

The message is straightforward. More the realist recognizes, with obvious regret, that England will not become Utopia. More the religious idealist wishes that his imagined better world would become real. One suspects that he chose the dialogic literary form to protect himself from just those charges—that his criticisms of England and his proposals for change reflected his true hopes and beliefs. If confirmed, these charges amounted to treason and heresy, crimes punishable by torture and death in the sixteenth century.

By having the fictional Hythloday explain how another land was superior to England, More the author distanced himself from criticism of his home country, then increased the distance by having the narrator More object to some of Hythloday's claims (More 1992, 108). Within the dialogue, More rejected arguments that private property must be abolished before "mankind [can] be happily governed"

---

4   Fineman herself uses the term to connote this idea: "the current politics in the United States are such that substantive equality arguments are likely to be *banished to the realm of utopian visions*" (Fineman 2003, 227; emphasis supplied).

5   Perhaps most pointedly, More was introduced to Hythloday in Belgium by Peter Giles, a fellow humanist and friend with whom More corresponded about *Utopia*, and who may have participated in a ruse claiming that *Utopia* was a travelogue, not a myth. See Adams 1992, 109–12, 123–5.

because in a private property regime "by far the largest and best part of mankind will be oppressed," arguing instead that individual pursuit of economic gain in a world of scarce resources was essential (ibid., 28):

> "But I don't see it that way," I replied. "It seems to me that men cannot possibly live where all things are in common. How can there be plenty of commodities where every man stops working? The hope of gain will not spur him on; he will rely on others, and become lazy. If man is driven by want of something to produce it, and yet cannot legally protect what he has gained, what can follow but continual bloodshed and turmoil, especially when respect for magistrates and their authority has been lost? I for one cannot conceive of authority existing among men who are equal to one another in every respect." (More 1992, 29)

These are arguments familiar to anyone living in a private property regime, which Hythloday acknowledges. But Hythloday's response also provides another clue to More's real purpose:

> "I'm not surprised," said Raphael, "that you think of it in this way, since you have no idea, or only a false idea, of such a state. But you should have been with me in Utopia, and seen with your own eyes their manners and customs as I did—for I lived there more than five years and would never have left, it had not been to make that new world known to others. If you had seen them, you would frankly confess that you had never seen a people so well governed as they are." (ibid.)

This passage could be nothing more than a literary character's script, but I think it is something else. Throughout the book Hythloday's role is to give voice to More's vision of the ideal society. Here Hythloday expresses the utopian's vision: *I have seen it!* Because he has. Utopia was the product of More's imagination. He transcribed what he saw when he imagined a just society embodying his Christian ideals. More was more than a satirist here; he was a social critic offering a radical vision of a better society.

This passage suggests another motive, as well. Having "seen with [his] own eyes" the Utopians "manners and customs," Hythloday, like a Christian missionary, was impelled to leave a society where he wished to remain to spread the good word, "to make that new world known to others." More was not merely imagining how the world could be remade; he was proselytizing a message of reform and salvation.

When contemplating whether More intended not only to provoke discourse but also to incite social change, it is worth remembering that More wrote at a time when the prospect of finding unique societies in remote places was not a fantasy for Europeans; it was an exciting new reality. More was born into the last generation of educated Europeans who came of age before fifteenth-century European explorers reached the new lands of the Western Hemisphere. More was fifteen when Columbus returned from his first voyage to the New World, and in the following decades

European explorers had repeatedly sailed west across the Atlantic and returned with reports of magnificent and terrifying places inhabited by unknown peoples, living according to exotic customs, mores, and rules. In the early years of European discovery, nothing could have stimulated the imaginations of Europeans more than fantasizing about these remote and unknown lands. It is far from implausible to imagine More could conjure up a society separated from the history and the sins of Europe not merely as a metaphor but also with the hope that, somehow, his dream could become real, if only because others believed that it was real.

Some of More's contemporaries did, in fact, believe that Utopia existed, that Hythloday had lived there for five years, and More was only reporting the facts of another expedition of discovery (Adams in More 1992, 108–33). Most surprising, perhaps, was that the arguments for abolishing private property and establishing a communist social, political, and economic regime received favorable responses from numerous educated, conservative, and privileged readers (ibid., 115–22).

Perhaps More viewed these readers as fools, unable to detect a good joke when they read it, but perhaps not. Recall More's wistful concluding sentence: "I confess there are many things in the Commonwealth of Utopia that I wish our own country would imitate—though I don't really expect it will" (More 1992, 85). Was More suggesting that such a society was possible, if not in England, then elsewhere? We do not know, but if ever a fantasy like Utopia could be taken seriously, it would have been Europe in the early sixteenth century.

I offer these speculations to raise the possibility that More was contemplating real solutions to the terrible conditions suffered by the poor and the dispossessed in England, conditions that inspired *Utopia*.[6] Most tellingly for this chapter, he was not concerned with the problems of the wealthy, the titled, the landed, but instead with conditions that made most Britons vulnerable to poverty, injury, disease, starvation, and despair. These conditions were made worse by the social, economic, and political injustice inherent in English society. Large numbers of people were executed for theft but

> [s]imple theft is not so great a crime that it ought to cost a man his head, yet no punishment however severe can withhold a man from robbery when he has no other way to eat [but] it would be much better to enable every man to earn his own living, instead of being driven to the awful necessity of stealing and then dying for it. (More 1992, 10)

Equally unjust was the landed aristocracy's mistreatment of their tenants. Hythloday offered a lengthy and detailed criticism of the economic, social, and legal injustices of English society, particularly those produced by the enclosure

---

6   On the feasibility of More's proposals, it is noteworthy that one "remarkable thing about Utopia is the extent to which it adumbrates social and political reforms which have either been actually carried into practice, or which have come to be regarded as very practical politics" (Chambers 1992, 137).

movement. Indolent and self-indulgent landowners—nobles, the gentry, and even the clergy—raised their tenants' rents to exorbitant levels (More 1992, 137). When even these rents failed to satisfy their greed, they enclosed "every acre for pasture" to raise sheep for the lucrative wool markets. Not satisfied by taking the land traditionally used by the lower classes for farming, some even destroyed the tenants' homes and villages and claimed that land as well (ibid.):

> Thus one greedy, insatiable glutton … may enclose many thousand acres of land within a single hedge. The tenants are dismissed and compelled, by trickery or brute force or constant harassment, to sell their belongings. By hook or by crook these miserable people—men, women, husbands, wives, orphans, widows, parents with little children, whole families (poor but numerous, since framing requires many hands)—are forced to move out. They leave the only homes familiar to them, and they can find no place to go. Since they cannot afford to wait for a buyer, they sell for a pittance all their household goods …. When that little money is gone (and it's soon spent in wandering from place to place), what remains for them but to steal, and so be hanged …or to wander and beg? …. They would be glad to work, but they can find no one who will hire them. (More 1992, 12)

The tragic consequences of English inequality supplied the rationale for Utopia, a society designed to eradicate as many of the horrors of English life as could be done by changing social, political, and economic structures, rules, and incentives. From this perspective, it is not farfetched to view *Utopia* not solely as fantasy, but also as an attempt to imagine social reforms for the real world. The economic organization, in particular, was designed to supplant a world in which after

> a barren year of failed harvests, when many thousands of men have been carried off by hunger, … if … the barns of the rich were searched, I dare say positively enough grain would be found in them to have saved the lives of all those who died from starvation and disease, if it had been divided equally among them. Nobody really need have suffered from a bad harvest at all. (More 1992, 83)

This begins to appear to be less a utopian fantasy than an attempt to imagine how to remake social institutions and values to solve problems inherent in More's own society. His diagnoses and remedies both anticipate ideas and arguments upon which Fineman's vulnerability theory rests.

Utopia and Reality

Fineman's writings developing her vulnerability theory are more straightforward than More's utopian tract. She does not use fictive dialogues or mythical islands to obscure her personal beliefs or the practical goals of her work. Fineman's policy goals are unambiguous:

> To richly theorize a concept of vulnerability is to develop a more complex subject around which to build social policy and law; this new complex subject can be used to redefine and expand current ideas about state responsibility toward individuals and institutions. In fact, I argue that the vulnerable subject must replace the autonomous and independent asserted in the liberal tradition. Far more representative of actual lived experience and the human condition, the vulnerable subject should be at the center of our political and theoretical endeavors. The vision of the state that would emerge in such an engagement would be both more responsive to and responsible for the vulnerable subject, a reimagining that is essential if we are to attain a more equal society than currently exists in the United States. (Fineman 2008, 1–2)

Even this succinct summary reveals similarities with More's utopian project, similarities that become more apparent when Fineman develops her thesis. First, like More, Fineman begins by reimagining how social institutions can be redesigned to create a more just society. Second, Fineman's imagined just society, like More's, offers comfort, security, and opportunity for its vulnerable members by eliminating entrenched advantages that benefit a privileged minority. Utopia was an egalitarian society. Much of Fineman's work is devoted to demonstrating that vulnerability theory can lead us to a better society in which the state and its institutions are responsible for ensuring substantive equality for everyone. Third, like More, Fineman's better society requires transformation of the fundamental values by which we envision the just society and the successful individual. Finally, like More, she imagines a society that emphasizes our interdependence, not our autonomy. I will discuss each of these elements of vulnerability theory, but first I want to point out fundamental distinctions between the utopian projects of these two authors.

First is the issue of genre. Perhaps the most popular utopian literature is fiction, and it is possible to conceive of utopian literature as consisting solely of famous fictional works like More's. Obviously, Fineman's work does not qualify for inclusion in that category. But if we use the more accurate and comprehensive concept of literature—"writings"—then Fineman's work fits comfortably within the extensive library of nonfictional utopian treatises. We may be most familiar with utopian fiction, but examples of its nonfiction manifestations are plentiful and important. It is possible to imagine an ideal society situated in reality, and not in myth.

Another noteworthy difference is that Fineman's ideas do not rest upon religious faith, and certainly not on More's sixteenth-century Catholicism. Her theories rest instead upon secularized values including justice, fairness, and empathy. Like More, she engages in the essential utopian task of imagining how the world could be different, but, rather than turn to theology for inspiration, Fineman's work is rooted in values and methods common to contemporary critical theory. For example, one of Fineman's self-imposed missions is to expose post-Enlightenment values of autonomy, self-sufficiency, and market efficiency as ideological myths that obstruct accurate understanding of the world.[7] Like a theologian explaining sin and its sources, this is a basic task for a critical theorist:

> Much of critical theory—from Marx and Engels to Althusser and Barthes—has equated ideology with *false consciousness* .... In order to disclose our social reality it was first deemed necessary to *expose our ideological fantasies.* One of the first steps in such disclosure was to demystify the ways in which ideology alienates human consciousness by attributing the origin of value to some illusory absolute outside the human. (Kearney 2004, 75)

Fineman attacks "illusory absolutes" like the Lockean "philosophy of liberal individualism" and the "liberal subject" who embodies that ideal, two foundational conceptions in the social and political traditions of the United States (Fineman 2008). Fineman reports accurately that this Lockean

> liberal subject informs our economic, legal, and political principles. It is indispensable to the *prevailing ideologies of autonomy, self-sufficiency, and personal responsibility*, through which society is conceived as constituted by self-interested individuals with the capacity to manipulate and manage their independently acquired and overlapping resources. (Fireman 2008, 10)

To establish the primacy of the vulnerability model and its related concept of dependency, Fineman first must demystify these post-Enlightenment ideals as inaccurate depictions of reality that harm individuals and society. The "vulnerable subject" will not replace the "liberal subject" as the organizing principle for our social and political institutions until these dominant values are delegitimized, or at least eroded. Fineman's most important task is to establish that vulnerability is the better device for explaining human existence and for constructing a just society.

This is the point where Fineman's work transcends mere social criticism. Her concepts of vulnerability and the vulnerable subject may be part of a utopian reimagining of the world, but they offer a succinct and remarkably practical model for radical reorganization of American society. Eschewing More's fictions, Fineman focuses on this place, the United States. Her imagined utopian society will not be in some remote location; it will not be at the margins of human life. Her better society will be this one remade. Recall how Fineman defines the scope of her project: "a reimagining ... *to attain a more equal society than currently exists in the United States*' (Fineman 2008, 2). As we will see, her vision of that society is utopian, but there can be no doubt it is focused on the heart of America.

---

7   More similarly argued that Utopia's just society rested upon mutual dependence, not individual autonomy. After More the narrator tried to justify basing a society on "market efficiency," Hythloday rebutted these arguments by protesting that he would not have believed communism would be so successful had he not seen it with his own eyes (More 1992, 29).

Fineman argues with devastating clarity why the universality of human vulnerability dictates that our dominant ideology of individual autonomy must be replaced. Her construction of vulnerability as both universal and particular provides a powerful secular model for reconstructing a society that extols individual acquisitiveness and control of social goods into one that thrives because its forms and norms rest on notions of interdependency.

Vulnerability provides a powerful mechanism for reordering social values and society because it arises

> from our embodiment, which carries with it the ever-present possibility of harm, injury, and misfortune from mildly adverse to catastrophically devastating events, whether accidental, intentional, or otherwise. Individuals can attempt to lessen the risk or mitigate the impact of such events, but they cannot eliminate their possibility. Understanding vulnerability begins with the realization that many such events are ultimately beyond human control. (Fineman 2008, 9)

The core of her argument rests upon this undeniably accurate insight—that we live under the constant threat of harm. Vulnerability is not our only reality, but it is one shared by all who are born. We all face the ultimate experience of vulnerability—we all die. And before that, everyone faces the threat of physical damage from injury or disease. Our physical existence is constantly at risk from

> disease, epidemics, resistant virus, or other biologically-based catastrophes. Our bodies are also vulnerable to other forces in our physical environment: There is the constant possibility that we can be injured and undone by errant weather systems, such as those that produce flood, drought, famine, and fires. These are "natural" disasters beyond our individual control to prevent. (Fineman 2010, 267)

Because of its universal nature and the costs it imposes on us individually and collectively, human vulnerability is a logically powerful heuristic device for social organization. Vulnerability, particularly of the poor and dispossessed, served as a fundamental principle for More's *Utopia*, of course. His distress about the precarious lives of most Britons helped motivate him to create that imaginary world. Fineman shares that ideal of organizing a society that offers support and security to its most vulnerable people, those possessing the fewest coping resources. But focusing on the most vulnerable people opens the door for the potent political objection that vulnerability is not universal, it is experienced only by some people, at some points in their lives, and many of these individuals are members of politically unpopular and stigmatized groups. Fineman addresses this objection by adding a second powerful element to her theory.

Vulnerability is universal, but it also is particular. Although all humans are vulnerable,

> [b]ecause we are positioned differently within a web of economic and
> institutional relationships, our vulnerabilities range in magnitude and potential
> at the individual level. [H]uman vulnerability is also particular; it is experienced
> uniquely by each of us and this experience is greatly influenced by the quality
> and quantity of resources we possess or can command. (Fineman 2008, 10; see
> also Fineman 2010, 263–4, 266)

This definition of vulnerability, as universal and particular, serves several
instrumental purposes for Fineman. Its universal nature supplies a grand theory
of human existence that challenges the hegemony of the "autonomy myth" and
also justifies Fineman's earlier work offering in its place a *dependency* model
for organizing society (Fineman 2004, 277). By recognizing that dependency is
the result of universal vulnerability, Fineman's theory washes away the stigma
associated with dependency in a culture that exalts self-sufficiency. It rebuts claims
minimizing the significance of dependency because it is temporary (childhood),
episodic (disability caused by injury or disease, followed by recovery), or
experienced only by some people, at least at any point in time. Because all humans
are vulnerable, all have at least the potential to become dependent, and in fact all
humans are dependent on others at points in their lives—childhood being only the
most obvious example.

Vulnerability's *universality* makes it an powerful concept for social organization,
but its *particularity* fuels Fineman's arguments for reconceiving our social values
and institutions to support the poor, the weak, the powerless, and the despised,
just as More imagined happened in Utopia. Fineman argues, for example, that our
commitment to the ideal of the liberal subject has produced theories of equality
and equal protection too "weak … to correct the disparities in economic and social
wellbeing among various groups in our society …. It does not provide a framework
for challenging existing allocations of resources and power" (Fineman 2008, 3).
Vulnerability theory does provide such a framework for social reform.

Individuals possess different abilities, of course, but Fineman focuses upon
the power of social institutions to distribute assets—physical (material goods,
wealth, and property), human (education and healthcare), and social (networks
of relationships) assets (Fineman 2010, 271–2). By arguing that the state must be
actively involved in distributing these assets, Fineman rejects the political ideal
of a restrained state that allows individuals to succeed and fail on their own. Just
as More demystified the economic and political structures in England, Fineman
demystifies the institutions and values that support the restrained state.

The fact that people "are positioned differently within a web of economic
and institutional relationships" means that, to some extent, the game is rigged
(Fineman 2010, 10). "Privileges and disadvantages accumulate across systems and
can combine to create effects that are more devastating or more beneficial than the
weight of each separate part" (ibid., 15). One inevitable result is that "systems of
power and privilege … interact to produce webs of advantages and disadvantages"
(ibid., 16). A person's "resilience in the face of vulnerability" depends in no small

part on the extent to which she has accumulated (perhaps inherited) physical, human, and social assets (ibid., 14).

The robust concept of equality Fineman advocates demands that we do not simply accept as inevitable that our institutions must continue to distribute assets according to the values currently dominant in our culture. At least to the extent that state authority is required for the creation and ongoing operation of institutions—as is true with corporations, schools, and hospitals—then the state must insure that these entities distribute assets in ways consistent with the public values she advocates, like equality and justice, rather than simply permit actions driven by the private values, like the profit motive, to dictate how distributions are carried out. The responsive state must replace the restrained state.

This means that the state and its institutions no longer would acquiesce in unequal distributions of these "public" assets, so that some are disadvantaged and others are privileged. The responsive state would be responsible for overcoming "existing systemic inequalities" resulting from the actions of its asset-conferring institutions (Fineman 2010, 272). The responsive state would provide medical care for all who needed it, just like More's sixteenth-century Utopia, where "the sick are carefully tended, and nothing is neglected in the way of medicine or diet which might cure them. Everything is done to mitigate the pain of those who are suffering from incurable diseases."[8]

This example suggests yet again that it is not unfair to conclude that More's attention was directed to the real world in which he lived, both in his critique of his society and even in his proposed recreation of society to better serve the needs of its most vulnerable subjects. No conjecture is required when we examine Fineman's writings. Her goal is not merely to imagine a society that cares better for its people; it is to change the place where she lives, now. Ironically, the primary obstacle to achieving that goal may be another universal for our species—human nature.

Utopia and Human Nature

Many would accept the derisive characterization of a utopia as a place inhabited by exemplary people "where few of us would feel quite happy; yet we go on using the word 'Utopia' to signify an easy-going paradise, whose only fault is that it is too happy and ideal to be realized" (Chambers 1992, 137). It is reasonable to conclude

---

8   More 1992, *supra* note 3 at 60. People suffering in agony from an incurable condition are urged to commit suicide by family, friends, the Senate, and the priests, "who are interpreters of God's will which ensures that it will be a holy and pious act." The primary purpose is to ease incurable suffering, but in a society devoted to interdependence and social responsibility, these advisors "remind him that he is now ... a burden to himself and to others ..." The decision rested entirely with the patient, however, who continued to receive care even though he had become a nonproductive social burden.

that the architect of such a plan must be an optimist about human nature. Who but an optimist would propose that an entire people could live lives of probity, order, decency, and modesty, without desiring to acquire personal property, in an ordered, secure, and supportive society?

I think this critique misunderstands More and the concept of human nature underlying *Utopia*. The book reveals that More was a pessimist about human nature, and not merely because he doubted that Utopian reforms would be adopted in his England. The perfect world he imagined limited individual freedom and required submission to society's commands. Utopia was an authoritarian society relying on strict rules to channel human behavior into socially acceptable forms. Utopia prescribed what work people did, where they lived and when they lived there, what time they ate dinner, and when they were allowed an hour of free time. False pleasures like gambling, drinking, and idleness were prohibited, and constant monitoring of each person's behavior ensured that they maintained tidy lives of muted conformity.

These constraints were necessary because people are inherently flawed—burdened with the original sins of Adam and Eve and the "mark" of their son Cain (Marius 1984, 166). This was the true import of More's Christian worldview.[9] In his world, Christ and the Church might save people from their sins, and complying with the rules of right reason and proper behavior might do the same in Utopia. But in both settings rigid institutional rules and punishments were needed to rein in the sinful nature of humankind.

If More had been an optimist about our human nature, those fortunate enough to live in his perfect society would have shunned sin, crime, or faithless conduct. But even Utopia was burdened with divorce, adultery, heresy, and criminal acts which could trigger harsh penalties. And criminal liability was not limited to the most heinous acts, or to *malum in se* crimes. A Utopian became a criminal by leaving "his district without permission" (More 1992, 45). When he was captured, he was "brought back as a runaway, and severely punished. If he is bold enough to try it a second time, he is made a slave" (ibid.). Utopians had to stay in their assigned districts to make it easy for the community to call on them to perform their assigned work for the commonweal. People who indulged in unregulated travel could not be found, allowing them to shirk their obligations to the collective. This was a crime against the society's well-being; it was a crime that Utopia would not tolerate.

Utopia's most significant limitation on freedom of thought and belief had similar instrumental functions. More has been praised for imagining a country that embraced religious toleration, where no state religion was established and where people were free to pursue and arrive at their own religious destinations (More 1992, 72–3). After King Utopus conquered the island and imposed his

---

9   One commentator has noted that "More simply did not believe that all the evil men do can be ascribed to the economic arrangements of society ... More's pessimism was ineradicable because it was part and parcel of his Christian faith" (Hexter 1992, 148).

ideas of the good society on its people, he "left the whole matter open, allowing each individual to choose what he would believe," with one noteworthy limitation (ibid., 74–5). "The only exception he made was a positive and strict law against any person who should sink so far below the dignity of human nature as *to think that the soul perishes with the body, or that the universe is ruled by mere chance, rather than divine providence*" (ibid., 75, emphasis added).

Like the rules requiring people to remain in their home districts, this religious restriction served an instrumental function. "Who can doubt that a man who has nothing to fear but the law, and no hope of life beyond the grave, will do anything he can to evade his country's laws by craft or break them by violence, in order to gratify his own private greed" (ibid.). Fear of punishment for eternity is needed to force people to behave properly on earth. Without fear of eternal unpleasantness, apparently everyone will violate laws, sometimes by violence, simply to satisfy their "private greed."

This was not a scheme that an optimist about human nature would devise, particularly for a society offering the greatest physical security and religious liberty that More could imagine. But Utopia's perfection resulted from the imposition of rules, not from individual freedom. Even when he imagined the ideal society, More concluded that some people were so flawed that they had to be controlled.

Social critics are often cynics, and anyone reading Fineman's *The Autonomy Myth* (Fineman 2004) with its extensive catalogue of the defects in American ideals and the damage caused in their name might consider her a pessimist about the inherent nature of people. By arguing for a more activist "responsive state," Fineman inevitably countenances the expansion of government authority. Like More's utopian schemes, her proposals would lead toward an authoritarian state. By placing faith in authoritarian policies and structures rather than in individual freedom, Fineman, like More, could be revealing a pessimistic attitude about human nature.

Fineman is aware of the criticism that her proposals could produce an autocratic state, but offers only a cursory—and rather utopian—response. She asks her readers to open their minds to—to imagine—the possibility of a non-authoritarian responsive state (Fineman 2010, 274).

Fineman's decision to sidestep this issue could have a number of explanations, and the one most relevant here is that, unlike More, Fineman is a human nature optimist. She does not need to address this issue because she believes that people can create activist, responsive states that are not authoritarian. She benefits, of course, from living in a constitutional democracy where ultimate power ostensibly rests with the people and not with a hereditary aristocracy. She benefits from living in a society where she can publish controversial ideas without fearing she will be subjected to anything more than criticism from those who disagree. She need not camouflage her personal views with fictions, and it may well be that had he written in this setting More would have appeared to be more of an optimist than was possible within an authoritarian sixteenth-century monarchy. It could be that living in a constitutional democracy makes the difference. Whatever the cause, close examination of Fineman's proposals suggests that optimism about human nature undergirds her work.

Fineman's optimism about human nature is confirmed by her belief that people will read her writings, have the capacity to understand her theories, have the intelligence to agree with them, and possess the commitment to social justice needed to bring them to fruition. More's Utopians did not create their ideal world, their conquering founder King Utopus did. Without him, they would not have adopted their operative values, implemented them with social rules and institutions, or even have completed practical tasks, like planning their cities. Fineman does not expect a great monarch to create a better world; she expects that the people can and will act to achieve that end.

Here is how she imagines such a people-driven reform process would happen:

> The realization that disadvantage is produced independent of racial and gender bias in many—but of course not all—instances provides an important political tool. Mobilizing around the concept of shared, inevitable vulnerability may allow us to more easily build coalitions among those who have not benefitted as fully as others from current societal organization. If we begin to operate from this perspective, institutional arrangements will be the targets of protest and political mobilizations, and interest groups need not be organized around differing identities. (Fineman 2010, 15)

Only a person optimistic about human nature would imagine that this combination of intellectual understanding, sustained and effective action, and self-interested altruism can be forged into a political movement capable of reinventing our society's institutions and its foundational values, stories, and myths. Fineman's belief that people can and will comprehend, organize, act, and ultimately prevail over the existing systems is the core of her proposal for implementing her ideas. This optimistic view of human nature may turn out to be an essential weakness in Fineman's theory.

The problem is not with her conception of vulnerability as a universal element of human existence. After studying her arguments, no honest reader could disagree with that claim. Rather the problem appears in her discussion of the competing values, myths, and theories she wants to replace. Her arguments underestimate their significance, and therefore their power, as elements of human nature.

Unlike vulnerability, which is "universal, inevitable, enduring aspect of the human condition" (Fineman 2008, 8), Fineman declares that the competing theory of autonomy "is not an inherent human characteristic, but must be cultivated by a society" (Fineman 2010, 260). Fineman contrasts her core concepts—vulnerability, equality, dependence—with those that she challenges—which I will refer to as collectively as independence or autonomy—by treating the former as universal attributes of human experience and the latter as socially constructed, arbitrary cultural phenomena. She argues that we should and can abandon our socially constructed values and replace them with universal realities. It is not too difficult to imagine that many people would willingly abandon culturally created, arbitrary values in order to organize our society according to the demands of our universally shared vulnerability.

The problem is that the concepts Fineman challenges are not just cultural innovations. They, too, can be considered universal in human nature, albeit in ways that differ from vulnerability. Consider autonomy; unquestionably, its American form is socially constructed, as are the forms it takes in other cultures. But that is the point; the drive for independence emerges in cultures around the world because it is a fundamental part of human nature. Just as most of us need (and desire) connections with society, its institutions, and its people, most of us also have some level of need for freedom from the constraints all societies impose.

It may be that vulnerability is more universal in human experience and human nature than is the need for autonomy. Virtually everyone becomes sick and suffers injuries at different points in their lives; of course we all die. In contrast, the importance of individual autonomy varies widely among societies and among individuals. We can rationally conclude, as Fineman does, that vulnerability is more universal and should be the centerpiece of our social systems. But this is just part of the story. Just as vulnerability is *particular*, affecting each of us in different ways at different points in our lives, so is the desire for autonomy. It varies among individuals and cultures, but it appears almost everywhere.

Similar analyses apply to each of the other values Fineman criticizes. Most relevant to this chapter is the desire to accumulate private property and social distinction. Rules governing private property are socially constructed, but that does not mean the desire to own property does not originate in human nature. The desire for individual distinction, for honors, accolades, and high social status—and for the accompanying material benefits—takes many different forms, but it appears in some form in virtually every human society.

The emphasis American society places on individual autonomy, high social status, and the private possession of wealth is defined and expressed in cultural terms, but the underlying impulses are universal. This reality does not mean that Fineman's proposals for reconstructing society are invalid or that vulnerability is not a universal characteristic of human existence.

It does mean, however, that it will be harder to persuade American society to replace the "liberal subject" with the "vulnerable subject" as a core concept around which society is organized. Fineman acknowledges that the Lockean values she challenges pose a powerful barrier to the adoption of her ideas, but she diminishes their power by characterizing them as social artifacts, not human universals like dependency and vulnerability. The barrier erected by individualistic materialism is higher if these values are inherent in human nature, as I believe they are. If the individualism and acquisitiveness emblematic of contemporary American society are not merely social creations, they will not disappear with the creation of new rules and institutions based upon substantive theories of equality. To replace them as America's foundational values requires a critique, implemented by social activism, that openly confronts this element of our humanity. Like good utopians, we can imagine a world in which that has been accomplished. Like Thomas More's Utopia, that better America may exist only there, in our imaginations.

But Fineman has imagined more than a mythical world like More's Utopia. Like More, she has written a muscular criticism of her society that challenges the legitimacy of its fundamental values. Like More, she has imagined a better society organized around values that transform how institutions treat individuals. But, unlike More, her better world is not so perfect that it can exist only in the creator's mind. Fineman imagines a better society created in the existing world, by living people employing the social and political processes available in American society. Fineman imagines more than a utopia—she imagines a better reality. If she can incorporate our innate need for autonomy into her theory of interdependence based on vulnerability, she may succeed in imagining a just society for the real world.

Chapter 6

After the Storm: The Vulnerability and Resilience of Locally Owned Business

Susan S. Kuo and Benjamin Means

Introduction[1]

In a market economy, the idea of an autonomous, independent, and self-sufficient business organization is not just false but incoherent. Unlike Henry David Thoreau, who made much of his retreat to Walden Pond (living on property owned by Ralph Waldo Emerson, but never mind), no business can reject its neighbors and survive. To be in commerce is to work with suppliers, distributors, and brokers, to entreat customers, and to coordinate the activities of employees, managers, and owners. That these various relationships are conventionally described through the economic metaphor of a "nexus of contracts" (Bainbridge 2006) only underscores the interconnection that makes business activity possible. In a disaster, each tie is vulnerable, but, if it holds, may also support a return to normalcy.

Thus, some crucial aspects of Professor Martha Fineman's critique of the "mythic dimensions" of rugged individualism (Fineman 2004, 8) apply to business organizations. Locally owned businesses, in particular, are "vulnerable subjects" because of their embodiment, their dependency, and their lack of self-sufficiency. None of this is to gainsay the hard work of individual entrepreneurs. Yet, just as human beings live in fragile bodies, exposed to a universe of insults, locally owned businesses are more than economic or legal abstractions; they are also brick-and-mortar institutions and depend upon the integrity of their physical location and the health and safety of their employees. The perpetual life available under the laws of business organization is no guarantee against the laws of nature, let alone supply and demand—even without a natural disaster most businesses fail and very few survive more than two generations of owners (Pieper 2007).

Identifying vulnerability, however, is not the same thing as decrying weakness. A locally owned business cannot stand alone, nor need it do so. As Fineman observes in broader context, "[w]e all exist in contexts and relationships, in social and cultural institutions, such as families, which facilitate, support, and subsidizes

---

1 We thank Bob Rees, Richard Simons, and Michelle Theret for research assistance. Portions of this chapter are reprinted from our "Corporate social responsibility after disaster," *Washington University Law Review*, 89/5 (2012).

us and our endeavors" (Fineman 2004, 50). A more pragmatic approach to disaster response, accordingly, would not seek to draw moral boundaries between those who provide aid and those who receive it: "[i]n complex modern societies no one is self-sufficient, either economically or socially. Whether the subsidies we receive are financial (such as governmental transfer programs or favorable tax policy) or nonmonetary (such as the uncompensated labor of others in caring for us and our needs), we all live subsidized lives" (ibid.).

This chapter contends that business entities, especially those that are locally owned, are both susceptible to harm and capable of resilience—and, in both dimensions, linked economically and socially to a broader community. Thus, a more nuanced understanding of vulnerability, building on Fineman's theory of the vulnerable subject, helps to broaden the inquiry into the role of businesses in disaster recovery. Current accounts tend to overlook locally owned businesses in favor of larger corporations that are capable of providing aid on a quasi-governmental scale in the immediate aftermath of disaster.

For instance, it is well known that when Hurricane Katrina caught the Federal Emergency Management Agency (FEMA) unprepared (Super 2011; Shughart 2006), Wal-Mart stepped in to help. Wal-Mart's own meteorologists had been tracking the storm and predicted landfall near New Orleans "more than 12 hours before the National Weather Service issued a similar advisory" (Leonard 2005, 158). Wal-Mart's Emergency Operations Center successfully routed trucks with "hundreds of thousands of cases of bottled water, Pop-Tarts, and generators to distribution centers" outside the city before the storm hit (ibid.). Within days, most of Wal-Mart's stores in the Gulf Coast region were operational (ibid.). Indeed, "Wal-Mart employees arrived so early in the disaster area that they often wound up running their own relief efforts" (ibid.). In addition to the goods, services, and employment made possible by its normal business operations, Wal-Mart contributed at least 17 million dollars to support disaster relief and recovery efforts (ibid.).

Wal-Mart is one of the world's largest corporations, and its highly visible and laudable contributions to disaster recovery in New Orleans and the Gulf Coast have become a focal point for discussions concerning the role of corporations in disaster. Some commentators contend that by enhancing public–private partnerships, government can incentivize the use of private distribution networks like Wal-Mart's in a coordinated effort with public disaster response agencies (Rhee 2009; Rosegrant 2007). A few scholars go further and argue that Wal-Mart's performance shows that profit-oriented corporations will not only provide necessary relief on their own but will do so efficiently, without the waste and mismanagement too often associated with public relief efforts (Horwitz 2008). Others contend that essential government disaster-relief functions should not be left in the hands of private industry and that large-scale private efforts can sometimes hinder effective disaster relief and recovery (McKendry 2007). Although the answers differ markedly, these scholars all ask variations of the same question: How can the economic resources of large corporations like Wal-Mart best be harnessed to support disaster relief and recovery?

We contend that the standard story concerning corporations and disaster relief is incomplete. While acknowledging the importance of large corporations like Wal-Mart, we focus instead on the role of smaller, locally owned business. In particular, we contend that locally owned businesses have social and economic importance and deserve attention in the formulation and implementation of disaster recovery plans. When business owners live in the same community as their customers, they have a deeper stake in the success of disaster recovery and the ability to influence not only the economic aspects of recovery but also the social connections that determine a community's overall resilience—its spirit. Yet, to a greater extent than larger corporations with far-flung operations, locally owned businesses are also highly vulnerable to disaster harm and may struggle to survive, particularly when disasters disrupt cash flow and force the owners to rely upon meager savings or difficult-to-obtain financing. Public disaster relief efforts can exacerbate the problem if they create bureaucratic obstacles to reopening shuttered businesses or stymie local business recovery by hiring outside contractors, poaching workers, and undercutting the market price for goods and services.

This chapter's argument proceeds as follows. The first section defines social capital and argues that a community's vulnerability and its resilience depend upon social as well as economic factors; without solidarity there can be no recovery. The second section contends that locally owned businesses are integral to community social capital and can drive disaster recovery. The third section contends that disaster law and policy should address the vulnerability of locally owned business in the aftermath of disaster in order to maximize their role in longer-term recovery and should avoid top-down relief measures that might inhibit the ability of locally owned business to re-establish their profitability.

Social Capital and Disaster Resilience

Social capital "refers to the trust, social norms, and networks which affect social and economic activities" (Nakagawa & Shaw 2004, 7; Putnam, 2000, 136–7). Among the most important social norms are "reliability, honesty, and reciprocity" (Jones 2000, 2080). Just as economic capital allows individuals to buy goods and services in a marketplace, social capital includes "the stocks of social trust, norms, and networks that people can draw upon in order to solve common problems" (Calmore 1999, 1953). In social networks characterized by high degrees of trust and reciprocity, "individuals and groups" are able "to accomplish greater things than they could by their isolated efforts" (Weil 2007, 3). Social capital is enhanced when individuals participate in group activities and organizations and when those overlapping relationships enhance the overall level of trust (Cross 2005, 1482).

According to the theory of social capital, strength and vulnerability depend in large part upon the nature and extent of a person's social connections. Thus, individuals are not simply autonomous rights holders of the sort envisioned by liberal political theory and neoclassical economics. As Fineman puts it, "[i]ndependence from subsidy and support is not attainable, nor is it desirable; we want and need the webs of economic and social relationships that sustain us" (Fineman 2004, 28). Further, because we are interdependent, human vulnerability is not a "pathological" condition but "a universal, inevitable, enduring aspect of the human condition that must be at the heart of our concept of social and state responsibility" (Fineman 2008, 8).

Effective disaster response depends upon the aggregation of individually vulnerable people into a resilient group. Thus, resilience to disaster appears to turn on social capital as well as economic capital: "Communities with more trust, civic engagement, and stronger networks can better bounce back after a crisis than fragmented, isolated ones" (Aldrich 2010, 4). To a greater extent than is commonly recognized, "[n]eighbors and friends—not government agencies or NGOs—provide the necessary resources for recovery after disaster" (6). Highlighting social context helps us to understand what motivates recovery and to avoid the mistake of assuming that the answer to a disaster is always simply "more resources" and markets. Even when markets are the answer, they depend upon some level of trust among the participants.

Social capital is crucial in the wake of disaster when state and municipal services such as fire protection, police services, trash collection, and home care for the elderly and disabled are disrupted. Individually rational, disconnected individuals might wait for others to take the initiative to establish these services and fail to "coordinate their efforts to bring about these desired outcomes" (Aldrich 2010, 7). Why contribute to group needs when others may do the work for you, and, if they do not, your own efforts will be wasted? This is the tragedy of the commons (Hardin 1968, 7). When disasters disrupt existing markets, potential participants cannot know if an investment of resources will be wasted unless they know if others will also contribute to a viable system of exchange. Communities that enjoy high levels of social capital may find that their members are willing to risk the consequences of others' noncooperation, although individual economic rationality might suggest a more conservative approach. Thus, more cohesive communities may be able to function and to maintain order even when the normal operation of the state has been suspended.

Social capital matters as well when individuals must decide whether to return to their community: "Survivors of Katrina did not want to return to be the only household on their blocks, as this could be risky due to both crime and a lack of social support" (Aldrich 2010, 6). Unless strong social networks and mutual trust can provide assurances that others will return, the individually rational choice is to leave or, at a minimum, wait to see what everyone else decides to do. Of course, if everyone is waiting for everyone else, then the lack of social coordination prevents a return that might have been the collective preference. As one survivor of the Tsunami in Japan told a reporter, "we don't want to leave … [b]ut if nobody else comes back, we can't stay. You cannot build a life by yourself" (Pittman 2011).

Strong social ties can influence decision-making, overcoming barriers to collective action, because economic decisions are embedded in a social context

(Fligstein 2001, 31). Put differently, loyalty can make exit less likely (Hirschman 1970, 77). Moreover, social capital predicts disaster recovery because "[n]eighbors with greater levels of social capital share information about bureaucratic procedures [how to apply for relief funds, how to get the electricity turned back on in your neighborhood] and upcoming deadlines, monitor public space to prevent dumping, and deter looting in their community" (Aldrich 2010, 7).

By contrast, communities that lack social capital may remain stagnant, regardless of whether they receive public resources. For example, in conducting a case study of Indonesia, researchers found substantial evidence that, in the wake of two major natural disasters—the Indian Ocean Tsunami of December 26, 2004 and the Central Java Earthquake of May 27, 2006, communities with higher levels of social capital experienced greater "life recovery" despite having received similar types and levels of disaster recovery assistance, including economic resources, as other communities (Sakamoto and Yamori 2010, 13–14).

We acknowledge, however, that the concept of social capital has not been accepted universally. The term captures a number of related phenomena and some scholars have criticized it for "over-versatility" (Nakagawa & Shaw 2004, 9). According to other commentators, the "capital" metaphor is potentially misleading when used to describe social phenomena and "at best" may be "useless and harmless" (Elster 2007, 456; see also Arrow 2000, 3–4). We hope to sidestep the academic debate here because we invoke social capital in connection with the basic proposition that individuals can accomplish a task in different ways. Sometimes they may spend money; sometimes they may draw upon social connections; further, social considerations may impact the use and the effectiveness of their economic resources. The shared label—"capital"—helps to clarify that social and economic power can substitute, cumulate, and otherwise overlap in accomplishing real-world tasks, such as disaster recovery.

However, it may be true that the underlying mechanisms involved in using economic capital and social capital to accomplish tasks differ and that it would be a mistake to assume that because they are both described as "capital" they must share a causal mechanism. For instance, money can be spent in a continuous fashion until it has been exhausted, and the last dollar is as valuable as the first dollar. By contrast, social capital turns on trust and can evaporate in an instant. Perhaps one could bolster the "social capital" metaphor by specifying that social capital is, in effect, printed in very large-denomination bills only, or perhaps one might point out the ways that economic capital is also and equally a metaphor—one can only use economic capital in the context of a great number of shared, cultural understandings that permit designated currency to hold value and to be exchanged for goods and services (Searle 1998, 126). Again, we do not intend to engage the debate concerning social capital theory because our argument does not turn on the precise mappings between interpersonal trust and capital (see, generally, Lakoff and Johnson 1980).

Rather, by highlighting the ways that economic behavior is situated in social context, we seek to help disaster planners avoid the mistake of assuming that outputs are connected to inputs by some mathematical, unvarying calculus. The test of recovery is not how fast the rubble gets cleared or how much money is allocated, but whether the social fabric holds and can be restored. After immediate life-threatening conditions ease, and outside aid has ameliorated the most severe harms, the longer-term repair of a community rests with the members of that community. Thus, some communities—even those more vulnerable to disaster harm—are more resilient than others because of the strength of their human connections. Without preexisting solidarity, there can be no solid basis for recovery.

The Social Capital of Locally Owned Business

Locally owned businesses are critical to bottom-up disaster recovery efforts because they are part of the social infrastructure, providing jobs that make return possible as well as a sense of community that makes return worthwhile. In Fineman's terms, a robust local business community should count among "the structures [that] our society has … to manage our common vulnerabilities" (Fineman 2008, 1). Every community is defined in part by its local establishments, and these markers of place are integral to achieving the normalcy required for the life recovery of disaster victims—"a primary aim of the disaster management process" (Fordham 1998, 130; see also Sakamoto and Yamori 2010: 82; de Ville de Goyet and Griekspoor 2007, 49).

Although local ownership does not constitute a category under US law, the concept is straightforward: a business in which the owners reside in the community. Such businesses will almost always be closely held (i.e., with relatively few owners and direct participation of most owners in management) (Bainbridge 2002, 797), whether they are organized as corporations, partnerships, or LLCs. We include locally owned franchises as well to the extent that key decisions are reserved to the local owners rather than to a corporate headquarters. Because local owners manage their businesses directly and answer only to themselves, they have the latitude to devote corporate resources to serve ends other than profit maximization. Further, based on their own social connections as well as the social networks of the business, owners have reason to consider the needs of the community in seeking to achieve both economic and social ends. This motivation is complex; neither profit seeking in a narrow sense nor purely altruistic.

The corollary to our thesis is that, despite their economic importance, public corporations are not as deeply invested in the communities in which they operate. Nor are the "owners" typically invested in the enterprise for anything more than its economic value: "Investors part with their money willingly, putting dollars in equities instead of bonds or banks or land or gold because they believe the returns of equities more attractive" (Easterbrook and Fischel 1989, 1419). (Some investors may choose to engage in socially responsible investing, placing explicit importance on goals other than financial return, but this is the exception that proves the rule.) Publicly traded corporations can operate on a larger scale because they aggregate capital from investors across the nation and worldwide. However, the shareholders, who are the residual beneficiaries of the firm, are unlikely to live in the same community and will be rationally ignorant concerning the firm's activities. This may be a boon for efficient capital allocation, but it does not build ties between a business and its community.

To see the value of locally owned business, consider an alternative account of business resilience in New Orleans during and after Hurricane Katrina. Here we are not concerned about putting Wal-Mart's emergency operations center and its fleet of trucks to good use. Nor are we interested in revisiting the longstanding debate as to whether public corporations can behave in a socially responsible fashion consistent with the obligation that managers have under law (as well as the market pressures they may face) to generate profits for the shareholders. Instead, we highlight the role of smaller, locally owned businesses. Although they lack economic resources on the vast scale of a Wal-Mart, local businesses are essential to the resilience of their communities.

For instance, there is much to learn from the example of "Johnny White's ... a Bourbon Street bar that never closes" (AFP Wire Service 2005). As noted in a number of news accounts, Johnny White's held true to its motto and stayed open through the storm, the power outages, and the looting that followed. In fact, the bar ignored official curfews: "Call it madness. Call it anti-authoritarian pigheadedness. Or call it dogged determination not to let a lifestyle die" (ibid.). Although presented as a human-interest story rather than as an example of disaster recovery, Johnny White's was an essential component of the community's resilience in the wake of disaster.

The owner, J.D. Landrum, seemed to recognize as much when he told a reporter, "You've got to have someplace open, even during the worst of times" (AFP Wire Service, 2005). Initially, "[t]he bar stools were filled with shell-shocked people who had swum out of their flooded homes to safety only to find that there was no help to be had from the powers that be" (ibid.). In the weeks that followed Katrina, "[t]he bar became a community center as a tight knit group of die-hards piled water and military rations up outside. It soon became a favorite among journalists and rescue workers who needed a place they could go to forget the despair and destruction" (ibid.).

One could as easily mention other local bars, restaurants, and businesses that committed to reopen whatever the cost and whose presence gave the community hope and a renewed sense of normalcy: the Camellia Grill; Emeril's; and Mother's, for example. Local owners who had a stake in their community refused to abandon restaurants and employees and, in some cases, went to great lengths in order to get back what they had lost: "Many restaurants set up FEMA trailers so employees could return to the city. Some workers lived in restaurant parking lots, even in the owners' homes for months after the storm" (Foster 2009).

The broader point is that a vision of corporate involvement in disaster recovery that focuses on the economic capital of large, public corporations leaves out the importance of bottom-up efforts that may be motivated by sound business reasons but that are also inescapably situated in the context of community ties and reciprocal obligations. Social capital explains departures from a simple economic framework wherein rational business owners benefit disaster-stricken communities only as a byproduct of profit-seeking activities (Benkler 2004, 326). Local business owners may also respond to their felt obligations as members of the community when deciding whether to invest in recovery or to seek more attractive investment opportunities elsewhere. In part, this may be a recognition of shared vulnerability—unlike the detached, rational actor of standard economic theory, a local business owner has connections to her community aside from those negotiated at arm's length.

After Katrina, pure economic rationality might well have led many restaurant owners to relocate. The choice to cut bait seemed clear, for instance, to "[h]igh-end steakhouse chain Smith & Wollensky," which decided "not [to] reopen its New Orleans restaurant" (Britt 2006). The chain is based in New York and its President, Eugene Zuriff, explained that the restaurant would "remain shuttered due to market conditions" (ibid.). Examining the same post-disaster environment as the restaurant owners who chose to stay, Mr. Zuriff's economic logic seemed impeccable: "There's no lunch crowd, no substantial convention business. It's going to be a while" (ibid.).

The benefits of social capital can be gleaned, in part, from its apparent absence in Mr. Zuriff's decision-making. Professor Angela Harris (2002, 1458) identifies three important aspects:

> First, social capital helps people resolve collective action problems: when people share social norms of mutual aid, free-riding is reduced. Second, social capital reduces transaction costs: "There is no need to spend time and money making sure that others will uphold their end of the arrangement or penalizing them if they don't." Third, social capital increases a distinctive set of virtues, such as tolerance and empathy for others. (See also Putnam 2000, 136–7)

Consequently, residents of communities with high levels of social capital are inclined to "work for a solution" rather than to leave, because they "have more at stake should the neighborhood not recover successfully" (Aldrich 2009). The owners of local businesses have a personal and a business stake in recovery.

Including Locally Owned Businesses in Disaster Planning

Locally owned businesses must survive before they can help their communities. Therefore, disaster plans should allocate financial assistance to help locally owned businesses surmount short-term cash-flow problems. The "disaster loans" made available through the Small Business Administration (SBA) are one example of this kind of approach (SBA.gov, economic disaster loans). The Gulf Zone Opportunity Act of 2005 ("GO ZONE") passed to help businesses damaged by

Katrina is another example (Pub. L. No. 109-35, 119 Stat. 2577 (2005); Smith 2008, 813–15).

By tying public funds to a commitment to rebuild in the devastated area (assuming that it is safe to do so), disaster plans can further incentivize locally owned business to stay put. This restriction on eligibility ensures that the money allocated will ultimately benefit the community. It might be objected that the intrusion of legal rules and incentives of this kind invariably diminishes social capital, supplanting social norms and networks with top-down requirements. However, the interplay of law and social relationships is more complex. As the example of marriage shows, legal structures can also reinforce community values:

> Consider a legal agreement associated with marriage. Viewed as "the province of the wealthy, the age disparate, the heartless, or the simply greedy, prenuptial agreements are often regarded with distrust and hostility." While prenuptial agreements may exemplify how law can undermine trust, the existence of marriage itself provides counterevidence—a marriage is itself a form of contract with important legal implications, but marriage is not generally viewed as a sign of the parties' mistrust. Rather, their willingness to commit to the legal implications of marriage can be taken as a sign of their trust and commitment to the relationship …. (Cross 2005, 1482)

Arguably, businesses that apply for special disaster loans or for other assistance in rebuilding are also, even in seeking aid, broadcasting an intention to remain in the community—a position that may galvanize others to return as well. In any event, locally owned businesses can do nothing for their communities if they relocate or go bankrupt.

In addition to financial resources, disaster planners should anticipate that local businesses may need help to cope with bureaucratic obstacles to restoring a previous business plan or developing a new strategy in response to changed needs in the community. In order to succeed, a business must find customers; disaster response that focuses on immediate vulnerability to harm and that discounts the importance of activities that sustain social connections can make local business less resilient and, therefore, less likely to recover. As a general principle, legal rules should be designed to encourage local businesses to adapt entrepreneurially to the post-disaster landscape. A recurrent complaint in recent disasters is that officials have been too slow to authorize reentry to damaged premises to recover important business materials and have failed to process applications for rebuilding in a timely fashion. For a small, locally owned business, delay can be fatal. For instance, local business owners in Tuscaloosa, Alabama were vocal in their opposition to a City plan that, in their view, posed impediments to rebuilding damaged businesses and did not adequately clarify zoning issues (Morton 2011).

Documents that guide disaster response, however, seem not to recognize the urgency. For instance, FEMA has recently circulated for comment a draft National Recovery Framework that recognizes a role for locally owned business in disaster recovery but appears to defer attention to the needs of such businesses until the last "economic recovery" stage of a multi-phase plan (FEMA 2010). According to the Framework's proposed timetable, disaster recovery efforts can be divided into stages: (1) immediate response; (2) stabilization activities; (3) intermediate recovery; and (4) long-term recovery. On this timetable, local business initiatives become significant only after intermediate-range recovery efforts take place, including population recovery: the long-term initiatives include as a goal, "[i]mplementing economic and business revitalization strategies."

Yet, locally owned businesses can help the members of a disaster-affected community overcome collective action problems in the earlier stages of recovery. As one commentator observes, local commercial activity is a kind of "[m]utual assistance" in that it "serves as a source of material support, but, more important, it sends signals that members of a community are committed to recovery and helps to restore the fabric of communities torn apart by disaster" (Chamlee-Wright 2007, 239). Therefore, "[o]nce … immediate concerns are met, the reestablishment of working social and economic systems ought to take priority because they are the foundation on which long-term recovery must be constructed" (253). Accordingly, the Framework's intermediate goals would seem to benefit from earlier, more sustained attention to the needs of local businesses. For many such businesses, recovery must be early or not at all. If permission to rebuild cannot be acquired swiftly, a business may run out of operating capital or decide to relocate.

Public officials can also help locally owned businesses by adopting guidelines that limit outside relief work when bottom-up recovery efforts can substitute for it. Otherwise, public disaster response may not only miss opportunities to support the social capital of locally owned business, but may also be at cross-purposes. In particular, disaster relief measures should strive to avoid duplication of tasks better left to local businesses and other community organizations. Advance planning is important in this regard because longer-term consequences may not seem as pressing in the midst of a crisis, but those potential costs must be weighed against shorter-term benefits. For instance, if a relief station gives away food in the parking lot of a local grocery store that has been struggling to reopen, the diminished ability of the locally owned business to reestablish itself in the market is a significant cost and not to be set aside lightly. Obviously, the first priority is to make sure that everyone has adequate food and water. However, once the immediate danger has passed, the goal should be to reestablish normalcy rather than to prolong dependency. Without a business sector, a community cannot restore the jobs and income, to say nothing of the supply of goods and services that make recovery possible.

This is not just a hypothetical concern. One study of small business recovery after Hurricane Katrina reported the negative reaction of business owners to outside relief efforts coordinated by FEMA (Runyan and Huddleston 2009). These reconstruction efforts focused on physical infrastructure and "exacerbat[ed] the shortage of workers in the area by providing 'too much' financial assistance to persons displaced by the storm, and 'poach[ed]' workers from local construction firms" (127). Short-term recovery efforts and disaster mitigation thus displaced longer-term rebuilding by starving local business of resources. According to one scholar, the slow pace of recovery in New Orleans may have been attributable to an excess of "orchestrated and centralized government effort" rather than a "lack of government resources" (Chamlee-Wright 2007, 237). On this view, by taking over recovery efforts, "public policy is distorting the signals emerging from markets and civil society that would otherwise foster a swift and sustainable recovery" (ibid.).

Part of the problem may be that the current focus in disaster planning and response is largely on physical infrastructure. Government, insurance, and other large businesses contribute resources to repair and rebuild roads, replace housing, and otherwise address physical damage in disaster-ravaged areas. Yet, as this chapter has argued, social networks are also crucial to recovery. If the ultimate goal of disaster relief efforts is to help a community recover fully from disaster, then a particular "hazard of in-kind charitable or volunteer activity is that it will compete with and harm still viable commercial enterprises, undermining the community's long-term economic viability" (Horwich 2000, 532). Accordingly, in order to take advantage of social capital and to foster bottom-up rebuilding, policymakers must reorient problem solving to include social infrastructure and should take care to avoid squelching the efforts of locally owned businesses.

Conclusion

Natural disasters offer repeated proofs of our shared vulnerability. Some commentators point out that the theory of vulnerability that applies in the context of disaster may be incomplete or, worse, selective in ways that reinforce existing ideas about privilege and responsibility:

> Ironically, at the same time that we stigmatize mothers on welfare, we commiserate with industries that experience other forms of "disaster" that we define as outside of individual control. American politicians apply differing standards of self-sufficiency to different situations. Hence we "bail out" some who run amok economically .... Sometimes ... the government is seen as playing the role of an insurer, such as when it responds to disasters that occur when houses built on floodplains or over fault lines are destroyed through predictable natural occurrences. (Fineman 2004, 33)

Even if our understanding of disaster is under-inclusive, however, the laws, regulations, and policies concerning disaster response show that it is possible "[t]o richly theorize a concept of vulnerability [and] to develop a more complex subject around which to build social policy and law" (Fineman 2008: 1). Within the parameters of a recognized disaster, the "vulnerable subject" does to some degree "replace the autonomous and independent subject asserted in the liberal tradition" (Fineman 2008, 2). Comprehensive disaster planning proceeds on the assumption that *everyone* is susceptible to harm and, at the same time, that a community contains many potential sources of resilience and recovery.

Locally owned businesses are an important part of this story: they contribute to the longer-term recovery of afflicted communities by building and supporting social networks that help individuals in a community to cope with shared vulnerability. Locally owned businesses will never match the Wal-Marts of the world in their ability to distribute vast quantities of blankets, portable generators, and, for that matter, Pop-Tarts, but they are essential to the disaster resilience of their communities.

Chapter 7
Housing the Vulnerable Subject: The English Context

Helen Carr

Introduction

This chapter explores Fineman's claim that 'vulnerability proves more theoretically powerful than the idea of dependency in arguing for a more just society' (Fineman, this volume, 19) by applying it to contemporary debates about British (and more particularly English) welfare provision, particularly those that support the overstretched homeowner or which question the future role of social housing. It concludes that Fineman's work not only enriches those debates, but that it has the potential to avoid the 'dead ends' of much British social welfare critique.

The chapter focuses on the British state's responses to the persistent and on-going crises of housing, to demonstrate that the post-World War II ambivalent and limited commitment to state provision of rental housing has been replaced by the aim of assisting citizens to achieve autonomy via homeownership. It is suggested that this reconfiguration of welfare makes Fineman's work especially relevant, notwithstanding its location in the specificities of the United States, because it has prompted a questioning of social obligations which until recently have been taken for granted.

The chapter begins by outlining some of the salient features of Fineman's vulnerability theory and suggesting its relevance for current British arguments about the allocation of housing resources. The substantive part of the chapter examines closely two contemporary questions relating to social responsibility for the provision of housing to ask if Fineman's vulnerability analysis can prove productive. The first question concerns those circumstances in which the state accepts responsibilities towards those who, having tried to buy their own homes, are threatened with repossession by their mortgagee (and who therefore might call upon the state via homelessness legislation). The second question is more complex and demanding; it relates to whether there is any longer a convincing argument in favour of the state providing a lifetime tenancy for some of its citizens. The chapter concludes by moving beyond these questions, understanding them as particular manifestations of broader governmental shifts from social to economic rationalities to suggest that Fineman's work can be used more generally to disrupt these trends.

Fineman's Vulnerability Theory

For British housing academics, vulnerability has a particular meaning within housing legislation. It operates as an apparently apolitical mechanism to sort homelessness claims and to allocate resources appropriately (see Carr and Hunter 2008). More generally, within welfare law and policy, vulnerability has been used to mark the distinction between the deserving and the undeserving poor. This has had several unfortunate outcomes. Firstly, it lends itself to audit, surveillance and confession as the primary tools through which welfare is governed, a phenomenon that has been extensively commented upon by housing academics (see, for instance, Cowan and McDermont 2006; Flint 2003). Secondly, new claims upon the state emerge through demonstrating the unmet needs of particular groups. This can result in an unseemly and unproductive competition for resources. Fineman notes a similarly perverse dynamic in the context of the United States where legal protections granted to particular discriminated-against groups 'has generated a politics of resentment and backlash on the part of those who fall outside of the protected groupings' (Fineman, this volume, 15). Finally, the neoliberal turn to economic rationality has meant that the special treatment accorded to such citizens becomes increasingly difficult to defend. This is reflected in the recently published British Social Attitudes Report (National Centre for Social Research 2011) which reveals increasing intolerance of state intervention to help the poor.

In contrast, Fineman, in the opening chapter to this book, provides a theoretically enriched understanding of vulnerability avoiding the corrosive consequences outlined above. For Fineman, vulnerability is primarily a characteristic of existence. It emerges from our embodiment, 'which carries with it the imminent or ever-present possibility of harm, injury, and misfortune' (Fineman, this volume, 20) and 'positions us in relation to each other as human beings' (13). Thus, in Fineman's work, vulnerability is universal and consequently carries with it the implication that the state should be 'more responsive to that vulnerability' (13).

Fineman's focus on vulnerability emerges from her concern with the limits of equal protection law in the United States – a doctrine with the limited claim that individuals be treated the same. As she points out, this 'ignores most contexts, as well as differences in circumstances and abilities on the part of those whose treatment is compared' (Fineman, this volume, 14). One troubling consequence of the dominance of the equal protection approach is 'that it distorts our understanding of a variety of social problems and takes only a limited view of what should constitute governmental responsibility in regard to social justice issues' (15). Understood in the way that Fineman proposes, vulnerability is so much richer than equal protection. Whilst vulnerability is a constant of our lives, it is out of our control, is complex and multiple in form and is experienced by each of us uniquely. Moreover, '[o]ur bodily vulnerability is compounded by the possibility that, should we succumb to illness or injury, there may be accompanying economic and institutional harms and disruption of existing social, economic, or family relationships' (20). Inevitably, there is significant variety in the personal resources available to us to respond to our vulnerability, dependent upon how we are situated. As a consequence societal institutions such as the family and have emerged. 'Together and independently, these societal institutions provide us with "assets"—reservoirs of capabilities, advantages, or coping mechanisms that cushion us when we are facing misfortune, disaster, and violence, as well as constituting the resources that we will need if we are to take risks and avail ourselves of opportunities as they arise' (22).

Institutions (including the state) are, of course, as Fineman makes clear, fallible. 'Societal institutions are not foolproof shelters, even in the short term. They too can be conceptualized as fallible. They may fail in the wake of market fluctuations, changing international policies, institutional and political compromises, or human prejudices' (Fineman 2010, 169). The extent to which institutions promote resilience to vulnerability should, Fineman suggests, form a significant measure of their effectiveness and of the justice of their operation. This would also serve to expose serious limitations to the utopian claims often made for such institutions. As Fineman points out, '[r]iddled with their own vulnerabilities, society's institutions cannot eradicate, and often operate to exacerbate, our individual vulnerability' (ibid.). Further, and usefully, the institutional focus supplements our understanding of the individual subject by placing him/her in social and historic context.

The recognition of vulnerability as a universal and particular human characteristic enables Fineman to disrupt the potent myth of the liberal autonomous subject. For liberal theorists, 'Society is conceived as a collection of self-interested individuals, each of whom has the capacity to manipulate and manage their independently acquired and overlapping resources' (Fineman, this volume, 15). This one-dimensional understanding has problematic consequences, for the liberal subject stands outside of both the passage of time and human experience. Its adoption as the centre of political theory positions dependency, for instance that of the child, the elderly or the disabled as different, perhaps inferior and not quite entitling the dependent to full human status. In contrast, '(T)he vulnerable subject is the embodiment of the realization that vulnerability is a universal and constant aspect of the human condition. Dependency and vulnerability are not deviant, but natural and inevitable' (Fineman, this volume, 17). Such an account of vulnerability thus enables claims to be made without the necessity of stigmatizing the claimant.

The insufficiency of equal treatment legislation in the United States seems a long way from debates about social housing in Britain. After all, Britain's social protections are far more extensive than those of the United States. Indeed, Britain is unique in placing statutory obligations upon the state to house the homeless and offers security of tenure (tenancies for life) to those to whom it grants local authority housing, suggesting that an implicit recognition of vulnerability in Fineman's sense has informed the allocation of scarce resources. However, contemporary welfare in Britain has been reconfigured in response to the prevailing neoliberal orthodoxy. This reconfiguration accommodates certain forms of policy interventions, such as those which promote equal treatment. It also – significantly for this chapter

– promotes homeownership as being essential to the economic citizenship that it valorizes. As a consequence, other forms of housing provision become at best marginal and at worst demonized. My argument here is that homeownership as a tool of social inclusion is limited in much the same way as the equality legislation which forms the starting point for Fineman's analysis. As Fineman observes, it 'ignores most contexts, as well as differences in circumstances and abilities on the part of those whose treatment is compared' (Fineman, this volume, 14). Like equal treatment, homeownership offers very different opportunities to different people depending upon where and when they purchase and what resources are available to them to support their new status (see Carr 2011). Before I expand upon the notion of homeownership as citizenship and its consequences, it is important to locate this analysis by reflecting upon the reconfiguration of British welfare, turning to what Dean describes as 'the charge led by Margaret Thatcher as she dismantled the British welfare state' (Dean 2009), a charge which had local authority housing as a principal focus.

Housing in the Reconfigured British Welfare State

The transformation of the post-war welfare state which took place in Britain (and elsewhere) from the late 1970s onwards has been well documented (see, in the particular context of housing, Forrest and Murie 1988; Cowan and McDermont 2006; Cowan 2011). In summary, the aspiration for social solidarity via redistribution of resources, which had been the hallmark of the Beveridgean welfare settlement, was gradually replaced by the promotion of 'individual responsibility'. Government interventions designed to promote full employment and to stimulate demand were abandoned, there was privatization of nationalized industries and assets, and wages were increasingly determined by the market rather than by collective bargaining. As a consequence, the focus of British welfare was no longer upon social insurance. Instead, its purpose was to enable each of its citizens to become a 'competent social actor capable of playing multiple and concurrent adult (formerly all-male) societal roles' (Fineman, this volume, 17).

Housing has played an important part in that transformation. Whilst the extent of the commitment to housing as a welfare objective has been contentious (see, for instance, Malpass 2003; Ravetz 2001), nonetheless much was hoped for from council housing. It was designed to eradicate squalor, to provide a safe haven for those in need and as a tool for integrating its residents into society. By the 1970s evidence of the failure of these utopian aspirations had been built into the post-war landscape via the crumbling tower blocks and the unpopular estates. Wright, for instance, notes that 'the tower block has become a kind of ideological bulldozer for discrediting local democracy and the local provision of services' (Wright 1991, 135), and, for Jacobs and Manzi, the tower block became 'a 'monument' for the state's failure appropriately to manage and maintain council housing (Jacobs and

Manzi 1996, 548–9). Moreover, council tenants somehow came to personify the dependency and immobility produced by welfare (see Thatcher 1993, 671).

Politicians and academics joined forces to demonstrate their radicalism by denigrating council housing. The position of politicians is epitomized by an article headlined 'Housing, room for a new view', written by John Patten, a cabinet minister, for the *Guardian* in 1987 (prior to, and presaging, the introduction of the Housing Act 1988 which provided for large scale transfer of council estates to the private sector): 'Council housing is a failed solution characterized by a whole array of deficiencies: poor design and layout, serious disrepair, rising rent arrears, increasing numbers of void properties and unmanageably large housing departments' (quoted in Malpass 1990, 11). Within academia, the work of Saunders (1990), extolling the virtues of homeownership, demonstrated a transformation in approach. As Forrest and Murie pointed out,

> [i]t may be that in the rather fashionable reaction to the statism of much previous social analysis there is a temptation to embrace the 'consumer's perspective' too easily and uncritically. Within this new realism is a dismissal of state provision as inherently unresponsive, undesirable and repressive. People should be given what they want through the enlightened manipulation of the market. And what they appear to want above almost all is an owner occupied house. (Forrest and Murie 1990, 618)

The introduction of the Right to Buy in the Housing Act 1980 therefore proved a popular measure by which to simultaneously dismantle state apparatus and promote the individual aspiration which was the goal of Thatcher's administration.

Housing Stratification

The implementation of the Right to Buy has, of course, had consequences. Whilst there is no doubt that many former tenants benefited from the massive transfer of resources from the state to the individual, and that for a time the percentage of homeowners was increased, the residualization of those who continued to rent from the state has become apparent. Harloe (1995) describes the concentration of low-income households, particularly those understood to be vulnerable (in the welfarist sense discussed above) within the sector, the increasing share of tenants dependent on welfare and the extensive pressure placed upon those who could to leave the sector. Particularly noted by social commentators has been the emergence of 'troubled' or 'problem' estates, which as Harloe puts it, are

> merely the most dramatic indication of a wider process of internal differentiation within social rented housing between the older established more socially and economically (but not ethnically) mixed tenants who had moved into the sector

in the previous era and the poor disadvantaged groups who increasingly looked to social housing as their principal form of accommodation. (Harloe 1995, 367)

The 2007 Hills report into the future of social housing updates and confirms Harloe's observations. It points out that, 'over the last quarter century the role of social housing has changed and although the social housing sector has become much smaller, nearly 4 million households still live within it' (Hills 2007, 6). Significantly, the report notes that as a result of constrained provision, new lettings are focused on those in greatest need:

> As a result, the composition of tenants has changed, with tenants much more likely to have low incomes and not to be in employment than in the past or than those in the other tenures. Seventy per cent of social tenants have incomes within the poorest two-fifths of the overall income distribution, and the proportion of social tenant householders in paid employment fell from 47 to 32 per cent between 1981 and 2006. Tenants have high rates of disability, are more likely than others to be lone parents or single people, and to be aged over 60. More than a quarter (27 per cent) of all black or minority ethnic householders are social tenants (including around half of Bangladeshi and 43 per cent of black Caribbean and black African householders), compared to 17 per cent of white householders. (Hills 2007, 54)

The concentration of poverty has unfortunate consequences for those who live in social housing. As Hanley, in her personal account of council housing, puts it,

> [f]irst there is the simple knowledge that you are surrounded by poor people – people who have drawn the short straw in life and can see no obvious way of lengthening it. The fact that you are living in a place populated almost exclusively by the poor makes those who are less poor unlikely to enter the area unless they have to, further entrenching its isolation and the stigma of living there. That isolation, in turn, limits the aspirations of those poor people by presenting few clear alternatives to the lives they see being lived around them. If those lives seem mad and chaotic, that madness and chaos will spread to those who arc most susceptible. So it spirals down. (Hanley 2007, 138–9)

There was nothing inevitable about these consequences. As Forest and Murie point out, 'the sale of council homes could have formed part of an imaginative and socially just restructuring of housing opportunities. Unfortunately they have been pursued as a political priority to the relative neglect of any significant compensatory or complementary politics' (Forrest and Murie 1988, 252). The political priority was ideological: a commitment to a form of individualized active and economic citizenship best delivered by homeownership.

Homeownership as Citizenship

Homeownership has, within those societies which promote it, somehow been endowed with magical properties. Kiviat provides (in the context of the United States) a useful summary:

> A house with a front lawn and a picket fence wasn't just a nice place to live or a risk-free investment; it was a way to transform a nation. Whether you were looking to promote personal responsibility, ease the postwar housing shortage for returning veterans, help the poor establish a financial foothold or drum up jobs in a labor-heavy industry, home ownership was the answer. (Kiviat, 2010)

As Ronald points out, homeownership's advance is not a natural phenomenon; instead it 'has been stimulated, constituted and reinforced by government practices, social discourses and the expansion of market relations' (Ronald 2008, 8). The Right to Buy provided one particular means of extending the magic beyond homeownership's typical aspirational middle-class constituency. But there was more that it could achieve, as Peter King's recent book *Housing Policy Transformed: The Right to Buy and the Desire to Own* (2010) suggests; in addition to extending the benefits of homeownership there was an intensification of its benefits once it was taken up by former council tenants.

> The Right to Buy connected with aspiration and altered expectations. It allowed people the perception and reality of greater control and to feel that they were achieving an independence, of becoming really private. But in doing so, they became part of some bigger whole through the responsibilities that their new rights brought with them. (King 2010, 44)

What is notable here is that King imbues the Right to Buy with double advantages: simultaneously, homeownership provides individualization and autonomy and has societal benefits as a mechanism of social inclusion via responsibilization. Indeed, the implication is that without responsibilities rights are somehow destructive – an unspoken reference perhaps to the corrosive effects of the irresponsibility of council tenure.

Gurney's careful analysis of the discourses of homeownership, which draws on Foucault, unpacks more of its normalizing and disciplinary effects. He identifies three particular strands:

> First, new forms of homelessness; the distinctive use of the word 'home' to differentiate between owners and tenants. Second, being good citizens, the association of home ownership with a set of desirable values. Third, being natural – the association between normal and natural behavior embodied in home ownership. (Gurney 1999, 171)

These discourses have effects:

> [I]t becomes normal for the majority of householders in great Britain to aspire
> to home ownership, it becomes normal for home ownership to be associated
> more closely than any other form of housing consumption with evocative and
> emotional ideas of home, it becomes normal for home owners to be represented
> as good citizens and good parents, it becomes normal for a preference for home
> ownership to be constructed as a fact of human nature. (ibid., 179)

However, the benefits of homeownership are not solely domestic. The coincidence
of an extension of homeownership with a neoliberal-inspired deregulation of
mortgage finance operated to transform its range. Martin describes the move
from 'a "locally originate and locally-hold" model of mortgage provision to a
securitised "locally originate and globally distribute" model' (Martin 2011, 595),
demonstrating the particular link between neoliberalism and globalization, and of
course meaning that the collapse of the local subprime mortgage markets in the
USA had global repercussions. This was tolerable because of the shift in what
homeownership was about. Dyal-Chand points out that:

> [i]mplicit assumptions about the fundamental *purpose* of homeownership
> changed quite radically … the market incentivized something markedly
> different: the use of home equity as a means of leverage, a means of risk taking
> in pursuit of greater wealth. (Dyal-Chand 2011, 47; emphasis in the original)

This neoliberal inspired use of the home to generate wealth promoted individualized
opportunity and risk taking and diminished collective interests in mutual security.
Owning a home gave the homeowner an asset to be exploited, which became more
significant than the security and responsibilization which had been the primary
aims of homeownership. The change reflected a shift in the relationship between the
state and the citizen – what was required of the state was to ensure that its citizens
were provided with opportunities for wealth, rather than the direct provision of
welfare. As Dyal-Chand puts it, '[t]he valorization of negative rights of access
to housing, defined primarily as access to the real estate and credit markets, over
positive rights to "shelter", … does not guarantee an improvement of welfare, but
merely provides opportunity for welfare enhancement' (Dyal-Chand 2011, 47).

This was particularly significant in the UK context. As Martin explains,
the mortgage bubble in the UK was less to do with the expansion of subprime
mortgages and more to do with 'treating housing as a capital asset capable of
yielding high rental income—hence the unprecedented expansion of the "buy-
to-let" market mentioned above—or as a means of funding future household
consumption via equity extraction' (Martin 2011, 600).

There are multiple outcomes of this emphasis on, and mutation of,
homeownership, not least the extraordinary differentiation in wealth between
those who are excluded from ownership and those who have successfully utilized

the home as a source of wealth enhancement and the differentially distributed global and national impact of the financial crisis (Martin 2011). In the rest of this chapter I focus on two particular consequences. The first concerns the character of the protections mobilized for the benefit of the marginal homeowner no longer able to afford to repay the mortgage and facing repossession; the second is the questioning of the benefits of the tenancy for life.

Safety Nets for Homeowners

The political risks of a downturn in house prices and consequent negative equity became apparent in the early 1990s when there were record levels of repossessions. These only began to fall following a voluntary deal between lenders and the government initiated by the then Prime Minister John Major (Clements 1999). Part of New Labour's electoral success in 1997 was due to revealing the brutality of the unmitigated consequences of repossessions. Academic work such as that of Nettleton and Burrows (1998) and Ford et al. (2001) argued that the economy appeared to be reliant on levels of homeownership that seemed unsustainable, and their work provided useful exemplifications of the vulnerability of marginal homeowners and the inadequacies of the public and private safety nets provided. When, despite promises to eliminate boom and bust, the global financial crisis erupted in 2007, resulting once more in negative equity and job losses, urgent moves to minimize the risks of repossessions were initiated. One particular move was the introduction of a pre-action protocol for mortgage possession proceedings.

The Pre-action Protocol for Mortgage Possession Proceedings

In October 2008, 40,000 repossessions were predicted in contrast to the 25,900 properties repossessed in 2007 – an increase of 54 per cent – and Britain was teetering on the brink of recession. In November 2008 the Council for Mortgage Lenders (the professional association) predicted that the following year would see over 75,000 repossessions (National Audit Office 2011). Gordon Brown, anxious to be seen to be responsive to a housing crisis, announced new guidance for judges hearing possession cases (Wintour 2008). This guidance took the form of a pre-action protocol for mortgage possession proceedings. The pre-action protocol is a set of guidelines issued by the Civil Justice Council and agreed with the Council for Mortgage Lenders. It formalizes good practice such as encouraging contact between lender and homeowner before they go to court, suggesting that lenders should take reasonable steps to ensure that information can be understood by the borrower, and proposing that lenders consider reasonable requests from borrowers to change the date of regular payment if that would help. Note that, although judges in possession hearings will scrutinize adherence to the protocol, it is not compulsory. Indeed, suggestions that the protocol be given teeth via costs sanctions or postponements of possession were strongly resisted by the mortgage industry

(Whitehouse 2009). The status of the protocol is perhaps best indicated by its second sentence, '[t]his Protocol does not alter the parties' rights and obligations' (see Alcock 2008).

Bright sets out the problems of this 'fuzzy' response: 'The impact of the protocol is … variable and the extent of compliance is affected by the identity of the mortgagee …. According to surveys conducted by advice agencies, not all lenders are following the protocol' (Bright 2011, 26–7). Positive effects, however, were noted: 'Surveys suggest that judges now ask more questions about whether lenders tried to reach agreement before taking court action, and there is a willingness by many judges to adjourn cases where the lender has not followed the protocol' (ibid., 27). The introduction of the protocol coincided with a significant fall in the number of possession orders granted and with a fall in the number of claims being issued, although no causal link between the protocol and these falls was established. Overall, considering the nature of the crisis, the impact was hardly substantial, although potentially detrimental. Whitehouse provides us with a useful analysis (Whitehouse 2009). The statutory protections for mortgagors set out in the Administration of Justice Act 1970, she argues, are based upon ensuring that the mortgagee does not exploit its power to dispossess the homeowner in circumstances when the homeowner could afford to discharge the arrears within a reasonable period. In order to access the protections of the statute and displace the inherent right to possession, the homeowner must show that the mortgage is affordable. It should be noted that the protocol not only leaves undisturbed the mortgagee's inherent right to possession, but by enabling judges to adjourn hearings when there has been a failure to comply with the protocol, costs are added to the borrower's account, reducing the likelihood of the debt being repayable within the reasonable period of time required.

The pre-action protocol demonstrates the limits of social intervention in contemporary England and Wales. Activated at a distance from the state and appealing to the best interests of the financial bodies, it demonstrates the limited responsibility that government is prepared to accept for the difficult circumstances faced by those who are marginal to its project of citizenship via homeownership. Moreover, based upon an understanding of the citizen as a freely contracting economic actor who should receive (time-limited) help only if the original decision to purchase the home was economically rational and sustainable, the protocol fails to address the vulnerabilities of those who have no alternative but to seek housing via homeownership, even if buying a home was neither rational nor sustainable. Equally significantly, the intervention took no account of the vulnerabilities of lenders to making decisions which underestimated the risks presented by particular applicants for mortgages – the risk of those poor decisions is being borne entirely by the borrower (see Harvey 2005, 74).

The Mortgage Rescue Scheme

Nor did the other protections mobilized by the state demonstrate any greater understanding of the vulnerabilities of those at risk of repossession. The mortgage rescue scheme devised by the then Department of Communities and Local Government in 2008 provides a useful example. It targeted households that, if repossessed, would be accepted as homeless, therefore obliging local authorities to secure accommodation for them. In an attempt to avoid this, and in order to sustain homeownership, the scheme provided a choice for eligible households – those that could demonstrate that they had exhausted all other options and were at imminent risk of repossession. The scheme could either make an equity loan to the household (the 'shared equity' option); or purchase the home at near-market rate, with the former owner remaining in the house on an initial three-year shorthold tenancy at up to 80 per cent of market rent (the 'mortgage-to-rent' option). The shared equity option, which was cheaper for the government, was anticipated to be the favoured option. However, it required households to have between 25 and 40 per cent equity in their home. No such requirements exist for mortgage-to-rent.

In 2011 the scheme was strongly criticized by the National Audit Office for failing to provide value for money. Its verdict was damning:

> The Scheme delivered 2,600 completed rescues between January 2009 and March 2011, less than half of those expected when the Scheme was launched. At its launch in January 2009, the Department expected the Scheme to help up to 6,000 households over two years. After six months, only 18 households had accepted a formal Scheme offer, but numbers subsequently picked up.
>
> The Department has spent on average £93,000 for each rescue completed – it expected to spend £34,000. The main reason for the higher-than-expected average cost is that most completed rescues have been the more expensive mortgage-to-rent type, with only a minority being shared equity. The Department had expected the opposite. The cost of the mortgage-to-rent rescues themselves is closer to plan, but rose from September 2009, when the Department sought to increase the availability of the Scheme by increasing the subsidy it provided to housing associations. On average, this type of rescue has cost £93,000 (19 per cent more than the £78,000 expected). Since this change was reversed in July 2010, the cost to the Department of each mortgage-to-rent rescue has averaged £81,000 (4 per cent more than expected). (National Audit Office 2011, 5)

The National Audit Office has a vision statement, 'to help the nation spend wisely', which betrays its particular perspective. It limited its task to the design, appraisal, implementation and management of the Mortgage Rescue Scheme and did not evaluate the wider effort to prevent repossessions more generally. Despite these limitations, it was able to conclude that the long-term costs of each rescue outweighed the measurable benefits. The Mortgage Rescue Scheme, analysed thus, provides a prime example of what Willse calls 'economizing the social', whereby a social problem, 'becomes a problem of inefficient use of resources. The solution becomes better management of social welfare administration through the application of business principles' (Willse 2010, 171). The Mortgage Rescue Scheme fails because it fails to apply proper business rigour to its operations.

I suggest that a vulnerability analysis could provide a far richer explanation of why government overestimated the number of families in danger of having their homes repossessed who would choose a loan and underestimated the number who would choose to sell their homes and then rent them back. A vulnerability analysis would have started from a elaboration of its own understanding of the vulnerabilities of those who were at risk of repossession, in particular the difficulties faced by those who had chosen to enter homeownership in the very recent past when prices were particularly high in relation to incomes and who were likely to be in the most insecure jobs. If recent purchasers are amongst the most vulnerable to repossession, it is not surprising that they chose to reject shared equity. Not only were they unlikely to have the requisite level of equity in their property, but their patent failure to manage the responsibilities of homeownership was very likely to make them choose to return to renting, particularly if it meant that they could stay in their own home. What government did was to overestimate the allure of homeownership – demonstrating government's vulnerability to its own ideological commitments.

Just as important, a vulnerability analysis would give much greater weight to one particular aspect of the scheme – the requirement that all alternative options had been exhausted. This ensured that those at risk of repossession – often those without sophisticated social resources at their disposal – sought professional advice. The scheme mobilized extensive resources, therefore increasing the resilience of those most vulnerable to the consequences of economic recession. The National Audit Office, not concerned with notions of resilience, underplayed this element of the scheme. Indeed, on reflection, surely the reality of our universal fragility has played some role in the design and construction of our societal institutions.

The transformation of homeownership from a secure to an insecure form of tenure had a consequence in addition to increasing the risk of repossessions for those at the margins of homeownership. It sharpened the debate about the tenancy for life provided for those who live in local authority housing. For, as security is diminished for the homeowner, the security provided to the social tenant looks increasingly anachronistic. It is to this debate that this chapter now turns.

The Tenancy for Life

The labelling of a secure tenancy, which is the type of tenancy given to tenants of local authorities, as a 'tenancy for life', derives from the fact that secure tenants can only be evicted on particular grounds and, in cases where alternative accommodation is not available, when it is reasonable to do so. So, for instance, if a tenant is proved to be in rent arrears, the judge has discretion whether or not to evict. This degree of security of tenure has only been a characteristic of local authority tenancies since 1980. Previously, local authorities had been able to evict their tenants almost at will; the belief was that local authorities would act in a benign fashion on behalf of the community. That paternalist position became untenable with the growth of civil rights in the 1960s and 1970s. Reform was promised by the Callaghan government in 1979, and its proposals were adopted by the victorious Thatcher government, which incorporated the 'Tenant's Charter', including security of tenure, into the Housing Act of 1980, alongside the Right to Buy. At that time security of tenure and the other rights provided for local authority tenants were useful to the government, as they served to decrease the power of local authorities – a prime target of the Thatcher administration. Nonetheless, the benefits of the 'Tenant's Charter' did not, nor were they intended to, compete with the allure of the Right to Buy.

One important consequence of the stratification of housing tenure, which was a consequence of the success of the Right to Buy, is highlighted by Gurney. The conclusion he reaches following his analysis of the discourses which construct homeownership as normal is that it creates, 'an out-group or a "shameful (housing) class" which exists beyond the frontier of abnormal behaviour. This exclusion is, strictly speaking, neither exclusively economic nor social. Instead it is cultural, linguistic and psychological' (Gurney 1999, 180). Flint makes a similar point about the construction of the local authority tenant as lacking in key characteristics of contemporary citizenship: 'Within housing, a conceptual differentiation emerges between owners of residential means of consumption (homeowners) and those who do not own such means of consumption but rather consume the collective means of consumption of public or social housing' (Flint 2003, 614).

These points are well made. The 'shameful' difference of the local authority tenant who is a drain on resources led to a questioning of the status of the secure tenant, particularly of his or her security of tenure. Its erosion started with an attack (via the Housing Act 1996 and the Anti-Social Behaviour Act 2003) on the security of tenure of the 'anti-social' tenant by extending discretionary grounds for possession in relation to anti-social behaviour, broadly defined; by expediting possession proceedings where anti-social behaviour was an issue; by introducing 'probationary' tenancies enabling easy evictions if a tenant does not behave responsibly, and by enabling local authorities to 'demote' secure tenants (see Smith and George 1997). This process has continued, with a variety of other devices, for instance the Family intervention tenancy, which has the purpose of rehabilitating allegedly anti-social families within the local community but which offers no security of tenure (see Morgan 2010). This is despite legal recognition that in certain (very limited) circumstances evicting the anti-social without considering the proportionality of that eviction may infringe their rights under the European Convention on Human Rights (see Cowan and Hunter 2012). Most recently (May 2012), the coalition government has proposed, in its White Paper

'Putting Victims First', a mandatory ground for possession where there is evidence of serious housing related anti-social behaviour.

The easy acceptance of the notion that the anti-social are disproportionally protected generated debates about security of tenure in general, with politicians and housing professionals proposing its replacement by tenancies which are regularly reviewed in order to ensure that the tenants continue to be in housing need. Despite considerable unease (see Hills 2007), the coalition government has moved to abolish automatic security of tenure. In 2011 it introduced provisions in its Localism Act that enable local authorities to offer renewable fixed-term tenancies. Current tenants will not lose their secure status, nor will local authorities be obliged to offer fixed-term tenancies. Nonetheless, something significant has changed; legal rights, which were unanimously supported less than 40 years ago, will no longer be automatic features of local authority tenancies. Furthermore, the change has met with relatively little opposition – this is in part because there is a shared concern that social housing estates result in social failure, and a belief that the state is not the best provider of housing.

The dissatisfaction with social housing is most clearly articulated in the Hills report, which suggests that outcomes for social housing are disappointing. In part, this is as a result of violence and crime, so for example,

> [m]ore than a fifth of social tenants in flatted-estate areas report the presence of drug user or dealers as a serious problem in their area, and nearly a fifth the general level of crime, fear of being burgled, vandalism and litter. These are all twice or more the levels reported by owner-occupiers and even private tenants on average. (Hills 2007, 93)

Equally telling was the evidence in connection with the poor employment outcomes of tenants of social housing:

> By Spring 2006 more than half of those of working age living in social housing were without paid work, twice the national rate. ... Even controlling for a very wide range of personal characteristics, the likelihood of someone in social housing being employed appears significantly lower than those in other tenures. There is no sign of a positive impact on employment of the kind that the better incentives that sub-market rents might be expected to give. Potential explanations of this include: the way those with the greatest needs even within any category are screened into social housing, but out of other tenures; particular fears about loss of benefits on moving into work within the social sector; the location of social housing and 'neighbourhood' effects from its concentration in deprived areas; possible 'dependency' effects of welfare provision; and the difficulty of moving home to get a job once someone is a social tenant. (ibid., 111)

However, it is not just the poor outcomes which have led to criticism. Somehow the insulation of the secure tenant from the risks of the market has become problematic. This is illustrated by the questions that the Chartered Institute of Housing asks in connection with the future of social housing:

> How can we move towards a more flexible system that allows the housing offer for individuals to change with their circumstances? Which can support the unlocking of the full range of housing ambitions and aspirations and supports choice and the pursuit of opportunity? Which incentivises individuals and which is fair for both those in and outside of the system? (Chartered Institute for Housing 2008, 21)

The shift in attitudes about security of tenure reflects the more general shift away from post-war welfarism and towards risk (see, for example, Ronald 2008). The extent of the rejection of collective welfarist values has left opposition to the move sounding hollow, resting mainly in a nostalgia for council housing, which fails to acknowledge criticisms of it as paternalistic and authoritarian. In contrast, proponents have available to them what appear to be convincing economic arguments.

Fineman's analysis becomes useful in helping identify the limitations of, and alternatives to, economic rationalities. There are at least three strategies through which the current debate could be enriched. First, the lifelong tenant should be understood, not as being a privileged or a dependent subject, but as being a vulnerable subject. That vulnerability is not specific to his or status as a social tenant but is shared with all who do not have sufficient resources to access the housing market in a sustainable way. The lifelong tenant's needs are therefore in common, not competing, with those of marginal homeowners. Second, Fineman's work enables us to understand that local authorities, the state institutions which bear primary responsibility for social housing, are themselves vulnerable – a vulnerability which they share with all institutions. The solution is not to dismiss them as authoritarian and failing, but to imagine new ways of increasing their accountability both to the public and to their own tenants. The third strategy involves reconceptualizing the lifelong tenancy as being an asset that assists in providing resilience to vulnerable subjects rather than as being something which depletes their economic vitality. The lifelong tenancy has the potential to be a particularly rich asset, which has human, social, physical, environmental and existential dimensions. Research with tenants, designed to flesh out these strategies, would be far more productive than forcing them to defend what has been deemed by others to be a privilege.

Conclusion

The contemporary discourse on welfare within England characterizes the tenancy for life, along with other state-sponsored protections such as the minimum wage, public sector pensions and unfair dismissal legislation, as an unjustifiable privilege, therefore legitimating its erosion. In addition, initiatives such as the mortgage rescue scheme are designed and judged on a narrow value-for-money basis. Only those state schemes, such as the mortgage possession pre-action protocol, which do not interfere with rights and responsibilities but operate by appealing to the best interests of commercial organizations are sustained. It is here that Fineman's work is of broader significance than the relatively narrow debates about social housing that this chapter has considered. Her understanding of the relationship between the state and the assets that individuals can draw upon to achieve the necessary resilience in order to manage their vulnerability has the potential to provide us with the necessary tools to reconceptualize the role of the state and rebut the prevalent neoliberal logic.

Fineman deploys a quite different logic. Once we accept that assets are distributed by institutions such as corporations, families and religious bodies, which are supported and legitimated in a variety of ways by the state, and that those institutions can almost invisibly produce or exacerbate existing inequality, then we must accept that 'their flaws, barriers, gaps, and potential pitfalls should be monitored and their operations adjusted when they are functioning in ways harmful to individuals and society. The values that should be applied in making such judgments and adjustments must be democratic and publicly oriented, reflecting norms of equality and open access and shared opportunity' (Fineman, this volume, 25). Such a vulnerability analysis lets structural inequality back into the political equation and provides the possibility for ethical scrutiny of legislative activity. Privileges are not eradicated within this vulnerability paradigm; instead, 'A responsive state would have to address the distortions that have arisen by privileging liberty over equality and advantaging some in society at the expense of others. This would necessitate looking at existing structures of privilege, as well as at entrenched disadvantage' (26). So, in the context of this chapter, any decision to remove the privilege of the 'tenancy for life' has to be justified and any justification would have to take into account the paucity of other assets that are available to provide the council tenant with resilience.

Whilst Fineman would insist on a similar accounting before any social protection is removed, it may be that it is in the arena of housing that the necessary paradigm shift is most possible. Harvey, in his seminal work on neoliberalism (Harvey 2005), alerts us to its political instability. Homeownership has become a means by which risk and possessive individualism can be enhanced, and this has placed it at the heart of the neoliberal project. But instability is inherent within the housing market. So Hamnett, for instance, describes homeownership as being akin to a casino: 'There have been big winners, but there have also been big losers. The last thirty years have been a roller coaster ride for owners: exhilarating, but potentially highly dangerous' (Hamnett 1999, 1), whilst Ronald points out the dilemma for government: 'Governments are having to take measures to sustain the system and are caught between ostensibly contradictory demands: to make housing more affordable to greater numbers of people *and* to make sure house prices go up in order to build capital equity amongst existing property owners' (Ronald 2008, 25).

Fineman's theoretical work on vulnerability can profit from this instability. There is the potential to enable arguments that disrupt the current neoliberalism-informed consensus that equality of opportunity is a more than sufficient basis for social provision. At the same time the juxtaposition of Fineman's work with current policy logic reveals the economic character of contemporary interventions that purport to be social. It achieves this productively, as it avoids potentially destructive comparisons between welfare groups, such as the marginal homeowner and the secure tenant. Most significantly of all, it may be that England's housing crisis will force a re-imagination of the state as responsive, enabling us to consider 'the possibility of an active state in non-authoritarian terms' (Fineman 2008, 19). Fineman makes clear that her vision is both participative and democratic: 'In a responsive state, individuals realize that we, too, are part of the state. We do not—cannot—stand outside of the state and we have a responsibility to participate—to be vigilant in seeing that the state is working effectively and in an egalitarian manner' (Fineman, this volume, 26). Fineman's work thus provides the scope to give substance to the desire for a meaningful collective life, which, for Harvey, poses the greatest threat to the neoliberal project.

Chapter 8

Assisted Reproductive Technology Provision and the Vulnerability Thesis: From the UK to the Global Market

Rachel Anne Fenton

Introduction: Fineman's Vulnerability Thesis[1]

Fineman's deployment of vulnerability arises out of her dissatisfaction with equal protection law in the US, which is founded upon sameness of treatment for recognised identity groups based on characteristics such as race, gender and religion. Fineman contends that the focus upon formal equality ignores differences and inequality in opportunity, possibility and circumstance and 'leaves undisturbed – and may even serve to validate – existing institutional arrangements that privilege some and disadvantage others' (Fineman 2008, 3). As a consequence, 'the state is not mandated to respond to those inequalities, nor does it have to establish mechanisms to ensure more equitable distributions of either social goods or responsibilities …' – indeed, the state is actually 'restrained from interference in the name of individual liberty, autonomy, and paramount values such as freedom of contract' (Fineman 2010, 252). Fineman therefore posits her concept of vulnerability as an alternative to formal equality, as a 'post-identity' analysis of what sort of protection society owes its members (Fineman 2008, 1). The vulnerable subject is positioned as a replacement for the liberal political and legal subject 'who is fully capable and functioning and therefore able to act with autonomy' and is therefore, as a competent adult, at the 'least vulnerable' stage in life – a trope justifying the restraining of the state in the name of privacy and freedom of contract (Fineman 2010, 262). The vulnerable subject, by contrast, 'embodies the fact that human reality encompasses a wide range of differing and interdependent abilities over the span of a lifetime' and that 'individuals are anchored at each end of their lives by dependency and the absence of capacity' (Fineman 2008, 12). Once we recognise the universal vulnerability of all, Fineman suggests, the vulnerability analysis has 'the potential to move us beyond the stifling concerns of current discrimination-based models

1   I wish to thank the editors for their invaluable critique and insights. I would also like to express gratitude to Sally Sheldon, Gayle Letherby, D. Jane V. Rees, Julie Kent and Helen Malson for their helpful comments.

toward a more substantive vision of equality' (Fineman 2008, 1). The concept of vulnerability may allow us to transcend contemporary ideological constraints in reconceptualising the role of the state in terms of responsiveness to, and the empowerment of, the vulnerable subject (Fineman, this volume, 24–6). Thus, the vulnerability thesis constitutes a 'powerful conceptual tool with the potential to define an obligation for the state to ensure a richer and more robust guarantee of equality' (Fineman 2008, 9).

The aim of this chapter is to explore infertility and the provision of Assisted Reproductive Technologies (ARTs) through the lens of Fineman's vulnerability thesis, adopting UK provision as its platform. Using infertility as an example of the embodied human condition, the chapter will examine how the liberal order's focus on autonomy has led to some gains in terms of formal equality provision, in the sense that this approach extends the category of liberal autonomous subject (partially) to embrace categories of identity previously excluded. However, by juxtaposing the 'gains' of formal equality with a vulnerability analysis of ART provision, the chapter reveals how a post-autonomy and post-identity analysis can expose the state's inadequacy in addressing the embodied vulnerability of the infertile – an inadequacy exacerbating conditions of privilege and disadvantage. In the light of this analysis, I argue that a more substantive vision of equality, as demanded by Fineman, can only be achieved by moving beyond autonomy – and beyond merely formal equality – to include an examination of the actual opportunities of access to ART provision. Such an examination, in the context of the UK, reveals that the state is unresponsive to infertility and that genuine equality is illusory.

The insights gained from a vulnerability analysis of the UK's ART provision, however, have implications lying far beyond the shores of the UK jurisdiction, as I will argue below. The chapter reflects on the fact that the consequences of unethical legislative behaviour and the evasion of a responsibility to provide genuine equality of access by a nation-state have ramifications beyond the limits of a domestic jurisdiction. Indeed, the consequences can be felt globally, especially in a situation where the establishment and reinforcement of global markets in fertility treatment and bio-material forms a veritable lion's den into which the unsuspecting infertile – and donors – may be thrown. Accordingly, I seek to show how the global market not only exacerbates existing vulnerability but also creates further vulnerabilities, perpetuating privilege and disadvantage along global geographic trajectories. Against this important backdrop, the chapter aims to illustrate how the vulnerability thesis can be used to call states to account, to make demands for genuine equality of opportunity and access to ARTs, to urge a deeper sense of collective and state responsibility for the creation of children as a social good and to address the global inequalities and vulnerabilities created and exacerbated as a result of blinkered unethical legislative behaviour in the global North.

The Meaning of Infertility

Clinical infertility is defined as being the failure to conceive after frequent unprotected sexual intercourse, that failure lasting for one to two years in couples in the reproductive age group (NICE 2004, 1, www.nice.org.uk/nicemedia/ live/10936/29269/29269.pdf). The cause may be pathological or unexplained and infertility is estimated to affect around one in seven couples in the UK (NICE 2004, 1). Yet infertility is not merely a result of clinical causes: a couple may be physically able to reproduce but need assistance to avoid passing on a hereditary genetic (or infectious) disease or to create a saviour sibling or a child of a particular sex. Likewise, individuals may be fertile but precluded from reproduction due to their sexuality or because they are single. To this end, then, I am using the word 'infertility' to describe a state of being whereby – for whatever reason (clinical or social) – a particular child cannot come into being without the use of ARTs. For the purposes of this chapter, the word 'infertile' will be used to designate *only* those who *want* to reproduce and *want* to use ARTs (or at least to have the choice of access to ARTs) in order to do so. My definition therefore does not encompass the voluntarily childless who do not want children (and have no use for ARTs) and are unlikely, in any case, to self-identify as 'infertile' (as 'infertility' is a term generally adopted only when an individual is seeking to reproduce but cannot). By adopting this definition, I am not suggesting that all people must or should want to reproduce, or to use ARTs. I am interested in the state provision of ARTs and its implications in the light of Fineman's vulnerability thesis. Therefore, feminist constructions of the desire to reproduce, motherhood and non-motherhood 'choices' and imperatives, and voluntary childlessness cannot be discussed in any great detail here for reasons of space (for a brief summary, see Fenton et al., 2011).

Infertility and the Human Condition

To be vulnerable is to be human; to be human is to be vulnerable. Vulnerability, says Fineman, arises 'from our embodiment' (Fineman, this volume, 20) and describes 'a universal, inevitable, enduring aspect of the human condition' (Fineman 2008, 8). Perhaps nowhere else is our humanity, and therefore our vulnerability, so keenly manifest than in our desires and decisions to bear or beget a child. Indeed, it can be argued that '… the need and desire to be a parent and make offspring can be considered one of the primeval and most elementary interests a person may have' (Sperling 2011, 375). The procreative instinct is not only 'a powerful human drive' (Storrow 2010b, 295) but has been argued to originate in 'guiding principles of evolution' (Silver and Silver 1998, quoted in Sperling 2011, 375). This need or urge or desire to reproduce, then, may be intrinsic to the essence of our humanity *even if* it is not universally felt and *even if* reproductive choices do not exist in a vacuum and may be socially constructed to some extent.

Reproductive health is defined by the United Nations as being 'a state of complete physical, mental and social well-being and not merely the absence of disease or infirmity, in all matters relating to the reproductive system' (1994 International Conference on Population and Development quoted in Csete and Willis 2010, 218). The impact of being unable to reproduce may be differentially experienced, but for some the human cost may be significant. One commonly used adjective used by writers and sufferers alike is 'devastating'. For example, in personal narratives collected by Pfeffer and Woollett one sufferer describes infertility as 'a major life crisis' (Pfeffer and Woollett 1983, 2) and another says of her situation:

> At first you try to think that it's not really happening. But this fear creeps up. This fear that the whole thing is so bad and the feeling so devastating that you don't know quite how devastating it's going to be. The depths of it are so great that somehow if you really open up, you might get out of control and you will never emerge again as a sane person. (Pfeffer and Woollett 1983, 24)

This is not to suggest that all sufferers of infertility are 'desperate' (see, for example, Letherby's work on women's differing experiences of infertility / involuntary childlessness (Letherby 2002)) but simply to recognise that, for some, it is 'a profound shock to [their] sense of self which often involves distress and represents a challenge to an individual's identity' (279). The *impact* of infertility may of course be felt differently in different societies or in different social groups within a society – depending upon how resilient the matrigno-idolatry (Meyers 2001) and procreation imperative is. In strongly pronatalist societies, in which cultural expectations not only endorse a procreation imperative (such as in Israel which 'sanctifies having children' – interviewee in Nahman 2011, 630) but which also isolate and ostracise infertile women who are subsequently at risk of domestic violence and other abuse (Csete and Willis 2010), infertility may incur an even more traumatic human cost.

Fineman uses the term 'vulnerable' to describe 'a universal and constant aspect of the human condition' (Fineman, this volume, 17), detaching the term '*vulnerable population*' from its association with 'victimhood, deprivation, dependency or pathology' (Fineman 2010, 266). To recognise infertility as being a state of vulnerability in Fineman's sense is therefore not to stigmatise it. From this perspective, what is important is that infertility is characterised by its very universality and ubiquity: it may genuinely affect anyone, male or female, black or white, rich or poor, disabled or able-bodied, religious or not, wherever they are globally situated. As humans, we are rendered vulnerable by infertility because it genuinely 'arises from our embodiment', from our very existence as humans, from our corporeality, and may well ultimately be 'beyond individual, or even human, control' (Fineman, this volume, 20). Infertility can therefore be said to be truly and utterly part of vulnerability as 'the human condition', perfectly demonstrating 'the limitations of human ability to avoid the ultimate consequences of our embodiment' (Fineman 2010, 267). Furthermore, Fineman recognises that humans are positioned differently whilst standing 'in a position of constant vulnerability' (268). Whilst infertility is universal, it, like vulnerability itself, is 'experienced uniquely' (269). Indeed, even the desire to reproduce (or not) is complex and may be influenced by particular social, cultural and religious contexts. (The provision of ARTs may in itself create pressures influencing reproductive choices.) These contexts may affect women more than men, and it is precisely within these contexts that infertility will be lived. Thus, those experiencing infertility are differentially and uniquely embodied, differently situated and will experience complex reproductive decision-making differently in a range of different contexts. Finally, it is worth noting that infertility is not recognised as being a form of inequality and, as such, no one is protected against discrimination on this basis. Indeed, what is particular about infertility is its transcendence of the traditional identity groups on the basis of membership of which equal protection claims may be made: Infertility may also render anyone in a traditionally protected category vulnerable on this count.

Historically, the decision to have a child within the traditional heterosexual family unit has been conceptualised as belonging to the 'private' sphere: reproductive decision-making only became part of the 'public' sphere and the concern of society when decisions were constructed as 'deviant' (Fineman 1995, ch. 5). Whilst what has been considered 'deviant' has shifted over time, the unassisted conception and birth of a child (and the rearing of that child absent any abuse or neglect) remains conceptualised as part of the domain of 'family' and therefore as private: such choices are deemed to be representative of our reproductive freedom and autonomy. As such, individuals are understood to bear children out of choice and to be responsible for that choice. As a corollary, the inability to reproduce is also conceptualised as being 'private' or even as being a 'choice', perhaps more so when it is not as a result of a clinical cause.

However, reproduction has implications that reach far beyond the 'private' zone of personal choice. Society must reproduce itself. Reproduction is also productive. We might go as far as suggesting that the state has an interest in reproduction because the creation of citizens and regeneration of society for the common good is an important and essential collective societal interest – as Chavkin says, 'societies must assume some social reproductive responsibilities if they want to self-perpetuate' (Chavkin 2008, 164). Further arguments for state interest may be made on the basis of sustained below replacement fertility in the developed world, and, increasingly, in the developing world as well (see Chavkin 2008; also Gallagher 2010, 165; Chavkin notes that 20 resource-poor countries have below replacement fertility). Declining birth rates are of concern 'because of the resulting skewed age distribution of the population and the consequences for the proportion of the population working, the ensuing tax base and economic productivity' (Chavkin 2010). Some states with very low fertility such as Italy have already offered financial incentives for having a child (see Fenton 2006). In her earlier work *The Autonomy Myth*, Fineman rejects the notion that having a child is a choice much like owning an expensive car, refusing to '… accept the basic premise that children are merely another commodity' (Fineman 2004, 43). She goes on to argue that 'a decision to have a child sets up a qualitatively different relationship between the decision maker and the collective or state … caring for dependents is a society-preserving task – care of children in particular is essential to the future of the society and all of its institutions … providing a social good as well as individual satisfaction' (43). Thus, if we reconceptualise the role of the family and recognise that 'the family is not separate and should not be segregated into the "private" sphere' (208), then not only the child-rearing role of the family but also its role as *creator* of future citizens essential to the preservation of society will become part of the interest of the state and societal institutions. Reproduction and the family will become elements of our collective interest for which the state can no longer exonerate its responsibility.

As noted above, vulnerability is not only universal but 'particular: it is experienced uniquely'; how it is experienced will depend on 'the quality and quantity of resources we possess or can command' (Fineman, this volume, 21). The vulnerability analysis thus requires a focus upon the state to ensure equality of opportunity and access in the distribution of its assets and to ensure that some citizens are not unduly privileged over others. As the alleviation of infertility is not an interest in fertility alone, but in becoming a parent, the responsiveness of the state in this regard pertains to the question of equality of opportunity in accessing ARTs (including surrogacy) in order to make possible the conception and birth of children (adoption is beyond the scope of this chapter). It might also be suggested that, logically, the more significant the social and cultural procreation imperative is in a society, the more proportionately responsive the state in question should be.[2] It should also be understood that the 'state' in this context includes societal institutions which, says Fineman, provide us with 'assets' which give us 'resilience' when faced with vulnerability (Fineman, this volume, 22–3). Such institutions are dependent on the state (narrowly understood) and the law for their legitimacy and operation as they 'distribute significant social goods' (Fineman 2010, 272). Thus, the state should 'be vigilant in ensuring that the distribution of such assets is accomplished with attention to public values, including equality or justice, or objectives beyond private or profit motivation' (ibid.). In the realm of ART provision, the most important societal institutions are healthcare providers. The vulnerability thesis therefore suggests that the state and healthcare providers – as societal institutions – have a duty to be responsive and '… a responsibility to structure conditions in which individuals can aspire to meaningfully realize their individual capabilities as fully as possible' (Fineman 2010, 274) – in this case, parenthood.

Against this broad theoretical background, the next part of this chapter will examine the responsiveness of the UK's regulation and the provision of ARTs in

---

2   Although this is inherently problematic in terms of state coercion of women into undesired motherhood.

the UK in terms of effectiveness, justice and 'equality of access and opportunity' (Fineman, this volume, 16). What I am attempting to do is to define 'what constitutes ethical legislative behaviour' (27) in the realm of ART provision using the concept of vulnerability, and to suggest what the 'ultimate ideals against which the state and its societal institutions and their actions are judged' (ibid.) might be for the vulnerable, infertile subject.

Infertility and the (Un)responsive UK state

General Healthcare Provision

'Health inequality' refers to disparities in terms of the general quality and level of people's health across the UK. According to the House of Commons Health Committee, 'health inequalities are not only apparent between people of different socio-economic groups – they exist between different genders, different ethnic groups …' (Health Inequalities 2009, 5). Whilst their causes are complex, there are some lifestyle-related factors which influence health inequalities in general, such as smoking, alcohol consumption, weight and sexual behaviour (21). Interestingly, these are also factors which may influence fertility, as evidenced by the fact that the National Institute for Clinical Excellence (NICE),[3] in its 'initial guidance to people concerned about delays in conception' (section 2.1, NICE 2004, 8) advises reducing body mass index (bmi), ceasing smoking and reducing alcohol consumption to aid conception. Female sexual health is also related to fertility. These correlations suggest that a state can indirectly protect and enhance reproductive health via general healthcare initiatives.

In the UK, the National Health Service (NHS), which provides healthcare free of charge to all, is a social asset, important in its provision of resilience and shelter against our vulnerabilities. In recent times the NHS has spent millions on anti-smoking, anti-alcohol and sexual health campaigns as well as on its general health campaign Change4Life, which tackles diet and exercise in particular (Change4Life, Mathieson 2011). Some of the lifestyle factors mentioned above which produce inequalities are more entrenched within the lowest socio-economic groups. This may mean that in effect the poorest in society are the most vulnerable, firstly, in terms of their general health and, secondly, as a corollary, in terms of their reproductive health. Such vulnerability is compounded by the fact that there is evidence suggesting that 'traditional public information campaigns are not successful with lower socio-economic or other hard-to-reach groups' (Health Inequalities 2009, 7). Furthermore, Earle and Letherby suggest that in the UK poverty and social exclusion remains the single most important factor in determining women's reproductive health (Earle and Letherby 2007, 234). And

---

3   Independent body providing guidance on promotion of good health and preventing and treating ill-health.

similar patterns of inequality are evident globally; in the US where healthcare is private, certain socio-cultural or racial groups may be more affected, for example, by their access (or lack of it) to basic medical care (Cahn 2009, 35), and Cahn reveals that '… there is some speculation that poor women have a higher rate of infertility than wealthier women because of their inadequate access to medical care that might prevent sexually transmitted diseases and other causes of infertility. Indeed, many causes of female infertility stem from problems with access to medical care' (35). The simple provision of healthcare or healthcare campaigns is therefore not enough.

A vulnerability analysis recognises that equal distribution of general healthcare resources does not simply mean the equal *availability* of provision by means such as a free healthcare system like the NHS, but also that provision must take into account the ability of differently situated groups in society to actually *access* them. The map of health inequality in the United Kingdom (UK) as it affects infertility is complex, but the patterned nature of the relationship between provision and access / lack of access suggests that there is a meaningful space for identifying and responding to the more subtle nuances of health inequality which affect fertility. These realities lend force to the argument that infertility patterns are an entirely appropriate concern of a responsive state. In terms of infertility, emphasis must therefore be placed on ensuring that the most vulnerable in society have equal access to both general and reproductive healthcare which may indirectly facilitate their fertility. Without genuine equality of opportunity and access, the least vulnerable in society (who are best placed to access healthcare) are further privileged. These are distinctively structural, and not merely individual, concerns and patterns – and implicate the state as mediator of social resources in the production of the general health-provision conditions under which fertility, or infertility, is facilitated. What then, of specific healthcare provision aimed directly at the treatment of infertility?

Specific Healthcare Provision

Under the spotlight: The Legal Regulation of ARTs   The UK regulates assisted reproduction by means of the Human Fertilisation and Embryology Act 1990, as updated by the amending statute bearing the same name in 2008 (hereafter, HFE Act). In general terms, the UK's regulation is liberal and permissive and can therefore be said to occupy a middle ground between countries which have restrictive regulation, such as Italy, Germany, France, and Turkey (Storrow 2011), and others which have no legal regulation, operating on a market basis, such as the US.

The constitution of the family as an institution is generally defined and regulated by the state, and entitlement to ARTs is often governed by the type of family that the state deems to be the appropriate and responsible place for the raising of children – which means that those who fall within the definition of the normatively preferred family are privileged whilst others are excluded. Indeed, 'unfettered choice in matters of assisted reproduction is not a feature of most developed countries, where the general conviction is that reproductive choice is justifiably constrained by legal regulation' (Storrow 2010b, 297). The desirable family for ART practices is identifiable from the access criteria that a state imposes on its citizens by means of some sort of regulation. In the UK, until the 2008 reform, the so-called 'welfare of the child' provision under s.13(5) HFE Act 1990 required clinics providing ARTs to consider 'the welfare of any child who may be born ... (*including the need of that child for a father*) ...' (my emphasis). In addition, the child born to a single mother was constituted as being legally father*less* by s.28 of the 1990 Act. The 'need for a father' paid homage to the patriarchal family, representing the homophobic and heteronormative expression of idealised parenting in the form of the sexually affiliated two-parent heterosexual family (although the Act did not go as far as requiring the legal status of marriage), and was thus used in order to justify the exclusion of single and lesbian women from infertility treatment by conceptualising them as deviant and 'other'. The regulation thus facilitated the privileging of the dominant heterosexual construct and the consequent marginalisation of any other type of family, mirroring the general concern of the liberal order with the 'dangerousness' of 'manless' mothers – evident within much of family law (see, for example, Fineman 1995, especially chs 4 and 5). Amid significant controversy, the 'need for a father' criterion was expunged from the legislation in 2008, in recognition of the positive findings of the literature on lesbian and solo parenting (MacCallum and Golombok 2004) and of the unacceptable discrimination that the original provision facilitated, now anachronistic in terms of the recognition of equality on the grounds of sexual orientation (for example, by the Civil Partnerships Act 2004). Furthermore, a new parentage regime now recognises second legal parent status for the civil partner or partner of the birth mother, thus bringing the legal position of lesbian couples into line with that of heterosexual married and unmarried couples. However, this alternative parenting model is set out in the legislation as a mirror image of the sexually affiliated heterosexual model and is symbolically suggestive of the notion that the alternative model is secondary or even 'other'. More radically, however, the reform also permits a non-sexual partner to be named as the father or as the second legal parent of a child. In this way, a child born to a single mother may not be fatherless and the family need not be premised upon sexual affiliation (something Fineman has argued for almost two decades: Fineman 1995, 2004). Nonetheless, even this more radical alternative family still conceptualises the family as being composed of two parents – as opposed to one or three for example – and thus maintains the primacy of the biogenetic two-parent model, upholding the normative priority of the sexual family so fundamental to the liberal order. Law appears unable to move away from the patriarchally-based image of family. Nonetheless, significant and positive recognition has been given to alternative family forms.

In terms of access, the 2008 Act embodies a liberality not found in many other jurisdictions. In Italy, for example, as in Turkey and France, access is restricted to heterosexual couples, who, in Turkey, must be married; in Italy, married or living together; in France, in a stable relationship (Fenton 2006, Gürtin 2011, Storrow 2010b). In the US, where there is little governmental regulation, 'the refusal of fertility treatment centers to serve lesbian couples and single women is a notable problem' and 'studies indicate that many infertility clinics will deny access to single men, gay couples and poor couples' (Storrow 2010a, 376–7). The UK's progress toward inclusivity in this respect is a result of the liberal order's rejection of discrimination against defined identity groups and of the steady march away from paternalism towards autonomy as being the predominant principle in medical law, which now includes even the (once unaccountably problematic) corporeal right to self-determination of pregnant women (*St George's Healthcare Trust v. S* (1998) 3 WLR 936). The 2008 reform is couched in the rhetoric of autonomy in the form of reproductive choice and therefore it is safe to say that the liberal order's focus on liberty has produced some valuable gains.

However, complexities and challenges remain. The central fulcrum of the idea of expanded access remains the idea of libertarian choice and access. As a corollary of this, the law mitigates vulnerability by granting access to previously excluded groups, a tendency suggesting that the state has become more responsive. However, such responsiveness to vulnerability is not by design and nor is it an adequate response to the vulnerable subject (or to the vulnerable infertile subject). The dynamic is more exclusory than it first appears – and infinitely more double-edged. What the law actually does is to extend the category of the liberal autonomous subject to those who were previously outside its remit: these single, male partnerless women begin to *look like* the liberal autonomous subject. The lesbian family begins to *look like* its heterosexual counterpart. The alternative non-sexual two-parent family begins to *look like* an accepted family form. Inclusion therefore *looks like* formal equality – at the price of a flattening conformity to the central liberal constructs and closures. As Fineman states, '[w]e have merely expanded the group to whom this version of equality is to be applied' (Fineman 2004, 24). Autonomy and choice under the 2008 Act are constructed through the lens of the liberal actor and the spotlight is shining brightly upon it. The symbolic recognition of previously excised groups *is* important but it lulls us into a false sense of security and into assuming that what is under the spotlight is all there is. A vulnerability analysis requires that we move away from the closure of this spotlight and examine what is lurking in the shadows in order to see whether this construction of the infertile as liberal autonomous actors can ever genuinely address equality of access and equality of opportunity in ART provision.

Lurking in the shadows – the 'welfare of the child' provision   The UK has, despite progress, retained a modified version of the 'welfare of the child' provision. By allowing clinics to consider 'the welfare of any child who may be born as a result' (s.13(5)), the Act provides a forum for state invasion of decisional privacy: the infertile are in essence subject to a discriminatory 'tax' from which the fertile are exempt. No control is exercised over the reproductive autonomy of the fertile on grounds of their future fitness to parent; autonomy is the reward for self-sufficiency in the procreation game. As a result, Jackson argues that 'the welfare of the child thus occupies a curious middle ground, in which it is always *less* important than fertile couples' bodily integrity and sexual privacy and *more* important than infertile couples' decisional privacy' (Jackson 2002, 184). This type of exclusionary provision, which purports to justify state intervention on the grounds of the best interests of the not-yet-conceived is not uncommon (see, for example, Cohen 2011 on the US). S.13(5) has been consistently criticised for its past deployment in order to justify subjective assessments of potential parenting (Probert 2004) and its unjustifiable discrimination against the infertile was recognised by the Select Committee (Science and Technology Committee 2005). The words 'need of that child for a father' have been taken out of s.13(5) in favour of a seemingly more neutral phrase, 'need for supportive parenting', which is now defined in the HFEA's 8th Code of Practice: 'It is presumed that all prospective parents will be supportive parents, in the absence of any reasonable cause for concern that any child who may be born, or any other child, may be at risk of significant harm or neglect.'

The Code also states that the assessment 'must be done in a non-discriminatory way … patients should not be discriminated against on grounds of gender, race, disability, sexual orientation, religious belief or age'. Here we can see the liberal construction of non-discrimination on grounds of identity, yet it is ironic that traditional identity groups cannot be discriminated against in the context of discriminating against a group that is *not* traditionally recognised as having an identity: the infertile. The 'welfare of the child' provision illustrates Fineman's vulnerability thesis in its critical mode: the focus on traditional identity groups ignores other inequalities and 'obscures the institutional, social and cultural forces that distribute privilege and disadvantage in systems that transcend identity categories' (Fineman, this volume, 16). As long as the welfare of the child provision *looks like* it cannot operate in a discriminatory fashion, then, viewed though the liberal order's lens, it is not discriminatory. But shining the spotlight on the welfare of the child provision reveals the state's failure to be responsive or to distribute social goods equally. The provision is therefore unethical in the light of a vulnerability analysis. Moreover, s.13(5) also begins to demonstrate how the access provisions' portrayal of the infertile as being autonomous, self-sufficient actors akin to the fertile is fallacious. Everyone requiring ARTs remains subject to the clinic's (and indirectly to the state's) assessment of the welfare of the child to be born: the provision is therefore paternalistic and unequal.

Hiding in the dark: Actual ART provision – resource availability and equality of access   Fineman's vulnerability thesis requires a consideration of whether the liberal subject, who is a 'competent social actor capable of playing multiple and concurrent adult (formerly all-male) societal roles' (Fineman, this volume, 17), is the appropriate construct of the subject to be placed at the heart of social policy. We have already seen how the category of liberal actor now 'includes' those previously excluded on the grounds of identity (to a certain extent). But genuine equality is unlikely to result from forced conformity to the model of the autonomous liberal subject, and, accordingly, we must engage in a post-autonomy, post-identity analysis to ascertain whether there is genuine equality in the provision of resources. One indicative factor is that, in ideological terms, it is in fact the interest of the 'demand for liberty on the part of the individual' that 'effectively operates as a restraint on the state' (Fineman, this volume, 17). Therefore, we might ask to what extent the restraining of the state is in the interests of the infertile. Accordingly, the discussion to follow here revolves around 'asset-conferring' (Fineman, this volume, 23) societal institutions – in particular, the NHS and healthcare providers who distribute ARTs as a social good. Is such provision responsive to vulnerability? Does it produce substantive equality?

It is worth emphasising that, unless resources are available, there can be no choice to access them. In the UK, some ART treatment is available under the NHS, at least theoretically. The National Institute for Clinical Excellence (NICE) guideline recommends that public healthcare should provide three full cycles of IVF for women aged 23–39 years who have identified fertility problems or unexplained infertility persisting for at least three years (NICE 2004). This guideline is currently under review (NICE 2012).

A recent report by the All Parliamentary Group on Infertility in 2011 found that 73 per cent of Primary Healthcare Trusts (PCTs) (regional healthcare commissioning bodies) do not provide the recommended three full cycles of IVF. Indeed, 3 per cent provided none, 39 per cent offered one cycle, 26 per cent offered two cycles and only 27 per cent provided three cycles (para. 4.2). Furthermore, PCTs have been found to employ a range of arbitrary and unsubstantiated non-clinical social criteria aimed at rationing treatment, such as: smoking criteria; no existing children; one partner has no living children; no children under 16 living with the couple; no children living in the household; no children in current relationship (Department of Health 2009). The use of such criteria to determine funding was not recommended by the NICE guideline and is not evidence based (Kennedy et al. 2006). What this has created is a 'postcode lottery' where access to treatment provision differs substantially according simply to geographic location within the UK. This demonstrates major inequality of access to public resources distributed by a societal institution, which unjustifiably exacerbates vulnerability.

NICE recommend a cut-off age limit of 39 years for women but no age limit for men. There is no age limit expressed by the 2008 Act and the issue is determined by clinics' discretion under the welfare principle. The imposition of an age limit of 39 years is itself problematic, as will be discussed below, but even more worrying is that some PCTs impose an age limit maximum as low as 35 years (and others a minimum of 38.5 years with a maximum of 40 years) for women whilst some impose maximum age limits for male partners varying from 46 to 55 years (Department of Health 2009). Some centres do treat women as 'old' as 40 years. The imposition of a specific age limit is justified on grounds of allocation of scarce resources: those who are more likely to succeed in a live birth are more likely to receive treatment and the chances of a live birth decline rapidly with age (NICE 2004). Yet there are other factors which affect fertility, such as obesity, but the NICE guideline does not state a specific BMI above which a woman should not be offered treatment in the way that it states a specific age. This method of resource allocation is not necessarily rational. A woman aged 36 years who fails to conceive has some potential access to NHS resources but a woman aged 39 years does not, simply by virtue of her chronological age. The 39-year-old, however, may have a potentially higher probability of success, in real terms, due to other indicators of fertility: age alone does not therefore provide a rational determination of outcome. Furthermore, there is evidence that IVF using donor eggs is no more efficient in the case of younger women than in the case of older women, because fertility problems are caused by aging ovaries (the decreasing frequency of ovulation and declining quality of eggs) rather than by the aging uterus – and nor does an older uterus increase birth defects (Parks 1999). Although medical research does cite evidence of increased health risks to older pregnant women, the risks are relatively low if the woman is in good health (Berryman et al. 1995). To choose 39 as being the cut-off age also appears at odds with social reality. The upward trends in the fertility of UK women in their thirties and forties over the last three decades (the number of live births in the 30–34 years and 35–39 years age range has risen steadily and there is a consistent increase in live births in the 40 years and over category ('Birth Summary Tables' 2011, 'Births to older mothers' 2010) indicate that women are choosing to conceive later in life. The woman who tries (but fails) to conceive after her mid-thirties is effectively penalised by the system because she must show three years of unexplained infertility in order to access NHS resources.

Were recognition of the vulnerable subject to be placed at the forefront of rationing decision-making concerning infertility and fertility patterns, there is a good argument for suggesting that it is actually older women who should be prioritised, as they need treatment more than younger women. Moreover, combined with the fact that women's choices to mother early are constrained by social and economic realities, the promise of ARTs means that the subsequent denial of NHS treatment amounts to a form of double jeopardy, exacerbating vulnerability. In Western society, the dominant cultural message sent out to women is that early pregnancy (before a career) is a form of failure (Goodwin 2005, 45) and that teenage motherhood is a social ill.[4] Thus the ideal medical age for pregnancy and childbirth (around 18–20 years old) 'no longer comports with social and cultural values and expectation' (45–6). Goodwin argues that 'soft' pregnancy and motherhood discrimination leads women to delay pregnancy and forces them into late mothering through a 'fertility penalty' (Goodchild and Elliot 2006) in terms of lost income and lost position on the career ladder. This creates a 'double bind' for women who believe that they have to choose between a career and early motherhood: 'If women truly possessed the right to choose motherhood without fear of discrimination, some might mother earlier when it is biologically safer to do so' (Goodwin 2005, 3). We might assume that with the gains made in terms

---

4   For example, in 1999 the UK government pledged to halve teenage pregnancy rates by 2010 and allocated £260 million to achieve this ('Teenage pregnancy' 2010, DCSF 2010).

of reproductive freedom and autonomy that women make their own reproductive choices, but we must remember that 'they [women] do not make [choices] just as they please; they do not make them under conditions which they themselves create but under social conditions and constraints which they, as mere individuals, are powerless to change' (Petchesky, in Earle and Letherby 2007, 233). The current economic crisis, which has precipitated cuts in resources across the board such as proposed cuts to child benefit, falling wages, falling employment, falling wealth, is likely to be a backdrop against which women postpone their childbearing.

A fertile woman's decision to have a child later in life is neither questioned nor opened up to scrutiny. Her self-sufficiency in terms of her fertility is rewarded with non-interference from the state. Autonomy in reproductive choice is shown to be a myth, however, when the vulnerable infertile subject is at the centre of our analytical frame. The infertile woman does not make autonomous choices. Frequently, she is differentially positioned in structural socio-economic terms and on the basis of other 'difference' markers – and she is most certainly not the liberal actor that the traditional identity-based formal equality analysis portrays her to be. Once public funding is required, moreover, potentially discriminatory resource allocation operates to deny autonomy in a noticeably patterned manner. In essence, the infertile woman is punished for her lack of self-sufficiency in her fertility and thus for her dependency upon the state. The guise of 'rationing' operates to mask the huge underlying inequality in opportunity affecting access to publicly funded ART.

The age limit imposed in the public sector appears all the more problematic in light of the fact that private clinics have the discretion to treat older and post-menopausal women. The maximum age for treatment varies according to the particular clinic, but it would appear that around 50 years is the currently accepted upper age limit in the UK. Furthermore, the reference to infertility made by the NICE guideline means that single and lesbian women who are, in themselves, fertile but rendered unable to conceive by simply being (male-) partnerless, may be excluded from publicly funded treatment. This pushes 90 per cent of patients into the private sector where a single round of IVF costs from £4,000 (Lord Winston 2007).

The public access criteria operate to create an excluded yet privileged class of infertile women – those with the economic resources to be able to pay for private sector treatment. It is particularly telling that it is only once the infertile woman attains economic self-sufficiency that she is rewarded by the reduction of external control over her choices. The non-economically self-sufficient infertile woman is, by contrast, in effect punished twice – she is punished for her initial lack of fertility and for her inability to buy herself out of the state's control. It might also be suggested that public funds are deliberately restricted to ensure that those who use ARTs can afford to raise any future child. The connection between financial self-sufficiency and use of ARTs was used by Jackson in the context of attempting to *further* equality by opening up access to ARTs to single women a decade ago: 'Women who choose to have fertility treatment on their own will be neither poor nor young, and they will not have had single motherhood thrust upon then as a result of either an unplanned pregnancy or a relationship breakdown' (Jackson 2002, 193). Ironically, this connection may now be being used to deny actual equality of opportunity.

The central problem of inequality of access to public funding reflects further elements of uneveness in the system: some infertile people are privileged simply by where they live – a pattern often reflecting socio-economic and demographic factors producing further inequality and privileging the rich who already have the resources to by-pass the state's restrictive provision. However, we must also consider that the rich may be rendered vulnerable by their position. Lord Winston suggests that 'exploitation is a real issue. The combination of desperation and high costs is corrosive not only to the patient but to medical practice' (Lord Winston 2007) because in the private sector these patients may be given IVF whether or not it is medically indicated. This also occurs in the US where clinics offer deals such as 'live birth or your money back' (Schmittlein and Morrison 2003). Privileging may therefore also create vulnerability in some respects, while ameliorating it in others.

Theoretically, law has widened the goalposts of access to ART but access, as we have seen, is not equal. In terms of reproductive autonomy, we have exactly the familiar liberal scenario described by Fineman: 'We gain the right to be treated the same as the historic figure of our foundational myths – the white, free, propertied, educated, heterosexual (at least married), and autonomous male. We do not gain, however, the right to have some of his property and privilege redistributed so as to achieve more material and economic parity' (Fineman 2004, 23). Healthcare institutions are not operating in a fair and just manner. The current NHS provision of ARTs is not a good manifestation of social responsibility and does not alleviate the vulnerability of the infertile. Yet the NHS as an institution *could* give protection against infertility by allowing equality of opportunity to resources. It *could* give us '... assets—reservoirs of capabilities, advantages, or coping mechanisms that cushion us when we are facing misfortune, disaster, and violence' (Fineman, this volume, 22). It *could* afford us 'resilience in the face of vulnerability' (23). Its ability to do so is dependent on the state, which has created the current system of privilege and disadvantage and which under a vulnerability analysis it must not do – indeed, the state 'has an obligation not to tolerate a system that unduly privileges any group of citizens over others' (Fineman 2010, 274). However, as Fineman suggests, institutions themselves are vulnerable, they are not 'foolproof shelters', but are 'potentially unstable and susceptible to challenges from both internal and external forces' (273). Indeed, at this time of economic crisis, the NHS is subject to reform, cost-cutting and political compromise. Several PCTs are reducing the already limited access to public funding (Beckford 2011). Fineman suggests that '(o)ne implication of recognising institutional vulnerability should be acceptance of the need for monitoring, evaluating, updating, and reforming our societal institutions when necessary […] consistent with the mandate of equality of access and opportunity and the obligation of the state to act with equal regard for the vulnerability of all' (Fineman 2010, 273). The responsibility of the state therefore needs to be reconceptualised, firstly, in terms of the resources made available for distribution by healthcare providers and secondly, if rationing were justified at all under a vulnerability analysis, in the establishing of a more equal and robust rationing system untainted by inequality and the privileging of the rich. In an alternative paradigm of state regulation and responsibility, equality demands 'that the state exercise some responsibility to ensure that each individual has the necessary basic resources to allow choices to be made and be meaningful' (Fineman 2004, 271). In the context of reproduction, the word 'meaningful' is paramount: formal autonomy is nothing without access to treatment. We need to create a paradigm in which 'the state is not a default (therefore stigmatized) port of last resort, but an active partner with the individual in realizing her or his capabilities and capacities to the fullest extent' (ibid.). In this instance, that includes becoming a parent.

Cross-border Reproductive Care (CBRC)

States do not exist in isolation. Neoliberal globalisation means that they are situated within a global market, and juridical globalisation means that state legislation and policies can have consequences beyond domestic jurisdictional borders. There is also a thriving global marketplace in gametes, embryos, surrogates and treatment providers. The vulnerability thesis, given the universality of its vision, also demands that we examine the vulnerabilities created by unethical legislative behaviour not simply at home, but also globally through cross-border reproductive care. It is to this that we now turn our attention. I will initially explore what an autonomy analysis of CBRC might look like and then demonstrate the problems inherent in this approach by positing a vulnerability analysis.

  CBRC denotes the movement of persons between jurisdictions in the pursuit of conception under different conditions from those available 'at home' and is facilitated by both globalisation and the commercialisation of assisted reproduction (Gürtin and Inhorn 2011). The reasons for choosing CBRC vary between individuals but there are identifiable trends in both the reasons for exodus from home jurisdictions and the trajectories that that exodus takes. Indeed, there are particularities of host or destination jurisdictions that make them attractive to particular groupings of fertility travellers and, furthermore, some states actively seek to 'encourage or further develop a lucrative reproductive tourism industry' and advertise accordingly (Storrow 2011, 539). South African official tourism, for example, advertises 'Baby-on-Safari' (Carbone and Gottheim 2010). In terms of accessing CBRC, the Internet is a social asset that provides a wealth of information and specific websites providing support, advice and information about treatment abroad (see websites such as 'Fertility Friends' and 'IVF world', Culley et al. 2011, 13).

An Autonomy Analysis of CBRC

Prima facie, it might seem that CBRC is an asset which provides us with resilience in the face of vulnerability caused not only by infertility itself but also by local restrictions/shortages that might affect us. This may also include the way in which states themselves construct CBRC. Indeed, Storrow points out that the knowledge of extra-state availability of ARTs can facilitate (and even be essential to) restrictive policy and practice in some Western countries: 'fertility tourism acts as a moral safety valve permitting national parliaments to express local sentiments while simultaneously acknowledging the moral autonomy of those who do not agree with those sentiments' (Storrow 2005, 305) to circumvent them when they are unresponsive to their own particular vulnerability. In the UK, for example, the availability of surrogacy elsewhere was acknowledged by the Warnock Report as a reason for not allowing it in the UK (see Storrow 2005, 305 and for a more recent example see *S.H. and Others v. Austria* (Cohen 2012)).

The circumvention of local restrictions is an important function of CBRC. Those who are excluded from local treatment by virtue of, for example, their sexuality, age, marital status, rendering them 'other', are able to access gametes, embryos, surrogates and treatment on the international market. In this way, as Spar points out, although markets are not designed to advance reproductive rights, they may actually do so: 'if we believe that one of the key aspects of reproductive freedom is access to reproductive choice, then markets – which tend naturally to produce both access and choice – are a natural ally of those who argue for reproductive rights' (Spar 2010, 179). The thriving global market, under this analysis, allows access by marginalised groups and facilitates alternative families by offering resilience against vulnerability. The buoyant cross-border trade within Europe exemplifies this. The first systematic data produced by ESHRE (on Europe) found, for example, that Italians go to Spain for oocyte donation and to Switzerland for sperm donation and that French single women and lesbians go to Belgium for sperm donation (Shenfield 2009).

CBRC also permits moral choices to be made and the exercise of autonomy: those who are not excluded from local treatment may nonetheless *choose* to go abroad if they disagree with the local conditions for treatment or if a treatment type (such as embryo sex selection) is simply not available. Donor gamete anonymity is a case in point. Those who desire anonymous gametes can purchase them in the marketplace. In Europe, for example, Denmark has become the 'fertility centre of choice for sperm donation' (Carbone and Gottheim 2010). The availability elsewhere also serves to reinforce the acceptability of that particular treatment (ibid.) and therefore may send an important symbolic message.

The global market also covers for shortages in local markets. Where local laws provide for donor gamete anonymity and payment restrictions, there is often a shortage of gametes and long waiting lists. This is the situation in the UK; gamete donation has been anonymous since 2004. According to the ESHRE study, the 'top' locations chosen by the British for egg donation are the Czech Republic and Spain. Culley et al. confirm that shortages of donor gametes in the UK is one of 'the four most commonly mentioned reasons for (the British) travelling abroad' (Culley et al. 2011, 10).

CBRC may also be used to cut costs, thereby allowing access to treatment to some poorer people, who cannot afford private treatment at home (but do have the means to purchase some treatment). Another of the main reasons for travel from the UK is the expense of treatment – with a cycle of IVF costing double that of some Eastern European countries. In order to tackle gamete shortages, 'there is some evidence of treatment using imported vitrified eggs now being available in the UK'; however, as Culley et al. point out, 'such treatment is very expensive and further reproduces existing inequalities in access to fertility treatment' (Culley et al. 2011, 18). As an asset, then, it is arguable that CBRC protects the vulnerable by allowing them to access cheaper treatment abroad.

On this analysis, CBRC is an important asset promoting reproductive freedom, autonomy and choice, ameliorating conditions of hardship for those facing forced or voluntary exclusions from local markets. However, problems remain and the market-based autonomy analysis reveals itself to be blinkered. CBRC as an 'asset' is premised on the notion of the market, and 'markets are entirely impersonal and mechanical constructs, bringing together buyers and sellers, supply and demand, in a chain of interactions mediated by price' (Spar 2010, 177). The CBRC market-model reflects a liberal construction of the parties as liberal autonomous actors able to contract for themselves from a position of equality in the market, without coercion. This assumption is only really defensible on the presumption of genuine equality and opportunity of the parties involved. However, as Storrow points out, '(t)he vulnerability of infertility patients, coupled with the lucrativeness of infertility care, raises concerns about the significant gaps in the regulation of the burgeoning CBRC industry' (Storrow 2011, 539). A vulnerability analysis therefore requires us to look beyond this idea of CBRC as being autonomous contracting in the marketplace, buying and selling commodities, and to recognise that 'because of the nature of what is being sold – reproduction dreams – this is the type of transaction that we, as a culture, want to regulate and where we might want to redefine efficiency to include access and equity' (Cahn 2010, 149). The vulnerability thesis then requires us to be more tuned into the fact that, 'the vulnerable human subject is systemically (and unevenly) disadvantaged by the *gap* between the juridical mythos and the uneven living real. This effect, moreover, is amplified in the context of the globalised neoliberal order' (Grear, this volume, 54). The autonomy analysis, therefore, requires careful balancing by a vulnerability analysis.

A Vulnerability Analysis of CBRC

CBRC, for all its positive elements and potential, may also exacerbate existing inequalities in access, opportunity and the power to exert one's own moral preference, whilst simultaneously exonerating states from the responsibility of ART provision. Whilst treatment abroad may be cheaper, the reality is that it remains the privilege of those who can afford both the travel and the treatment, and it allows states to rationalise their failure to respond to vulnerability in the knowledge that cheaper treatment is available elsewhere. But what this dynamic is actually permitting is the subversion of the ethical preferences espoused by the home state. This in itself is problematic: take, for example, the use of anonymous sperm donation abroad which flies in the face of a nationally recognised principle of biological truth – of the possibility for a child to know its genetic origins. If this principle were considered sufficiently important, then there might be criminal sanctions (or other 'techniques' such as non-recognition of the child born) applied to the use of anonymous donor gametes abroad, but, in the absence of criminal responsibility or such like, a dual regime is created because the rich can contract out of local laws but the poor cannot. The poor are subject to rules and restrictions (which are not even considered important enough to carry criminal sanctions) and the rich are free to subvert them. CBRC, in this sense, exacerbates the vulnerability of the poor, who do not have equality of access or opportunity to bypass such local laws. Carbone and Gottheim note that, '[i]f the state healthcare system offers financial advantages over those services available abroad, the state may be in a better position to lock in its ethical preferences' (Carbone and Gottheim 2010, 209). This is certainly true and could be a reason to tempt the state to examine its responsiveness to reproductive vulnerability. However, it might also be a double-edged sword: the locking in of ethical preferences is only positive if those ethical preferences are themselves based upon genuine equality.

A vulnerability analysis requires the examination of three aspects of CBRC: first, the potential vulnerability of the fertility tourist, who is not necessarily the freely contracting liberal actor as so easily conceptualised under the CBRC autonomy analysis; secondly, the vulnerability of the home state upon the return of the fertility tourist; thirdly, the potential exploitation of the economically vulnerable and disempowered in the host state, commodification concerns, and the pricing of locals out of their own local market as higher prices are paid by foreigners. The vulnerability of the resulting child in some CBRC arrangements is also clearly an issue, but beyond the scope of this chapter.

The personal narrative of Ekaterina Aleksandrova reported in the *Guardian* (30 July 2008) exemplifies the reality of the vulnerabilities at play in CBRC. Aleksandrova bought anonymous donor sperm online from Denmark, which was shipped to India at a cost of £800 to fertilise the anonymous donor eggs of an Indian woman (bought for £500). Five embryos were implanted into Aleksandrova in India, resulting in a singleton pregnancy. In the UK, Aleksandrova, at age 42, would have been unlikely to qualify for NHS treatment, would have faced a long wait for donor gametes which would not be anonymous, would have paid significantly more for treatment and would not have been able to have five embryos transferred. The allure of the Indian market-based option where the UK rules are subverted becomes clear. Yet the vulnerabilities it creates are also clear.

We can observe the risks to Aleksandrova in terms of the lack of safety standards such as the potential multiple pregnancy (and which could have had a correlative impact on NHS resources had a multiple pregnancy ensued – for example, University College London Hospital has seen an increase in high-order multiple pregnancies from treatment abroad; see Shenfield 2009). Additionally, questions about the vulnerability of the egg donor in terms of the health risks of donation and her possible exploitation need to be raised, as India is one of the cheapest places to buy gametes in the global market. Egg donors can be paid as little as £70 (by contrast, in the US, '[t]he price of a desirable egg may be more than fifty thousand dollars' (Cahn 2010, 147)), and it is unclear whether donors are informed of the risks and whether their ovaries are over-stimulated to maximise profit. What is apparent is that the egg donors are hidden from view; this is a theme also evident in Nahman's work on the 'reverse traffic' of the human egg trade between Romania and Israel, which 'heightens, rather than diminishes, inequalities among differently situated women globally' (Nahman 2011, 3) and 'turns some women into available resources and others into consuming bodies' (10). Romania, the source of eggs, is 'still marked by sharp socio-economic inequalities' and is 'notorious for being one of the centres of "bioavailability" in Europe' (7). The egg trade can result in doctors setting up clinics in 'donor' countries to take back eggs to their country of origin so the women recipients do not have to travel. In this 'reverse traffic repro-migration', Nahman suggests that 'tissues/embryos/ eggs and recipients are prioritised over the well-being of the oocyte seller herself', perhaps more than in other forms of CBRC (11). Such reverse traffic in eggs has been reported as happening in the UK with eggs being imported from Moscow (Templeton 2010). This invisibility of women donors and the commodification of their eggs is of *particular* concern at the intersection between developed and developing countries in the global market, and the general direction of traffic in reproduction facilitation from poor to rich, from global South to global North. The vulnerability analysis must then ensure that these global donors *do* become visible – and accounted for – by states when they make domestic arrangements for ART, ensuring that part of ethical legislative behaviour is the consideration of the impact on humanity itself.

For those unable to attain pregnancy at all, surrogacy may be the only solution. Many states, including the UK, place restrictions on commercial surrogacy or outlaw it completely, leaving their citizens to negotiate surrogacy arrangements abroad. Where it is permitted in the developed world it is generally the privilege of the very rich. The allure of developing countries such as India for cheap surrogacy is therefore unsurprising – surrogacy costs just one-tenth of the price in Anand in India compared to Canada or the US (Pande 2009, 149). The choice of India as a source of cheap bio-availability illustrates how '[t]he poorest peoples and nations of the earth are forced disproportionately to bear the deepening social costs of capitalism' (Grear, this volume, 51). Pande suggests that Eurocentric 'portrayals of surrogacy cannot incorporate the reality of a developing-country setting – where commercial surrogacy has become a survival strategy and a temporary occupation for some poor rural women' (Pande 2009, 144). For the women themselves (egg donors and surrogates), hunger (among other things) is referred to in their defence of this type of 'work': 'You wouldn't ask me why I did it if you'd ever lived on one meal a day' (Prasad 2008); 'This is not work, this is *majboori* (a compulsion)

... if your family is starving what will you do with respect? Prestige won't fill an empty stomach'; '[p]eople who get enough to eat interpret everything in the wrong way' (Pande 2009, 161). Pande goes on to argue that, 'in such a setting, surrogacy cannot merely be seen through the lenses of ethics and morality but is a structural reality, with real actors and real consequences' (144).

Some facts are inescapable, including the extreme poverty, degrees of illiteracy, the lack of (the Westernised concept of) informed consent and the high stigma surrounding surrogacy and egg donation. It is difficult to see how the concept of free choice can operate in this context. Furthermore, '[t]he added attraction for clients is that the clinic runs several hostels where the surrogates can be kept under constant surveillance during their pregnancies' (Pande 2009, 149). The documentary *Google Baby* (2009) visually demonstrates Indian surrogates living communally in rooms with beds lined up close to one another, provoking an image of battery baby farming. If such conditions were replicated in the West, there would be moral outrage. Moreover, feminists in the West have been fighting against the medicalisation of pregnancy for decades – notions of surveillance are anathema to the basic concepts of bodily autonomy and dignity which the developed world is privileged to enjoy. Globalisation therefore permits the exploitation and commodifcation of women and gametes in the name of the free global market, and the unresponsive developed nation-state creates this market through its own restrictions on treatment availability or type. Furthermore, states may leave children vulnerable, stateless and parentless because of conflict of laws issues, refusing to recognise the children born through surrogacy arrangements. States are not only unresponsive to the vulnerabilities of their own citizens but, as a consequence, they create additional vulnerabilities for people in developing countries through such unethical legislative behaviour. Indeed, Storrow suggests that '... countries considering bans or restrictions on certain forms of reproductive technology have an *ethical obligation* to consider and address the effects that those laws will have on infertile couples and gamete donors in countries that have become the destinations of fertility tourists' (Storrow 2005, 299, my emphasis). Western inequality combined with corporeal vulnerability creates and perpetuates disadvantage and vulnerabilities for other human populations mainly in the global South, amplifying, in this sense, embodied global vulnerability.

Conclusion

The reformulation of the politico-legal subject as vulnerable (and, in this case, infertile) allows us to require not only the elimination of inequality, privilege and disadvantage created by our own state's local provision but also calls upon states to be responsive to structural inequalities in the context of neoliberal globalisation. In the case of the UK's local provision, its relatively progressive and seemingly inclusory legislation creates the semblance of equality under the guise of autonomy and choice. However, an application of the vulnerability thesis to UK ART policy reveals that the reality is very different and what is discovered is an unresponsive and unethical state and healthcare system which perpetuates privilege and disadvantage through real inequality of access and opportunity for ART provision. The corollary of such actual inequality and unethical legislative behaviour is the bolstering of an unregulated global market in which reproductive material can be bought and sold regardless of home state ethics and commodification concerns, and in which the exploitation of the conception-pursuer and the globally socio-economically disempowered is probable if not inevitable. Additionally, then, the vulnerability thesis can be used to require that states be made accountable for the vulnerabilities created externally by their own internal legislation: we could demand that legislative processes should include the carrying out of a sort of 'global vulnerability impact assessment' in the search for a more responsive, just and equal global social order. Indeed, as Grear points out, 'Fineman's call for the responsive state, when placed within the neoliberal globalised context, implies that states need now to become fully responsive, not to the current imperatives of voracious and apparently illimitable forms of consumer and corporate capitalism, but to the implications of multiple forms of vulnerability located within the substantive, material conditions of globalisation' (Grear, this volume, 52).

What the vulnerability thesis cannot do, however, is address with easy solutions the many ethical nuances which the area of assisted reproduction raises. It is not suggested that all states must regulate assisted reproduction in the same way, but, minimally, the vulnerability thesis could be used to argue for the implementation of global standards, ethics and regulation that all states should adhere to in recognition of our universal embodied vulnerability. Certainly, the approach has particular sensitivity to the patterned forms of inequality and disadvantage imposed by unresponsive states and health providers failing to respond to the implications of universal human vulnerability in the context of fertility injustice.

Chapter 9

A Quiet Revolution: Vulnerability in the European Court of Human Rights

Alexandra Timmer

> The technique is to focus on a concept or term in common use, but also grossly under-theorized, and thus ambiguous. (Fineman 2008, 9)

Introduction[1]

A revolution is quietly taking place in the case law of the European Court of Human Rights ('ECtHR', 'the Court' or 'the Strasbourg Court'). Without occasioning much comment, the Court is increasingly relying on vulnerability reasoning. The aim of this chapter is to analyse that development and discover what potential the concept of vulnerability has to improve the legal reasoning of the ECtHR. By 'improving the legal reasoning' I have something specific in mind, namely the question of how to include more fully and consistently the specific concerns of marginalized people into the legal tests used by the ECtHR.[2]

Martha Fineman's vulnerability thesis opens up new ways of thinking about the Court's reasoning. At its most fundamental, she argues that vulnerability is the universal human condition, and that it is this condition that grounds the social contract. Vulnerability, she goes on to reason, requires a (more) responsive state. Her thesis was initially developed for an American audience. In the United States – where, as Fineman (2008, 2) underlines, 'the rhetoric of non-intervention prevails in policy discussions' – her claims are radical. But the thesis also holds purchase in the European context, even though Europe has traditionally been more interventionist in its orientation and practice. In fact, I am struck by the transformative potential of the vulnerability thesis precisely in the European human rights context. Through the lens of this thesis, previously overlooked elements of ECtHR case law suddenly come to the fore.

---

1   The research for this chapter was conducted within the framework of the European Research Council (ERC) Starting Grant project entitled 'Strengthening the European Court of Human Rights: More Accountability through Better Legal Reasoning'.
2   This is one of the topics within the Court's case law that Eva Brems has identified as being in need of urgent redress. See Eva Brems, *Research Proposal European Research Council*, at 5–6 (manuscript on file with author).

In a previous article, Lourdes Peroni and I have shown that 'vulnerable groups' is an emerging concept in the case law of the ECtHR (Peroni and Timmer 2013). The present chapter builds on that work and complements it by exploring vulnerability as a judicial tool of the Strasbourg Court in a broader sense. My intention is to analyse the tensions and the synergies between Fineman's vulnerability approach and the Court's vulnerability case law, in order to draw out the potential of the Court's reasoning. Part I will lay the foundations for the case law analysis by briefly discussing the vulnerability thesis and the ways in which various commentators have conceptualized its relationship to human rights. Part II will then chart and critique the ways in which the ECtHR reasons in terms of vulnerability. Next, part III will explore what kind of ability vulnerability reasoning has to change human rights law, and part IV will take an institutional perspective to show that the Court is vulnerable itself. Part V concludes the chapter with some reflections about the extent to which the ECtHR, in effect, adopts an approach that is consistent with the vulnerability thesis – and to what extent it has the possibility to do so.

I. The Vulnerability Thesis and Human Rights

In the specific context of this chapter, I think of the vulnerability thesis as a conceptual way to bridge the gap between the legal subject as currently conceived of and real human beings.[3] The vulnerability thesis is an invitation to reimagine the 'human' of human rights as a vulnerable subject, and to 'redirect' (Grear 2010) human rights law in his/her image. My analysis builds primarily on the work of Martha Fineman, Anna Grear and Bryan Turner. First of all, I will briefly discuss how these authors conceive of vulnerability. Then I will move to the human rights context and explore what light the vulnerability thesis sheds on some of the (liberal) suppositions informing human rights law subjectivity.

Real human beings – Fineman, Grear and Turner argue – are vulnerable due to their embodiment. This ontological fact forms the foundation of the vulnerability thesis. As embodied beings we are vulnerable both due to our physical openness to hurt and due to our inevitable dependence upon others (including the state) for survival (Neal 2013, 10). We cannot escape the vulnerable condition and so, as Fineman emphasizes, vulnerability is universal and constant (Fineman 2008, 1; Fineman 2010, 266–7). As such, vulnerability is not something that only attaches to specific population groups. Fineman terms her inquiry 'post-identity' (Fineman 2008, 1). However, while vulnerability is universal, our experience of it is particular. This experience is profoundly affected by social institutions; since each and every one of us is situated in 'a web of economic and institutional relationships' (Fineman 2008, 10). At the same time, these social institutions are 'vulnerable entities in and of themselves' (Fineman 2008, 12–13) – this is a point

---

3   The vulnerability thesis is a broad and ambitious framework. Inevitably, I lift just some aspects out of it for this chapter.

that Fineman and Turner both underline. I will return to this point in my analysis of ECtHR case law.

Vulnerability theorists – and in this sense I can count myself among them – do not conceptualize vulnerability as being a purely negative condition. In fact, they attempt to reclaim 'vulnerability' from its negative connotations; they warn against reducing vulnerability to 'harm' and 'injurability' (Butler 2004, xii). Vulnerability is also in many ways *generative*: it forges bonds between human beings and leads us to create institutions (Fineman 2012). This is the basis for the normative claim (most strongly formulated in Fineman's work) that vulnerability can be turned into 'a powerful conceptual tool with the potential to define an obligation for the state to ensure a richer and more robust guarantee of equality than is currently afforded' (Fineman 2008, 8–9). A vulnerability analysis does this by turning critical focus towards the institutional production of both privilege and disadvantage (Fineman 2010, 274).

How has vulnerability been deployed as a conceptual tool in the human rights context? In different ways, both Turner and Grear have conceptualized embodied vulnerability as being *foundational* to human rights. From a sociological perspective, Turner takes ontological vulnerability as the foundation for a defence of the universalism of human rights (Turner 2006). His work sheds light on one of the difficulties facing vulnerability theorists: the fact that (the experience of) vulnerability does not by itself have prescriptive force. The problem is that, without more, vulnerability is ethically ambiguous: our corporeal vulnerability can invite care and empathy, but also violence and abuse (Butler 2004; Murphy 2009). Turner adds to the vulnerability thesis by recognizing that vulnerability does not automatically produce sympathy. He conceptualizes human rights law as a form of institution-building that attempts to answer this dilemma (Turner 2006, 39–43).

Grear argues that vulnerability is presuppositional to human rights as both an historical and conceptual matter (Grear 2010). She submits that human embodiment and its attendant vulnerability have played a foundational role both in the creation of rights discourse in the eighteenth century and in the creation of the Universal Declaration of Human Rights after World War II (Grear 2010, 137–49). But the human rights story is not straightforward. Grear shows that the relationship between vulnerability and human rights is complex and contested, and that the individual that human rights law seeks to protect is not necessarily always the vulnerable subject.[4] On the contrary, through tracing a 'genealogy of quasi-disembodiment' in human rights law, Grear makes a convincing case that the abstract liberal subject is comfortably ensconced within the human rights paradigm (Grear 2010, 96–113). One notable offshoot of this reality is that corporations now enjoy human rights – something Grear argues against. Human rights, she suggests, need 'redirecting' towards a full appreciation of human embodiment (as opposed to quasi-disembodied understandings of persons and, in particular, the corporate form) and suggests that we can redirect human rights precisely by drawing on the presuppositional role of vulnerability.

---

4   Anna Grear, email to the author, 24 May 2012.

In light of Grear's argument, it is worth pausing for a moment to consider more explicitly the figure in the background of the vulnerability thesis: the 'liberal subject'. Fineman, Grear and (to a lesser extent) Turner all present their vulnerability analysis as an answer to the ills associated with liberal notions of (legal) personhood.[5] The liberal subject is the one currently dominating both legal and political discourse in the United States and Europe: as an archetype, 'he' (for this subject is male) symbolizes autonomy, independence, personal responsibility and self-sufficiency (Fineman 2004, 34; Fineman 2008, 10–11). This is also a familiar figure in human rights law; indeed, he is a key target of critical human rights scholars (Douzinas 2000; Otto 2006; Grear 2010). I do not have the space here to do justice to the complexity of their arguments nor to develop a full account of legal subjectivity in the case law of the ECtHR.[6] In a nutshell, the difficulty is that the human rights universal is often premised on a mythical *in*vulnerable subject, who is male, white, rational, autonomous, etc. (Bergoffen 2012, 109). This subject, moreover, is 'unable to survive without the existence of an "Other"' (Kapur 2006, 675; also Douzinas 2000, 357–66 and Mutua 2001); who is everything the supposedly universal subject is not. Thus, the point is that the 'allegedly neutral subject of human rights law' reproduces time-worn hierarchies of gender, race, nation, socio-economic status, religion and sexuality (Otto 2006, 318).

At the heart of the idea of universal human rights subjectivity is the notion of human dignity. Despite the voluminous scholarship on this topic (Grant 2007; McCrudden 2008; Habermas 2010), the *positive* links between vulnerability and dignity are not often explored. Indeed, dignity is often associated with *in*vulnerability (Waldron 2009, 11; Neal 2013, 13). According to classic Kant-based readings, dignity is about overcoming vulnerability through the use of reason (Waldron 2009, 15–16; Neal 2013, 20). However, some scholars – notably Mary Neal, Anna Grear and Debra Bergoffen – offer very different readings of the relationship between dignity and embodied vulnerability. In different ways, their project is to align dignity with vulnerability. Their work recognizes that both dignity and vulnerability are inherent in the human condition: the vulnerable subject is a subject with dignity. According to Grear, vulnerability is the 'presuppositional' core of human dignity (Grear 2010, 196–98). Neal takes the analysis of the relationship between these two concepts a step further, by arguing that '[d]ignity ... treats vulnerability as a *source* of value. ... all valid uses of "dignity" reflect a valuing of the sense in which human existence (perhaps uniquely) embodies a union between the fragile/material/finite and the transcendent/sublime/immortal' (Neal 2013, 21). I summarize these arguments here, because the Court seems to increasingly connect vulnerability and dignity (as the next parts of this chapter will show).

---

5   See generally about the different constructions of legal subjectivity Naffine 2003.

6   That would be a fascinating topic for future research. Others have persuasively suggested that the ECtHR fails to respond adequately when applicants do not fit the template of the liberal subject (e.g. Brems 2012).

To conclude these reflections, it should perhaps be clarified that the scope of this chapter is theoretically less ambitious than the work of Turner, Grear and others: this chapter does not seek to proffer a rereading of the foundations of human rights. The comments that are offered here are anchored in human rights practice, in the sense that they take the case law of the ECtHR as their focal point. I draw on vulnerability theory primarily to inform my reading of the ECtHR's practice. At the same time, I hope that my reading of this practice will contribute – even if only in a small way – towards refining and developing the theory. In that context, I note that the case law of the ECtHR sheds light on the theoretical question – originally raised by Turner (2006, 36–7) – as to whether the vulnerability thesis is directly relevant for all human rights, or just for socio-economic rights. Turner maintains that the thesis is more directly pertinent to socio-economic than to civil-political rights. Grear disagrees, because in her view all categories of human right presuppose embodied vulnerability (Grear 2010, 134–5 and 156–61). Anticipating the next part of this chapter, which assesses the case law of the ECtHR, I wish to emphasize that the ECtHR employs vulnerability considerations to great effect both in cases that turn on socio-economic issues[7] and in cases that concern more classic civil and political rights.[8] From the perspective of Strasbourg, therefore, Grear seems to be right.

Lastly, it should be emphasized that the ECtHR is by no means developing its vulnerability reasoning in a vacuum.[9] Care for human vulnerability is part of the culture of human rights both in the Council of Europe[10] and in the United Nations system (Morawa 2003; Chapman and Carbonetti 2011) – as evidenced by the frequent references to vulnerability in the output of these organizations. Regrettably, this chapter will not be able to address the cross-fertilization between the vulnerability reasoning of these different bodies: it will now proceed to trace how the ECtHR (and the ECtHR alone) uses vulnerability considerations.

II. Vulnerability in the Case Law of the ECtHR: Thematization and Critique

This part explores how the Court conceives of vulnerability. As vulnerability is such a little-known concept of ECtHR jurisprudence, the aim here is first of all to chart the Court's vulnerability case law. By asking the question of what

---

7   Such as housing or the provision of medical treatment for prisoners. See *infra* Part II.

8   Such as the right to a fair trial: see Salduz v. Turkey (GC), App. No. 36391/02, 27 November 2008, (2009) 49 Eur. H.R.R. 19, and *infra* Part II.4.

9   As Lourdes Peroni and I discussed in our joint paper, the Court often refers to these other instruments of human rights law when it makes a vulnerability-claim (Peroni and Timmer 2013).

10   This is evidenced, for example, by the work of the Committee of Ministers; the European Committee of Social Rights; the Council of Europe Commissioner for Human Rights; and the European Commission on Racism and Intolerance (e.g. Committee of Ministers 2011; Hammarberg 2011).

renders people vulnerable in the eyes of the Court, I explore how the case law fits or fails to fit with the vulnerability thesis. In order to do this, I find it useful to keep Grear's argument in mind that the historical development of the human rights movement yields two different stories: one story adopts a liberal quasi-disembodied subject and the other story adopts a human embodied vulnerable subject as the central figure of human rights. Keeping this ambivalence in mind allows one to see that the Court often struggles between these competing narratives and produces contradictory impulses in relation to outcomes. On the one hand, it will quickly become apparent that the Court does not, like Fineman, conceptualize vulnerability as universal and constant. Instead, 'vulnerable' is an epithet that the Court attaches to some (groups of) applicants but not to others. I will argue that the result is that, in many ways, the Court's vulnerability reasoning does not disturb the assumptions underpinning the liberal subject.[11] On the other hand, even though the Court's vulnerability reasoning might not signal a complete paradigm shift, this part of my argument shall show that it does spur many sensitive and substantive case-assessments.

A. Thematization

1. Inherent vulnerability: children and persons with mental disabilities   The Court comes closest to embracing Fineman's vulnerability thesis in its case law concerning children and people with a mental disability. Fineman's thesis has origins in her earlier work on the inevitability of dependency: 'All of us were dependent as children, and many of us will be dependent as we age, become ill or suffer disabilities' (Fineman 2004, 35). Fineman's vulnerability approach is therefore responsive to the fact that abilities differ over the course of a lifespan (Fineman 2008, 12; Fineman 2012). The Court is responsive to this too; at least when it concerns children and people with a mental disability. These are the two types of applicants that the Court considers to be inherently and constantly vulnerable. The Court does not often make it explicit why it conceives of their vulnerability in this way, but the case law contains many references to their dependency upon the care of others,[12] and their difficulty or inability to complain of abuse or of their treatment more generally.[13] It is noteworthy that the Court

---

11   See *infra* Part II.B.

12   See, for example, Mubilanzila Mayeka and Kaniki Mitunga v. Belgium, App. No. 13178/03, 12 October 2006, (2008) 46 E.H.R.R. 23, ¶ 51.

13   M.C. v. Bulgaria, App. No. 39272/98, 4 December 2003, (2005) 40 E.H.R.R. 20, ¶ 183 and 58 (rape of young girl); Juppala v. Finland, App. No. 18620/03, 2 December 2008, (2010) 51 E.H.R.R. 4, ¶ 41-42; M.B. v. Romania, App. No. 43982/06, 3 November 2011, ¶ 52 (rape of a woman with mental disabilities); Keenan v. United Kingdom, App. No. 27229/95, 3 April 2001, (2001) 33 E.H. R.R. 38, ¶ 111 (imprisonment and subsequent suicide of person with a chronic mental disorder). The Court has recognized that the same can apply to elderly people: Heinisch v. Germany, App no 28274/08, 21 July 2011, ¶ 71.

has not really applied vulnerability reasoning yet in cases concerning elderly applicants. There are a few judgments in which the Court has recognized that an elderly person was in a vulnerable situation,[14] but the Court has not developed a jurisprudence that reflects the fact that people are differently vulnerable towards the end of their lives (cf. Fineman 2012).

For children and people with a mental disability, however, the Court's vulnerability reasoning has had a real effect, both in participation-related and protection-related cases. Mostly via the doctrine of positive obligations (about which the next part of this chapter will say more), the Court has developed a jurisprudence that requires states to pay attention to the specificities of children (Kilkelly 2010) and of people with a mental disability and thus to provide them with adequate protection from human rights abuses. An example is the case of *C.A.S. and C.S. v. Romania*, concerning the failure of the authorities to investigate the sexual abuse of a seven-year-old boy:

> Concerning notably the weight attached to the victim's reaction, the Court considers that the authorities were not mindful of the particular vulnerability of young people and the special psychological factors involved in cases concerning violent sexual abuse of minors, particularities which could have explained the victim's hesitations both in reporting the abuse and in his descriptions of the facts.[15]

Similarly, the Court has emphasized that 'the vulnerability of mentally ill persons calls for special protection'.[16]

Both children's rights theorists and disability rights theorists have long insisted that human rights discourse is disempowering if vulnerability is stressed to the exclusion of agency (Vandenhole and Ryngaert 2012). The Court shows that it is aware that vulnerability and agency go hand in hand. The Court knows how to rely on vulnerability in a way that is empowering, especially in participation-related cases. This passage from *Stanev v. Bulgaria*, a case concerning the placement of a mentally disabled man in a social care home, is an example:

> The Court considers that any protective measure should reflect as far as possible the wishes of persons capable of expressing their will. Failure to seek their opinion could give rise to situations of abuse and hamper the exercise of the rights of vulnerable persons. Therefore, any measure taken without prior consultation of the interested person will as a rule require careful scrutiny.[17]

---

14   See, for example, Mudric v. The Republic of Moldova, App. No. 74839/10, 16 July 2013, ¶ 51 (concerning violence by an ex-partner against a 72-year-old woman).

15   C.A.S. and C.S. v. Romania, App. no. 26692/05, 20 March 2012, ¶ 81.

16   Renolde v. France, App. No. 5608/05, 16 October 2008, ¶ 109.

17   Stanev v. Bulgaria (GC), App. No. 36760/06, 17 January 2012, ¶ 153.

2. Vulnerability due to state control: persons in detention   The paradigmatic image of the vulnerable person who cannot protect himself from the power of the state is found in the case law concerning detainees. It is firmly established in the Court's case law on Articles 2, 3 and 5 that people who are deprived of their liberty by the state are in a vulnerable position.[18] The Court considers persons in custody to be vulnerable because they are within the control of the authorities and, as such, their physical well-being depends on the state.[19] This has had one spectacular effect, namely that the burden of proof is reversed in detention cases: when death or injury occurs in prison, it is for the authorities, and not for the applicant, to establish what happened.[20]

Conceptualizing vulnerability so narrowly that state control is the only criterion has significant limitations, however. The Court's exclusive focus on physical state control does not allow for a response to the political vulnerability of prisoners and ex-prisoners, for example. In *Scoppola v. Italy (no. 3)* the Court paradoxically held that disenfranchising certain prisoners for life could serve the legitimate aim of ensuring the proper functioning and preservation of the democratic process.[21] If prisoners and ex-prisoners are not allowed to vote, who will represent them? It is relatively obvious that disenfranchising prisoners renders them more vulnerable. Another example of the Court's narrow notion of vulnerability is found in *Stummer v. Austria*; a case concerning the non-affiliation of prisoners to the pension system for work they performed while imprisoned.[22] The seven dissenting judges held that ex-prisoners are vulnerable too, as they have less access to social services.[23] The majority disagreed: apparently, once outside the prison walls and therefore beyond the physical control of the state, ex-prisoners cannot count on a responsive state (or a responsive court).

---

18   Foundational cases include Kurt v. Turkey in which the Commission held: 'Article 5 (Art. 5) aims to provide a framework of guarantees against abuse of power in relation to persons taken into custody. Such persons are vulnerable to a wide range of arbitrary treatment and infringements of their personal integrity and dignity.' Kurt v. Turkey (Com.), App no 24276/94, 5 December 1996, ¶ 201. See also the Grand Chamber case of Salman v. Turkey: 'Persons in custody are in a vulnerable position and the authorities are under a duty to protect them.' Salman v. Turkey (GC), App. No. 21986/93, 27 June 2000, (2002) 34 E.H.R.R. 17, ¶ 99.

19   Denis Vasilyev v. Russia, App. No. 32704/04, 17 December 2009, ¶ 115. The same rationale applies to conscripted servicemen, and more generally 'in other situations in which the physical well-being of individuals is dependent, to a decisive extent, on the actions by the authorities', such as when the police finds an unconscious person on the street. *Id.* ¶ 115–16.

20   See, for example, Salman v. Turkey (GC), App. No. 21986/93, 27 June 2000, (2002) 34 E.H.R.R. 17, ¶ 99–100.

21   Scoppola v. Italy (no. 3) (GC), App. No. 126/05, 22 May 2012, ¶ 91.

22   Stummer v. Austria (GC), App. No. 37452/02, 7 July 2011, (2012), 54 Eur. H.R.R. 11.

23   *Id.* (Tulkens, Kovler, Gyulumyan, Spielmann, Popović, Malinverni and Pardalos J. dissenting, ¶ 10).

3. Vulnerability due to gender: women in domestic violence or precarious reproductive health situations In recent cases concerning domestic violence the Court has come close to adopting a vulnerability approach. Fineman advocates that we should shift our attention to 'the individual's location within webs of social, economic, political, and institutional relationships that structure opportunities and options' (Fineman 2012, 129). In line with this, the Court acknowledges that the vulnerability of female victims of domestic violence is both physical and psychological,[24] and that this is the result of a combination of individual and social circumstances. The following quote from *Opuz v. Turkey*, the Court's ground-breaking domestic violence case from 2009, is in this respect illustrative:

> The Court considers that the applicant may be considered to fall within the group of 'vulnerable individuals' entitled to State protection … In this connection, it notes the violence suffered by the applicant in the past, the threats issued by H.O. following his release from prison and her fear of further violence as well as her social background, namely the vulnerable situation of women in south-east Turkey.[25]

In this case, the Court found a violation of the Convention because the state failed to comply with its positive obligation to take effective measures to protect the applicant from the violence of her husband.[26] In the cases of *Bevacqua and S. v. Bulgaria* (2008) and in *Hajduová v. Slovakia* (2010) the Court went a step further, categorically declaring that victims of domestic violence as such are particularly vulnerable.[27] This could also be conceptualized as a form of *ex-post* vulnerability; a person is particularly vulnerable after (and because of) suffering this kind of human rights abuse.[28] The Court's approach, however, is not consistent. In some recent domestic violence cases the Court did not acknowledge the particular vulnerability of the applicant.[29]

---

24 Opuz v. Turkey, App. No. 33401/02, 9 June 2009, (2010) 50 E.H.R.R. 28, ¶ 132.

25 Id. ¶ 160.

26 The link between vulnerability reasoning and positive obligations will be discussed in the next part of this chapter. See *infra* Part III.B.

27 Bevacqua and S. v. Bulgaria, App. No. 71127/01, 12 June 2008, ¶ 65; Hajduová v. Slovakia, App. No. 2660/03, 30 November 2010, (2011) 53 Eur. H.R.R. 8, ¶ 46 ('The Court notes in this respect that the particular vulnerability of the victims of domestic violence and the need for active State involvement in their protection has been emphasized in a number of international instruments'). See also ¶ 41 and 50. Similarly Eremia and Others v. The Republic of Moldova, App. No. 3564/11, 28 May 2013, ¶ 73.

28 Understood this way, torture victims also suffer from *ex-post* vulnerability; Aydin v. Turkey, App. No. 23178/94, 26 August 1997, (1998) 25 Eur. H.R.R. 251, ¶ 103.

29 See, for example, A. v. Croatia, 55164/08, 14 October 2010.

The other area of case law in which the Court increasingly often – but not always[30] – reasons from gendered vulnerability[31] concerns reproductive health. In three well-known judgments against Poland concerning access to abortion, *Tysiac v. Poland* (2007), *R.R. v. Poland* (2011) and *P. and S. v. Poland* (2012), the Court held that the applicants in these cases were in a vulnerable situation.[32] It seems that their vulnerability is a result of their physical condition, their distress on account of their own (in the case of *Tysiac*) or their foetus's health (in the case of *R.R.*),[33] and their dependence upon their doctors to provide them with timely and correct information about their health and access to abortion. The first applicant in *P. and S.* was a 14-year-old girl who was pregnant as a result of rape, so these were additional factors that exacerbated her vulnerability. Dependency on doctors was also stressed as a vulnerability factor by Judges Sajó and Tulkens in a dissenting opinion in a case that concerned the question whether women should have the right to give birth at home.[34] Thus we see that the theme of dependency – which is also very important in the work of Fineman – recurs throughout different areas of the Court's vulnerability reasoning.

4. Vulnerability due to a legal power imbalance: persons who are accused and persons who lack legal capacity   One of the Court's successful deployments of vulnerability reasoning is found in the influential[35] case of *Salduz v. Turkey*.[36] In *Salduz*, the Court has held that 'an accused often finds himself in a particularly

---

30   The Grand Chamber abortion case of A,B, and C v. Ireland, for example, makes no mention of vulnerability. A, B, and C v. Ireland (GC), App. No. 25579/05, 16 December 2010, (2011) 53 Eur. H.R.R. 13.

31   But see also B.S. v. Spain, App. No. 47159/08, 24 July 2012, ¶ 71 (a case concerning police violence against a sex-worker of African descent).

32   Tysiac v. Poland, App. No. 5410/03, 20 March 2007, (2007) 45 Eur. H.R.R. 42, ¶ 127; R.R. v. Poland, App. No. 27617/04, 26 May 2011, (2011) 53 Eur. H.R.R. 31, ¶ 159; P. and S. v. Poland, App. No. 57375/08, 30 October 2012, ¶ 110 and 162–166.

33   In *R.R.* the Court held that 'the applicant was in a situation of great vulnerability. Like any other pregnant woman in her situation, she was deeply distressed by information that the foetus could be affected with some malformation.' The Court shows great empathy for the situation that this woman was in and recognizes that she suffered 'painful uncertainty' and 'acute anguish' and that she was 'humiliated'. R.R. v. Poland, App. No. 27617/04, 26 May 2011, (2011) 53 Eur. H.R.R. 31, ¶ 159–60.

34   Ternovszky v. Hungary, App. No. 67545/09, 14 December 2010 (Sajo J and Tulkens J dissenting) ('the expectant mother has to interact during the period of pregnancy with authorities and regulated professionals who act as figures of some kind of public authority vis-à-vis the pregnant person, who is understandably very vulnerable because of her dependency').

35   As a result of this ruling, many European states had to amend their laws (Brants 2011).

36   Salduz v. Turkey (GC), App. No. 36391/02, 27 November 2008, (2009) 49 Eur. H.R.R. 19.

vulnerable position' in the investigative stage of criminal proceedings.[37] The Court continued: 'In most cases, this particular vulnerability can only be properly compensated for by the assistance of a lawyer whose task it is, among other things, to help to ensure respect of the right of an accused not to incriminate himself.'[38] This has since become the standard under Article 6 § 3 (c) of the Convention (right to a fair trial). This is a sound instance of vulnerability reasoning, because the Court convincingly diagnoses the reason why people who are accused of a crime are particularly vulnerable – they could easily experience pressure to incriminate themselves – and, subsequently, the Court requires that a 'responsive State' (Fineman 2010) 'counter[s] the power imbalance'[39] by giving the accused the right to legal assistance.

In the same line of successful vulnerability reasoning concerning legal power imbalances is *Zehentner v. Austria*.[40] In fact, the applicant in that case had no legal power at all, as she had a legal guardian appointed for her. Her complaint at Strasbourg related to the fact that she had not been able to institute legal proceedings against the forced sale of her house. The Court holds that: 'persons who lack legal capacity are particularly vulnerable and States may thus have a positive obligation under Article 8 to provide them with specific protection by the law'.[41]

5. Vulnerability due to espousal of unpopular views: demonstrators and journalists   In the context of Article 11 of the Convention (the right to peaceful assembly and association), the Court has held that: [the positive obligation of the state to secure the effective enjoyment of these freedoms] 'is of particular importance for persons holding unpopular views or belonging to minorities, because they are more vulnerable to victimisation.'[42] This reasoning comes from the judgments in *Baczkowski and Others v. Poland* and *Alekseyev v. Russia*, both concerning applicants who wanted to organize a demonstration to draw attention to discrimination against gays and lesbians. The Court has also been known to recognize the vulnerability of Ukrainian journalists 'who cover politically sensitive topics' and who thereby 'place themselves in a vulnerable position *vis-à-vis* those in power (as evidenced by the death of eighteen journalists in Ukraine since 1991)'.[43]

---

37   Id. ¶ 54.

38   Id.

39   Paskal v. Ukraine, App. No. 24652/04, 15 September 2011, ¶ 76.

40   Zehentner v. Austria, App. No. 20082/02, 16 July 2009, (2011) 52 Eur. H.R.R. 22.

41   Id. ¶ 63.

42   Baczkowski and Others v. Poland, App. No. 1543/06, 3 May 2007, (2009) 48 Eur. H.R.R. 19, ¶ 64. See also Alekseyev v. Russia, App. Nos. 4916/07, 25924/08 and 14599/09, 21 October 2010, ¶ 70.

43   Congadze v. Ukraine, App. No. 34056/02, 8 November 2005, ¶ 168; and Gazeta Ukraina-Tsentr v. Ukraine, App. No. 16695/04, 15 July 2010, ¶ 51.

What makes these various people who espouse unpopular views vulnerable? One way of looking at these cases is that they all concern human rights defenders.[44] Another way of looking at them is that these cases all concern people who are isolated from the mainstream. The theme that was just discussed – vulnerability due to a power imbalance – also clearly plays a role here.

6. Vulnerability in the context of migration: detention and expulsion of asylum seekers   The Court's vulnerability reasoning with regard to 'irregular' migrants is complex and problematic. Regrettably but not surprisingly, the Court often fails to respond to the vulnerability of asylum seekers.[45] However, there are also positive developments in the jurisprudence. The Court now struggles between a classical liberal human rights discourse – a discourse bound up with Westphalian sovereignty (Cornelisse 2011) – and a discourse that is more receptive of real lived vulnerability. I will illustrate the Court's difficulties with formulating an appropriate response to the vulnerability of asylum seekers through an analysis of the case law concerning detention conditions and *non-refoulement*.[46] Both these types of cases are litigated under the prohibition of inhuman and degrading treatment (Article 3).

The Court's deportation cases, in particular, are inconsistent and distressing from a vulnerability perspective. The question the Court seems most concerned with in such cases is the question of *which state should bear the responsibility* of taking care of migrants: the receiving state or the state of origin. When defining the scope of the term 'ill-treatment' under Article 3 in deportation cases, the Court makes a distinction between future harm that would emanate from 'the intentional acts or omission of public authorities or non-State bodies' and the kind of harm that emanates from 'a naturally occurring illness and the lack of sufficient resources to deal with it in the receiving country'.[47] Only when a rights-holder is in danger of suffering the first kind of harm – namely political persecution – is there a chance[48]

---

44   This reading sits well with human rights soft law which calls for the special protection of human rights defenders. See, for example, G.A. Res. 53/144, U.N. Doc. A/RES/53/144 (8 March 1999).

45   There is a lot of literature discussing the failure of human rights to include (the vulnerability of) migrants and refugees in its system (Douzinas 2000, 141–4; Grear 2010, 150–56; Dembour and Kelly 2011).

46   That is not to say that vulnerability does not play a role in other types of migrant cases; I just think that in these cases vulnerability considerations are most pronounced.

47   N. v. United Kingdom, App. No. 26565/05, 27 May 2008, (2008) 47 Eur. H.R.R. 39, ¶ 43; Sufi and Elmi v. United Kingdom, App. Nos. 8319/07 and 11449/07, 28 June 2011, (2012) 54 Eur. H.R.R. 9, ¶ 281.

48   But no guarantee: the Court has often held that an applicant is not so vulnerable in his or her home country as to make deportation incompatible with the prohibition of inhuman treatment. See, for example, Samina v. Sweden, app no 55463/09, 20 October 2011, ¶ 62–5; S.S. v. UK, inadmissible, 24 January 2012, app no12096/10, ¶ 74 ('the Court finds that in the present case the applicant, a healthy male of 27 years of age, has failed

that the ECtHR will interfere. In other words, only when a migrant is vulnerable to political persecution in her home country can this put a responsibility on the receiving European country not to deport her. Within these narrow confines, the expulsion case that is most promising from a vulnerability perspective is *Salah Sheekh v. Netherlands*.[49] This case is promising because the Court's vulnerability analysis combines both individual elements (concerning the applicant's own history of victimization and his family's) and group-based elements (concerning the vulnerability of the Ashraf minority).

(In)famously, in *N. v. UK* the state-oriented approach that only recognizes vulnerability on the ground of political persecution,[50] led the Court to approve the expulsion of a woman who suffered from AIDS after she had lived in the UK for ten years.[51] The woman was in a stable condition thanks to the medication that she had received in the UK, but the Court knew that deportation to her native Uganda would quickly lead to her death due to lack of available medication. Fineman's vulnerability thesis calls attention to the utter inadequacy of conceiving of vulnerability in this truncated manner: embodied vulnerability to sickness, drought, and food shortage cannot be separated from embodied vulnerability to – say – violence and government-led exploitation.

However, as I suggested at the start of this sub-paragraph, there are also glimmers of hope that the Court is moving towards a fuller recognition of lived vulnerability.[52] Most significant in terms of developing a vulnerability thesis that can do justice to asylum seekers is the Grand Chamber case of *M.S.S. v. Belgium and Greece* from 2011, concerning an Afghan asylum seeker who entered Europe through Greece where he was first held in detention and later released on the streets from where he eventually made his way to Belgium.[53] As regards the conditions of his detention, the Court held: 'In the present case the Court must take into account that the applicant, being an asylum seeker, was particularly vulnerable because of everything he had been through during his migration and the traumatic

to submit any evidence to the Court to indicate that he would be unable to cater for his most basic needs in Kabul or that he has any particular vulnerability ... to suggest that his removal to Kabul would subject him to destitution or engage Article 3 of the Convention').

49   Salah Sheekh v. Netherlands, App No. 1948/04, 11 January 2007, (2007) 45 Eur. H.R.R. 50. See particularly ¶ 140 and 146.

50   D. v. UK (1997) is the one – and so far exceptional – case where the Court stopped the deportation of a man on ground of his illness. D. v. United Kingdom, App. No. 30240/96, 2 May 1997, (1997) 24 Eur. H.R.R. 423.

51   N. v. United Kingdom, App. No. 26565/05, 27 May 2008, (2008) 47 Eur. H.R.R. 39.

52   Some voices on the Court – notably the dissenters in N. v. UK – call for an 'integrated approach' that combines civil-political rights with their social dimension. Id. ¶ 6 (Judges Tulkens, Bonello and Spielmann J., dissenting).

53   M.S.S. v. Belgium and Greece, App. No. 30696/09, 21 January 2011, (2011) 53 Eur. H.R. Rep. 2.

experiences he was likely to have endured previously.'[54] Moreover, as regards his living conditions once he was released from detention, the Court held:

> [T]he Court considers that the Greek authorities have not had due regard to the applicant's vulnerability as an asylum seeker and must be held responsible, because of their inaction, for the situation in which he has found himself for several months, living in the street, with no resources or access to sanitary facilities, and without any means of providing for his essential needs.[55]

In this context, the applicant's dependency on the state was certainly a consideration for the Court.[56]

On top of this, the Court held that Belgium violated Article 3 of the Convention, by sending M.S.S. back to Greece and thereby back to such appalling detention and living conditions. That makes this case directly relevant for future expulsion cases. *M.S.S.* represents an important step towards an embrace of the vulnerable subject in asylum law. Lourdes Peroni and I have extensively analysed this case in our article on vulnerable groups (Peroni and Timmer 2013) so I will not discuss it here any further, except to say that, in some cases that have been delivered since *M.S.S.*, the Court finds it difficult to reconcile the traditional approach epitomized in *N v. UK* with the vulnerability approach of *M.S.S.*[57]

7. Vulnerability due to group-membership: Roma, people with impaired health, and (to some extent) asylum seekers   M.S.S. leads to the next strand of case law in which the Court reasons from vulnerability: the cases that concern discrimination on account of group-membership. The Court has used the concept of 'vulnerable groups' in relation to Roma,[58] people with mental disabilities,[59] people living with HIV[60] and – to a limited extent – asylum seekers.[61] Lourdes Peroni and I have discussed this concept in our joint paper (Peroni and Timmer 2013), but I just mention it here in order to be as complete as possible in this thematization of vulnerability in the Court's case law. We came to the conclusion that the Court's use of the 'vulnerable group' concept does not chime well with Fineman's

---

54   Id. ¶ 232.

55   Id. ¶ 263.

56   Id. ¶ 253.

57   See Sufi and Elmi v. United Kingdom, App. Nos. 8319/07 and 11449/07, 28 June 2011, (2012) 54 Eur. H.R.R. 9, ¶ 278–83.

58   See, for example, D.H. and Others v. the Czech Republic (GC), App. No. 57325/00, 47 Eur. H. R. Rep. 3 (2007); and V.C. v. Slovakia, App. No. 18968/07, 8 November 2011.

59   Alajos Kiss v. Hungary, App. No. 38832/06, 20 May 2010; and Z.H. v. Hungary, App. No. 28973/ 11, 8 November 2012.

60   Kiyutin v. Russia, App. No. 2700/10, 10 March 2011, (2011) 53 Eur. H.R. Rep. 26.

61   The example is M.S.S. v. Belgium and Greece, App. No. 30696/09, 21 January 2011, (2011) 53 Eur. H.R. Rep. 2.

vulnerability thesis – which explicitly rejects an identity-based focus – but we have nevertheless welcomed the concept as a positive move towards a more robust notion of equality.

8. Compounded vulnerability   The Court's docket includes a high number of complaints of people considered to be vulnerable due to a combination of the reasons mentioned above, such as children who are held in asylum seekers centers;[62] physically and/or mentally disabled persons who are held in prison[63] (or who died there and whose cases are judged with regard to their vulnerability while alive[64]); female detainees who have been subjected to a forced gynaecological examination;[65] and, more generally, particularly vulnerable women (read: young, old, imprisoned, disabled, etc.) who have been sexually abused.[66] Analogous to the idea of compounded discrimination,[67] I would call this 'compounded vulnerability'. In such situations, the Court sometimes speaks of 'extreme vulnerability',[68] 'double vulnerability',[69] or 'great vulnerability'.[70]

It appears that when the Court is of the opinion that an applicant is vulnerable on multiple grounds, the Court is inclined to attach great importance to this fact. Indeed, compounded vulnerability has been known to *trump* other considerations. This is most clearly stated in a case concerning the detention of children in a Belgian asylum centre. The Court held in *Muskhadzhiyeva and Others v. Belgium*:

---

62   See, for example, Mubilanzila Mayeka and Kaniki Mitunga v. Belgium, App. No. 13178/03, 12 October 2006, (2008) 46 E.H.R.R. 23.

63   See, for example, Raffray Taddei v. France, App. No. 36435/07, 21 December 2010; Slawomir Musial v. Poland, App. No. 28300/06, 20 January 2009, ¶ 96 ('Undeniably, detained persons who suffer from a mental disorder are more susceptible to the feeling of inferiority and powerlessness. … The Court accepts that the very nature of the applicant's psychological condition made him more vulnerable than the average detainee').

64   See, for example, Keenan v. United Kingdom, App. No. 27229/95, 3 April 2001, (2001) 33 E.H. R.R. 38; Jasinskis v. Latvia, App. No . 45744/08, 21 December 2010.

65   Juhnke v. Turkey, App. No. 52515/99, 13 May 2009, (2009) 9 Eur. H.R.R. 24, ¶ 76–7.

66   See, for example, M.B. v. Romania, App. No. 43982/06, 3 November 2011, ¶ 52 and 57 (rape of a woman with mental disabilities); Aydin v. Turkey, App. No. 23178/94, 26 August 1997, (1998) 25 Eur. H.R.R. 251, ¶ 83–4 (rape of a Kurdish girl in prison); X.Y. v. Netherlands A 91 (1986); (1986) 8 Eur. H.R.R. 235 (rape of a 16-year-old girl with mental disabilities); M.C. v. Bulgaria, App. No. 39272/98, 4 December 2003, (2005) 40 E.H.R.R. 20, ¶ 183 (investigation of twice-raped 14-year-old girl).

67   Defined 'as a situation in which discrimination on the basis of two or more grounds add to each other to create a situation of compound[ed] discrimination' (Makkonen 2002).

68   G. v. France, App. No. 27244/09, 23 February 2012, ¶ 77 (prisoner with mental disorder); Kanagaratnam e.a. v. Belgium, App. No. 15297/09, 13 December 2011, ¶ 62 (detention of mother and three children); Mubilanzila Mayeka and Kaniki Mitunga v. Belgium, App. No. 13178/03, 12 October 2006, (2008) 46 E.H.R.R. 23, ¶ 103.

69   De Donder en De Clippel v. Belgium, App. No. 8595/06, 6 December 2011, ¶ 75.

70   M.S. v. United Kingdom, App. No. 24527/08, 3 May 2012, ¶ 44.

'*la situation d'extrême vulnérabilité de l'enfant était déterminante et prédominait sur la qualité d'étranger en séjour illégal*' (which I would loosely translate as: 'the extremely vulnerable situation of the child was decisive and took precedence over her status as an illegal immigrant').[71] This reasoning is very promising, as the Court explicitly distances itself from a sovereignty approach in favour of a vulnerability approach.

B. Critique

Does this overview of the Court's quite extensive vulnerability reasoning show that the Court has adopted the vulnerability thesis? No. The Court does not conceptualize vulnerability as universal and constant, nor does it fully move beyond liberal notions of legal subjectivity. The crux of the problem is that the Court's vulnerable subjects (prisoners, people with a mental disability, migrants, etc.) are examples of marginalized and stigmatized subjects: they do not function as an alternative to the liberal subject, but are classic examples of liberalism's 'Others'.[72] Labelling only these subjects as vulnerable does not challenge the idea that there is such a thing as an *in*vulnerable subject (who does *not* suffer from all the impediments described in the paragraph above, such as dependence), nor does it challenge the hold of this fictional creature on human rights law. In other words, the Court does not really disrupt the vulnerable/invulnerable binary – nor for that matter the related binary of autonomous/dependent (Otto 2006, 354).

Drawing on the work of Fineman and of Otto, the somewhat bleak suggestion presents itself that as long as the Court does not do something radical, namely jettisoning the liberal subject and putting the universally vulnerable subject in its place, it is doomed to reinforce the marginalization of the very people it seeks to protect (Otto 2006, 351). I am, however, not prepared to draw the conclusion that the Court's vulnerability reasoning is a failure (see also Peroni and Timmer 2013): on the contrary, my analysis so far has shown that this reasoning has resulted in many context-sensitive judgments. The next part of this chapter will explore this further. On a more ideological level, the Court does in some ways move beyond liberal assumptions, in my opinion. The results of the Court's vulnerability reasoning in the context of existing human rights theory and practice will also be discussed below.

III. The Ability of Vulnerability

So far, this chapter has noted that in important ways the Court's vulnerability reasoning does not fit Fineman's thesis, but that there are aspects to it that are

---

71   Muskhadzhiyeva and Others v. Belgium, App. No. 41442/07 41442/07, 3 May 2012, ¶ 56. This is actually the Court's summary of Mubilanzila Mayeka and Kaniki Mitunga v. Belgium, App. No. 13178/03, 12 October 2006, (2008) 46 E.H.R.R. 23, ¶ 55.

72   See *supra* Part I. I am grateful to Anna Grear for emphasizing this point.

encouraging and constructive. The present part of this chapter will further unpack the power and transformative promise of the Court's reasoning. How does vulnerability add to the Court's existing jurisprudence? My analysis will show that proportionality and positive obligations are the primary jurisprudential conduits through which vulnerability is leaving its mark. The result is, I argue, (A) a prioritization among the different claims on the ECtHR, and (B) an extension of rights.

A. Prioritizing among Different Claims

This sub-paragraph will show that vulnerability considerations lead the Court to prioritize both in its workload and in its case-assessments. Vulnerability's potential to prioritize – and the role that the judiciary can play in this respect – has not been much explored in the work of the theorists that was discussed in Part I. This is therefore an area in which the ECtHR's practice could inform the vulnerability thesis.

1. Workload prioritization: vulnerability and the priority policy determining the order of cases   Vulnerability considerations play a role in the Court's arrangement of its work schedule. This is evidenced by the Court's 'priority policy'. This policy is designed to allow the Court to face its massive caseload crisis by giving precedence to the cases that are most urgent. The policy has devised seven categories of cases. A case that is classified in one of the lower categories is likely to 'remain on the docket virtually eternally' (Buyse 2010) and so this classification carries huge practical significance. Vulnerability considerations are not mentioned in any of the categories but in my opinion they are implicit in the first – as well as pertinent to the third:

> I. Urgent applications (in particular risk to life or health of the applicant, other circumstances linked to the personal or family situation of the applicant, particularly where the well-being of a child is at issue, application of Rule 39 of the Rules of Court).

> III. Applications which on their face raise as main complaints issues under Articles 2, 3, 4 or 5 § 1 of the Convention ('core rights'), irrespective of whether they are repetitive, and which have given rise to direct threats to the physical integrity and dignity of human beings.[73]

---

73 ECtHR, *The Court's Priority Policy, available at* http://www.echr.coe.int/NR/rdonlyres/AA56DA0F-DEE5-4FB6-BDD3-A5B34123FFAE/0/2010__Priority_policy__Public_communication.pdf.

The first category makes specific mention of two groups that are considered *especially* vulnerable:[74] children and applicants who have requested an interim measure – these are often 'irregular' migrants who face deportation (ECRE 2012).[75] The third category mentions physical integrity and dignity of human beings together; thus linking dignity to embodiment. In different ways, therefore, embodied vulnerability is key to both categories.[76]

2. Substantive prioritization: vulnerability and proportionality   By substantive prioritization I mean the kind of prioritization that occurs in the case law itself: a prioritization between claims. Here, a distinction should be made between Article 3 cases, concerning the absolute prohibition of torture and inhuman and degrading treatment, and cases that concern qualified Convention rights (which permit a relative balancing of rights). In the first type of case the central question is whether treatment reaches 'the minimum level of severity' in order to engage Article 3. In this test, vulnerability weighs heavily and can have absolute prioritizing force. The case of *Muskhadzhiyeva and Others v. Belgium* is a good example.[77]

The focus here is on the second type of case; namely the type that concerns rights which – by virtue of their formulation in the Convention – can be restricted. As is well known, the ECtHR performs a proportionality analysis in such cases. The virtues of proportionality analysis in human rights law are contested (Tsakyrakis 2009), as is the Court's application of the analysis (Gerards and Senden 2009). From the perspective of the vulnerability thesis, the Court's proportionality reasoning – with its attendant discourse of 'conflicts of rights' – is troubling. The problem is that harm to real and vulnerable individuals gets reduced to harm to 'conflicting rights and interests' (Cohen-Eliya and Porat 2011, 470), while, in the meantime, the vulnerable human being risks getting 'lost in translation' (Otto 2006).[78]

Leaving aside the conceptual critique for a moment, vulnerability does play an increasingly prominent role in the Court's proportionality analysis. To quote from a dissent by Judge Power: 'vulnerability is a factor to be weighed in the balance.'[79] How much weight the Court attaches to vulnerability is ambiguous, however. Nevertheless, a *bottom line* has emerged: the Court insists that – at the very least – the state should take the particular vulnerability of the persons it is

---

74   See *supra* Part II.A.

75   The former President of the Court, Judge Costa, has noted about these cases that 'the application of Rule 39 has preserved the physical integrity, the liberty and even the lives of many people who by definition are vulnerable' (ECtHR 2012, 40).

76   I am grateful to Anna Grear for sharing this insight.

77   See *supra* Part II. A.8.

78   This is again the question of who is law's subject: see *supra* Part I. Suzanne Baer has made an analogous critique of the language of 'conflicts of rights' (Baer 2010, 63–4).

79   F.H. v. Sweden, App. No. 32621/06, 20 January 2009 (Power and Zupančič J., dissenting).

dealing with into account. *Whenever a Government completely omits to consider the particular vulnerability of an individual rights-holder, it will not be able to pass the Strasbourg proportionality analysis.*[80] In other words, paying attention to the particular construction of vulnerability has turned into a procedural requirement.[81] This insistence on an appreciation of particularity is very promising and I see no reason why this kind of analysis cannot inform more than the marginalized subjects cases described in Part II, above. Once the state can prove that it has complied with the minimum (procedural) requirement of not ignoring particular vulnerabilities, then it will depend on the circumstances of the case – and of the sort of vulnerability in question – how far the Court will go in prioritizing the protection of particularly vulnerable people over other (often economic) considerations.[82] There is no readily available formula that determines the weight – and thereby the prioritizing force – of vulnerability.

B. Extending Rights (via the Doctrine of Positive Obligations): The Court as an Asset-Conferring Institution

Christopher McCrudden has argued that one of the uses of human dignity in human rights law is to 'justify the creation of new, and the extension of existing, rights' (McCrudden 2008, 721–2). Vulnerability reasoning is put to similar use by the Strasbourg Court – sometimes alone and sometimes explicitly in conjunction with dignity reasoning. It is mainly through the doctrine of positive obligations (Mowbray 2004) that the Court has repeatedly extended existing rights on the ground of vulnerability considerations.

In the first place, the Court has relied on vulnerability considerations to legitimize the gradual extension of positive obligations into the socio-economic sphere. The asylum case of *M.S.S. v. Belgium and Greece*, which was discussed

---

80 See, for example, Zehentner v. Austria, App. No. 20082/02, 16 July 2009, (2011) 52 Eur. H.R.R. 22, ¶ 63–5; Yordanova v. Bulgaria, App. No. 25446/06, 24 April 2012, ¶ 129 (concerning an 'outcast community of Roma' who the Court acknowledges to be vulnerable: 'In the context of Article 8, in cases such as the present one, the applicants' specificity as a social group and their needs must be one of the relevant factors in the proportionality assessment that the national authorities are under a duty to undertake.')

81 This requirement also applies in the context of the absolute prohibition on torture and inhuman or degrading treatment. See, for example, Okkali v. Turkey, App. No. 52067/99, 17 October 2006, (2010) 50 Eur. H.R.R. 43, ¶ 70 ('the authorities could have been expected to lend a certain weight to the question of the applicant's vulnerability.') (concerning a child who was beaten in custody); and B.S. v. Spain, App. No. 47159/08, 24 July 2012, ¶ 71.

82 See also Vandenhole 2008 (arguing that in case of conflicts of socio-economic rights with serious resource implications, priority should be given to the rights of the most vulnerable groups).

in the last part, is a good example.[83] Another example comes from a Roma rights case (which is reasoned from group-vulnerability), namely *Yordanova and others v. Bulgaria*. The Court held:

> Article 8 does not in terms give a right to be provided with a home … and, accordingly, any positive obligation to house the homeless must be limited … However, an obligation to secure shelter to particularly vulnerable individuals may flow from Article 8 of the Convention in exceptional cases. (citations omitted)[84]

Secondly, the Court has also responded to vulnerability by deepening existing positive obligations; for example by turning an obligation of care into an obligation of result. In the case of *M.S. v. UK*, the Court has held that the authorities are under an obligation to ensure detainees with mental health problems are given adequate treatment.[85] This is a good example of a case in which obeying the minimum rule of heeding particular vulnerability was not enough:[86] even though the police showed 'real concern'[87] for the detainee, the Court still found a violation of the Convention. The Court held the government responsible for degrading treatment, because:

> [T]he applicant was in a state of great vulnerability throughout the entire time at the police station, as manifested by the abject condition to which he quickly descended inside his cell. He was in dire need of appropriate psychiatric treatment, as each of the medical professionals who examined him indicated. The Court considers that this situation, which persisted until he was at last transferred … early on the fourth day, diminished excessively his fundamental human dignity.[88]

In these paragraphs, the Court relies on vulnerability to create a richer understanding of what it means to respect human dignity. By underpinning dignity with vulnerability considerations, the Court creates a holistic picture of the sufferings of the applicant: a picture that includes contextual factors such as embodiment, location, mental state and material realities. These vulnerability considerations lead the Court to insist on a substantive obligation (the authorities should have arranged for timely psychiatric treatment) rather than just a procedural obligation of care.

The positive obligation cases that were quoted in this paragraph, *Yordanova and others v. Bulgaria* and *M.S. v. UK*, illustrate that vulnerability reasoning can

---

83   M.S.S. v. Belgium and Greece, App. No. 30696/09, 21 January 2011, (2011) 53 Eur. H.R. Rep. 2, ¶ 263. See also Peroni and Timmer 2013.

84   Yordanova v. Bulgaria, App. No. 25446/06, 24 April 2012, ¶ 130.

85   M.S. v. United Kingdom, App. No. 24527/08, 3 May 2012.

86   Another example is Mubilanzila Mayeka and Kaniki Mitunga v. Belgium, App. No. 13178/03, 12 October 2006, (2008) 46 E.H.R.R. 23, ¶ 52.

87   M.S. v. United Kingdom, App. No. 24527/08, 3 May 2012, ¶ 31.

88   Id. ¶ 41 and 44.

be understood as the Court's way of specifying what rights mean to differently situated people. At the same time, these cases are examples of the ways in which the Court interprets the Convention in an evolutive manner. Commentators usually focus on the 'the Convention as a living instrument' concept when discussing the Court's progressive manner of interpretation (e.g., Letsas 2013); but it is time to acknowledge that vulnerability is also part of the Court's toolbox of concepts that it uses to create its dynamic approach.[89]

Importantly, the Court's reliance on vulnerability considerations to deepen positive obligations and to extend them into the socio-economic sphere is perfectly consistent with Fineman's thesis. Fineman does not use the term 'positive obligations' (which is not surprising as this is human rights law jargon), but when she describes 'the responsive state' I think this is an important part of what she has in mind. Indeed, she has argued that the current American antidiscrimination paradigm is not delivering real equality, and that 'some more positive state action is required' (Fineman 2010, 257). This comes close to the way Alastair Mowbray has characterized positive obligations: 'the duty upon states to undertake specific affirmative tasks' (Mowbray 2004, 2). Through the concept of positive obligations the Court has achieved some of the things that Fineman advocates a 'responsive state' should do. For example, the Court has deployed vulnerability reasoning to lay down positive obligations that bridge the traditional public–private in the domestic violence case of *Opuz v. Turkey*.[90] This is in line with Fineman's argument that 'a particular strength of a vulnerability analysis is its institutional focus that blurs the line between public and private' (Fineman 2012, 130). In Fineman's vocabulary, the Court becomes an asset-conferring institution; providing applicants with the assets that give them resilience in the face of vulnerability (Fineman 2008, 19; Fineman 2010, 272).

To summarize the argument so far: this chapter has identified two ways in which the Court's vulnerability reasoning is changing the face of its case law. Firstly, both as a matter of caseload-management and as a matter of jurisprudence, vulnerability has developed prioritizing force in Strasbourg. Secondly, vulnerability considerations result in the extension of rights through the doctrine of positive obligations. These two functions combined make for a human rights law that is more responsive to vulnerable and often marginalized people.

IV. The Vulnerability of the Court Itself

One of the central tenets of both Fineman's and Turner's vulnerability analysis is that social institutions are vulnerable in and of themselves (Fineman 2010, 273; Turner 2006, 25–34). The Strasbourg Court is no exception, as torrents of criticism

---

89   See also Donald, Gordon and Leach 2012, 110–12 ('the value of a dynamic approach: protection of the vulnerable').

90   Opuz v. Turkey, App. No. 33401/02, 9 June 2009, (2010) 50 E.H.R.R. 28, ¶ 143–4. See *supra* Part II.A.3.

leading up to the Brighton Declaration of April 2012 have painfully revealed (for a discussion of the Brighton Declaration, see Helfer 2012). Withdrawing from the Convention has seriously been discussed in Russia and the UK, because many voters and politicians feel that the Court is unduly infringing on their state's sovereignty (e.g., Pollard 2012). The former President of the Court, Judge Costa, identified several factors that led to this criticism of the Court: the fight against terrorism; the current financial and socio-economic crisis; the rise of populist movements in Europe; and the rise of Euroscepticism (Costa 2011). Especially in places where these last two developments converge, the Court is vulnerable (Costa 2011, 12). Costa notes:

> [H]uman rights are becoming less popular, especially seen from the point of view of a Court which treats equally all human beings, including 'unpopular' categories of the population: the prisoners, the criminals, the aliens, the asylum seekers, the immigrants, the vagrants, people belonging to minorities. (Costa 2011, 12)

In other words, the Court's very protection of especially vulnerable and unwanted people renders the Court vulnerable and unwanted itself.[91] At times, the response to the Court is even virulent. The idea of giving prisoners voting rights makes UK Prime Minister Cameron 'physically ill', for example (Cameron 2010).

The Court's case law in relation to immigrants and asylum seekers, specifically, is provoking a lot of indignation. Marc Bossuyt, President of the Belgian Constitutional Court, has been among those who vocally object to what I have described in the last paragraph: extending certain rights on the basis of vulnerability considerations. He is of the opinion that the ECtHR is on a slippery slope when it comes to asylum seekers, because in his view the Court is continuously lowering the threshold of Article 3 (Bossuyt 2010). Responding to the ruling in *M.S.S. v. Belgium and Greece*, he has literally asked how many more vulnerable groups we can expect.[92] Bossuyt appeals to what Kenji Yoshino has aptly termed our 'pluralism anxiety'; apprehension of 'new' kinds of people and 'newly visible' kinds of people' (Yoshino 2011, 751). In doing so, Bossuyt re-enacts the very us-against-them discourse that the vulnerability thesis seeks to challenge. Grear's work enables us to see that this kind of resistance to the ruling in *M.S.S.* is resistance to the idea of replacing the liberal subject with the vulnerable subject in human rights law.

Again, this confirms that the Court's adoption of the vulnerability thesis – even if only partially – renders the Court itself more vulnerable. This diagnosis leads

---

91   That is not to say that vulnerability and unpopularity necessarily go together: children are especially vulnerable but very popular.

92   Marc Bossuyt, Professor and co-President of the Belgian Constitutional Court, Remarks at the 'How to Deal with the Criticism of the European Court of Rights?' Conference (The Hague, 13 April 2012).

to the conclusion that there are limits to the Court's ability to affect a revolution through its vulnerability reasoning. The fact is that the Court is part of a liberal paradigm (Grear 2007, 535–8). Its vulnerability reasoning is therefore not going to do the full extent of the transformative work the supporters of the thesis (including myself) want it to do – mostly because no state would listen anymore.

V. Conclusion

The ECtHR has clearly not fully embraced the vulnerability thesis. Lourdes Peroni and I have argued that, 'while scholars like Turner and Fineman support vulnerability for its potential of capturing the universal, the Court does it for its ability to capture the particular' (Peroni and Timmer 2013, 5). Still, I do not believe that these two approaches are necessarily at odds with each other. In my understanding, the Court's focus on specific vulnerability can go hand in hand with universal vulnerability as the (implicit) presupposition of human rights law.[93]

By delineating the Court's case law, this chapter has shown that, when vulnerability is explicitly used in human rights jurisprudence, it functions as a prioritization or as an extension/specification tool. Vulnerability is thus an important judicial concept that helps create a more inclusive human rights law: in other words, a human rights law that is more responsive to the needs of vulnerable people. At the same time, the quiet revolution that I have analysed in this chapter is definitely accompanied by struggle. The work of Fineman and Grear illuminates the fact that the Court struggles between a liberal subject approach and a vulnerability approach. Somewhat ironically, their thesis also helps to see why the Court is attacked by critics in the process. The vulnerability thesis thus predicts its own limits in the ECtHR context: as a social institution the Court is vulnerable in and of itself, which is a reality that the Court will have to take seriously in order to survive as a supranational human rights court.

At this point, a sceptic might object that the Court is just taking the old approach of 'cautious incrementalism' (Bartlett et al. 2007, 256) and that no real revolution is taking place at all. In response, I would point out that some of the rulings analysed in this chapter are not 'cautious' in the least; think for example of *M.S.S. v. Belgium and Greece*, *Opuz v. Turkey*, *Salduz v. Turkey*, *Yordanova v. Bulgaria* and *M.S. v. UK*. On a more profound level, I wish to connect the Court's reasoning to what Costas Douzinas has famously claimed: 'human rights have only paradoxes to offer' (Douzinas 2000, 21). The same holds true for vulnerability. Ontologically,

---

93   The judges of the ECtHR might intuitively link their work to universal vulnerability. When Lourdes Peroni and I asked a judge about the Court's reasoning, he replied: 'All applicants are vulnerable, but some are more vulnerable than others.' In this one sentence, the judge neatly reconciled the apparent tension between universal and particular vulnerability in human rights law.

vulnerability is both particular and universal;[94] as a thesis it concerns both the 'is' and the 'ought'; and as human rights reasoning it sits between law and critique (Grear 2010, 169). In short, the Court's vulnerability reasoning is partly a genuine shift in discourse (a revolution), and partly a manifestation of the status quo. The title of this chapter is an attempt to capture the paradoxical nature of the role of vulnerability in human rights law.

Revolution or no revolution, vulnerability is a concept to keep an eye on. Vulnerability considerations are at the frontlines of the Court's case law: this is where it happens, especially in case law concerning migrants. The vulnerability thesis promotes a radical restructuring of societal institutions and also of our way of thinking about the foundations of law. It invites a reimagining of the human of human rights law. '[T]he challenge is to think beyond current ideological constraints' (Fineman 2010, 274). The vulnerability approach celebrates a shared humanity instead of casting us as antagonists in a bitter fight over limited state resources (see contra Xenos 2009). Surely, this appeals to the heart of the human rights project.

---

94 Compare Bergoffen 2012, 30 ('Our bodies, in establishing the boundaries that separate, distinguish and individuate us from others, are also the source of our connection to them.')

Chapter 10

Animals as Vulnerable Subjects: Beyond Interest-convergence, Hierarchy, and Property

Ani B. Satz

I. Introduction[1]

Human relations with domestic animals—companion, factory farm, and laboratory animals—are based on contradiction. We coddle them, eat them, leave our estates to them, experiment on them, buy them designer collars and clothes, wear them, risk our lives for them, and abandon or kill them. These contradictions are entrenched in a sprawling body of law regulating human use of animals as property.

Animals receive legal protections only when their interests align with human interests. Consider the following examples. Animals are not slaughtered before being "rendered insensible" because of the cruelty involved as well as the reduced hazard for slaughterhouse workers, efficiency in processing, and economic gains associated with decreased bruising of flesh foods (Humane Methods of Livestock Slaughter Act (HMLSA), 7 U.S.C. §§ 1901–1907). Downed pigs and sheep (animals too sick to stand) are not dragged or hauled to slaughter unless an inspector deems them fit for human consumption (21 U.S.C. § 603). Animals in laboratories are entitled to enough shelter and food to keep them alive to facilitate research (Animal Welfare Act (AWA), 7 U.S.C. §§ 2131–2159). Companion animals are protected against cruelty in every state because of a desire to prevent harm to them as well as the value humans place on their relationships with them and the link between animal cruelty and violence against humans.

Derrick Bell famously described this phenomenon—of a privileged group providing legal protections to a disadvantaged group when it supports the interests of the privileged—as interest-convergence (Bell 1980, 523). Bell argued in the context of desegregation that whites opposed segregation "not simply [because of] the immorality of racial inequality, but [because of] … the economic and political advances at home and abroad that would follow abandonment of segregation" (524). Whites knew that desegregation would aid US foreign policy, black soldier morale in the wake of World War II, and the economic development of the South

---

1   This chapter is an excerpted and revised version of a chapter that appeared in Volume 16 of the *Animal Law Review* and is reprinted with permission.

(524–5). When the interests of whites and blacks diverged, the reach of *Brown v. Board of Education* and school desegregation was limited (525–6). In 1977, a mere 23 years after *Brown*, the US Supreme Court held that segregation could be justified if it was not intentional or condoned by the school (527). This decision undermined busing plans vital to the implementation of *Brown*, and desegregated schools began to re-segregate (531–2).

Animal laws are also the product of interest-convergence. Despite their nomenclature, animal welfare and anti-cruelty statutes protect human as well as animal interests. The problem with providing animal protections in this manner is that when human and animal interests conflict, animal protections are reduced or eliminated to facilitate human use of animals. Even one of the most basic animal interests—avoiding suffering—is ignored. Animals are anally shocked to death, drowned, suffocated, or gassed, so as not to damage their furs for fashion garments; subjected to invasive experiments without appropriate pain relief or sedation to prevent drug interference with experimental results; tethered on short leads without sufficient shelter, food, or water for the entirety of their lives as guard animals; and intensively confined in dark, windowless warehouses for efficient meat production after being routinely castrated, de-beaked, and de-toed without anesthesia.

When human and nonhuman animal interests diverge, the natural baseline for the legal protection of animals—premised on their inherent capacities—is redrawn to facilitate human use of animals. *All* protections for animals are placed in jeopardy. Unlike protections for other disadvantaged groups, there is no constitutional or other legal floor guarding the basic liberties of animals.

In addition to undermining fundamental protections for animals, diverging interests create moral and legal inconsistencies. Animals with the same capacities, often within the same species or legal class, are treated differently. These inconsistencies undermine the form and function of animal law, making it difficult for owners, users, and advocates of animals alike to understand the legal boundaries of human behaviors affecting animals.

The problems created by interest-divergence are not easily remedied. While existing law might be refocused on enforcing the interests of a protected, disadvantaged human group (Bell 1980, 532–3), nonhuman animals have no baseline of rights upon which to refocus. Instead it is necessary to reestablish fundamental legal protections for animals based on their inherent capacities.

Various scholars, recognizing that animal welfare laws do not adequately protect animals, propose frameworks to offer more meaningful protections (Dillard et al. 2006; Francione 1996; Regan 2004; Singer 2002a; Wise 2000). However, such scholarly efforts are unable to overcome significant problems. First, under rights- and interests-based approaches, a hierarchy problem arises: Due to the higher capacities of humans, their rights or interests in using animals will always trump the rights or interests of animals, even with regard to avoiding suffering in some contexts. Second, existing scholarship is entrenched in a paralyzing debate about whether categorizing animals as "persons" instead of "property" will improve their legal protections.

Thus, current law and scholarship fail to provide mechanisms to protect animals sufficiently and to avoid legal inconsistencies in their treatment. In this chapter, I propose a new legal paradigm for the regulation of human interaction with domestic animals based on the principle of equal protection that "like beings should be treated alike" to resolve these problems. I combine the insights of vulnerability theorists with the equal protection principle and capability theory to create an approach that recognizes the equal claims of human and nonhuman animals to protections against suffering. To be clear, my paradigm does not invoke an Equal Protection Clause argument. Such an argument would require that animals are recognized as persons, and I do not argue that the property status of animals should change.

To develop my proposal, Part II discusses as a threshold matter arguments for the moral status of animals and why laws must protect animals. Applying aspects of Martha Fineman's vulnerability thesis to nonhuman animals, it establishes a novel approach to the moral status of animals based on universal vulnerability to suffering. Parts III–V critique current animal welfare laws and proposed legal solutions. Part III argues that interest-divergence results in differential treatment of animals with the same capacities in three contexts: (1) the same legally defined class, (2) the same species, and (3) across species. Part IV discusses the failure of the humane food movement as well as other compromises regarding animal well-being to treat equally morally relevant human and nonhuman animal capacities. Part V examines existing proposals for law reform, ranging from changing the legal status of animals from property to persons or "living property," to a nondiscrimination approach that recognizes the right of all animals to noninterference.

Working from the premise that animals are vulnerable subjects, Part VI presents a new paradigm for the legal regulation of human use of domestic animals that combines the equal protection principle and capability theory to allow animals equal claims to certain basic capabilities. It is a nondiscrimination approach that creates a presumption against use of animals who have the capacity to suffer. Part VII addresses the implications of my proposal for dominant social views and practices, the ability of the paradigm to address possible conflicts between human and nonhuman animal capabilities, and the changes to legal structures it requires.

II. Moral Obligations to Animals

The moral status of animals informs whether they should receive legal protections, and, if so, the nature of those protections. Moral status may be understood generally as the ability to be wronged by the actions of others (Jamieson 2002, 122). Laws such as the AWA and state anti-cruelty statutes operate from the premise that animals are part of our moral community, though they do not protect animals accordingly (AWA, 7 U.S.C. §§ 2131–2159). This part underscores inconsistencies between the stated purpose of animal laws and the protections they confer.

A. Current Approaches

Animals may be wronged by a variety of human uses and other human acts. It is helpful to view animals as possessing interests, rights, or vulnerabilities that entail something akin to negative and positive freedoms under Isaiah Berlin's classic account, though Berlin himself does not include animals in such account (Berlin 1969, 118–34). Animals may have a claim to freedom from interference as well as to affirmative obligations to assist them in achieving certain states, which, for domestic animals, stem from their inherent dependency on humans for survival.

The view that animals possess either interests or rights is based on the notion that they have capacities that are morally relevant. In 1789, utilitarian Jeremy Bentham argued that: "The question is not, Can [animals] reason? nor, Can they talk? but, Can they suffer? Why should the law refuse its protection to any sensitive being?" (Bentham 2001). Contemporary utilitarian Peter Singer develops this view, arguing that animals are sentient beings based on their capacity to suffer and thereby entitled to equal consideration of their interests (Singer 2002a, 8). Under Singer's view, the suffering (or happiness) of nonhuman sentient animals should be considered equally with the suffering (or happiness) of human animals (ibid.). To argue otherwise, Singer suggests, would be speciesist, or would unjustifiably privilege human suffering over that of other species (18–20).

Singer argues under a "properties view" (as distinguished from viewing animals legally as property) that, while all animals have the capacity to suffer, some animals have additional morally relevant interests because they possess higher properties or capacities (Singer 2002a, 20–21; Singer 1996, 73–4, 110–11). According to the properties view, animals with higher capacities—such as the ability to see themselves existing over time, to be autonomous, to have conceptions of themselves, or to have relationships with others—possess interests that must be weighed within the utilitarian calculus (ibid.). As a result, not all sentient beings have lives of equal worth (ibid.).

A common criticism of the properties view is that it results in a hierarchy problem because it privileges animals with the greatest capacities and may therefore justify harmful human use of nonhuman animals (ibid.). Although Singer argues that no animal's interest in avoiding suffering is to be displaced by a higher-order interest—such as an interest in eating a ham sandwich as compared to the suffering of a factory-farmed pig—humans have higher-order interests that may privilege their suffering over that of nonhuman animals. For example, the suffering of a human with cancer may be greater than that of a nonhuman animal with the same type of cancer, given the human's knowledge of the effect of cancer on long-term plans and complex familial relationships (Singer 2002a, 15–16). If scientists must sacrifice 100 million mice to find a cure for a common cancer that affects 2.5 million people (a proposition Singer believes to be untrue, given computer modeling and other alternatives to animal experimentation) (25–94), a balancing of interests could result in experimenting on and killing the mice. Balancing interests also may deny nonhuman animals a right to continuous existence. Assuming some nonhuman animals do not have a concept of a future, if they could be raised without suffering and killed painlessly, they could be sacrificed for a human purpose (17–20). Despite these possibilities, current uses of animals in laboratories and factory farms cannot be justified, according to Singer, because the suffering they cause outweighs inferior interests in experimentation and flesh food consumption (25–158).

Deontological or rights-based views, on the other hand, are derived from the tradition of Immanuel Kant, a contemporary of Bentham, who believed that rights are possessed by, and duties are owed to, beings capable of mutual justification and reason-giving (Kant 1993, 7–17). While nonhuman animals do not possess these capacities and therefore cannot themselves be rights-holders, Kant believed that humans have indirect duties towards animals (Kant 1979, 239–41). Cruelty to animals, Kant argues, offends humanity: "A master who turns out his ass or his dog because the animal can no longer earn its keep manifests a small mind" (241). Under Kant's view, it is likely that the cruelties of factory farming and some animal experimentation would offend our humanity, though farming and experimentation could be justified if they could be performed humanely.

Tom Regan offers a stronger rights-based view that animals' inherent value situates them within our moral community and affords them universal rights (Regan 2004, 150–94). Regan argues that humans have obligations of noninterference as well as affirmative duties to prevent harm to animals in most situations (ibid.). Regan's framework requires vegetarianism for humans (since humans have alternative food sources) and the end of hunting, animal experimentation, and presumably most other uses of domestic animals except for companionship (150–94, 330–98). The problem with Regan's view is that conflicts will arise between humans and animals who possess inherent value and have competing rights claims. As with interests, rights may be weighed and protections for lower-order animals undermined.

Other arguments for including animals within our moral community are based on vulnerability. These approaches are not rooted in moral theory like utilitarian or deontological approaches; rather, they provide independent moral arguments for the status of animals. One such view, which might be termed a holistic or ecological view, is that animals are part of our moral community because they are a constitutive part of our environment and contribute to its diversity (Bryant 2007, 239–43; Bryant 2006, 162–93). Thus, animals within our ecosystem are vulnerable to disturbances and possess claims to noninterference regardless of sentience, or the ability to suffer (ibid.). This view is the most inclusive approach to the moral status of animals because it creates a presumption against harm to all animals regardless of mental properties. Applied to the domestic animal context, this view would prohibit almost all current uses of animals, with the possible exception of animals used as companions, so long as conflicts between the interests of domestic companion animals and wild animals could be minimized.

B. Animals as Vulnerable Subjects

This chapter argues that animals are part of our moral community based on a different type of vulnerability approach. Human and nonhuman animals share universal vulnerability to suffering with respect to certain basic capabilities. In developing my position, I apply Martha Fineman's concept of vulnerability to nonhuman animals (Fineman 2008).

Fineman understands vulnerability as a universal and constant aspect of the human condition (8). All individuals are vulnerable as a result of their biology (for example, sickness) or environmental or social forces (such as natural disasters or war, respectively) (9). The counterpart to vulnerability is resilience, which may take the form of biological resilience or resilience through social supports, or, arguably, serendipity (13). In the absence of resilience, vulnerability may be realized, and individuals may become impaired or dependent. Dependency may be episodic or permanent, and the potential for it is universal; thus, vulnerable subjects are interdependent in this way (9–10). Fineman argues that current legal structures privilege individuals whose vulnerability is not realized (13–14).

Social and legal institutions are also vulnerable to the extent that they may be controlled by the interests of individuals who are privileged (12–13). As a result, substantive inequalities may be embedded within the institutions that seek to address vulnerability (18–19). Fineman argues that the state must restructure its social institutions to "reflect … an affirmative obligation not to privilege any group … over others …." (21).

Fineman's concepts are easily extended to domestic nonhuman animals. Domestic animals are vulnerable due to both their biology (limited capacities compared to most humans) and their environment (social and legal constructs that support their use for human benefit). Further, domestic animals and humans are interdependent. Animals are dependent on humans to provide them care and shelter, and humans depend on animals in a variety of contexts including companionship, protection, service, and rescue. Unquestionably, our legal and social structures favor human capabilities over those of domestic animals and are susceptible to further control by human interests. As a result, domestic animals are vulnerable to severe deprivations of basic capabilities, like the ability to receive sufficient food and hydration, to engage in natural behaviors of movement, and to maintain bodily integrity.

Unlike most human animals, however, the dependency of nonhuman domestic animals is permanent. Throughout their lives, domestic animals rely on humans to provide them nourishment, medical and other care, and a place to live. The permanent dependency of domestic animals is created and controlled by humans, rendering such animals uniquely vulnerable to exploitation. Domestic nonhuman animals are, for this reason, perhaps the most vulnerable of all sentient beings.

While a theory of animals as vulnerable subjects warrants development elsewhere, for present purposes it is sufficient to say that my argument for the moral status of animals is based on a number of premises that combine vulnerability concepts with long-standing views about animal capacities discussed in Section A. First, animal capacities for suffering are morally relevant, as are higher-order capacities such as the ability to see oneself existing over time. Second, it is speciesist to privilege human over nonhuman animal suffering. Third, human and nonhuman animals are universally vulnerable to suffering, and their most basic capabilities must be treated equally before nonhuman animals may be used to support higher-order human capabilities. State institutions must not privilege humans in responding to universal vulnerability affecting certain basic capabilities. Before developing my proposal further, it is necessary to discuss both the scope of current legal protections and existing proposals for improving animal protection.

III. Human Use of Animals and Interest-divergence

Domestic animals are property under the law. As such, they are gifted, traded, sold, transported, stored, abandoned, and discarded. They are valued at market price. They are owned by individuals as well as by government and corporate entities.

Legal protections for animals are based primarily on their value to their owners. Unlike most other forms of property, however, animals have protections by virtue of being living organisms. For example, companion animals must be provided food and hydration (Ga. Code. Ann. § 16-12-4(a)(3), 2009), laboratory animals with food and space to stand and turn around (9 C.F.R. § 3.6(a)(2)(xi), 2008), and factory farm animals with blows or electric stunning to render them unconscious prior to slaughter (HMLSA, § 1902(a)). The animal property holder determines the animal's use, operating under weak constraints imposed by animal welfare and anti-cruelty laws, and, in some cases, public health laws and regulations.

Animals may be either the primary or secondary subjects of laws. Animals are the primary subjects of laws purporting to prevent human cruelty to them as well as laws with the stated purpose of regulating human use of animals for both animal welfare and human safety. Every state has statutes criminalizing the abuse and neglect of companion animals. Federal statutes that address animal welfare pertain to animal dealing (AWA, §§ 2131–2159), confinement of laboratory animals (ibid.), livestock slaughter (HMLSA, §§ 1901–1907), and, most recently, animal fighting (Animal Fighting Prohibition Enforcement Act of 2007, Pub. L. No. 110-22, §§ 1–3, 121 Stat. 88, 89, 2007). Human uses of animals also are regulated directly to guard against threats to human health. The most notable example is the prohibition of the slaughter of diseased cattle for flesh food (Martin 2008).

Animals are the secondary subjects of laws that focus on humans. For example, animals may be used as disability accommodations under the Americans with Disabilities Act of 1990 (as amended) (ADA) (ADA, 42 U.S.C. §§ 12101–12213), the Fair Housing Act (42 U.S.C. §§ 3601–360), and parallel state disability and housing statutes. Animals also may be police or military property.

A consequence of the property status of animals is that they do not have standing to sue (Sunstein 2000, 1334, 1359). Animal advocates have limited ability to bring suit on behalf of animals, and many federal animal cases are dismissed for lack of standing (Dillard et al. 2006). While standing may be statutorily granted, the AWA, the HMLSA, and the Marine Mammal Protection Act of 1972 do not contain a private right of action. Further, animal advocates experience difficulty demonstrating injury for abuses to animals they do not own. Advocates attempting to meet the constitutional requirements for standing of a concrete and particularized injury advance with limited success theories of economic, aesthetic, and informational harm, each of which supports a human interest (Sunstein 2000, 1343–52). Whether animals are the primary or secondary subjects of laws, or regulated for their own or human welfare, their legal treatment is defined by human interest. This results in interest-convergence, which both undermines fundamental protections for animals and creates legal inconsistencies.

A. Undermining Fundamental Protections

Interest-convergence that undermines legal protections arises in three contexts. First, it occurs in the development of laws focusing on animals. Second, it results when existing laws are reinterpreted to accommodate new or to maintain existing human uses of animals. Third, it occurs when human interest in using animals resolves conflicts between human legal rights. While animals receive some protection in the last situation, they are considered a means to an end rather than as beings possessing legally relevant capacities. In each of the three contexts, basic protections for animals based on their capabilities are undermined.

1. Privileging human over animal interests in the development of laws focusing on animals   Even a superficial examination of laws focusing on animals reveals that, despite their terminology, they largely protect human rather than animal interests. For example, the AWA addresses the confinement of laboratory animals with requirements only sufficient to sustain animal life to facilitate research (AWA, §§ 2131, 2143(a)(1)–(2), (4), 2143(a)(2)(A)). When humane treatment conflicts with scientific or other human interests, even these minimum standards may be sacrificed (§ 2143(a)(3)(D)). In addition, the AWA regulates animal dealing to protect owners of companion animals against theft of their property (§ 2131(3)). The "Findings and Declaration of Policy" of the HMLSA addresses the conditions of slaughterhouse workers, improved flesh foods, economy of production, and other benefits to "producers, processors, and consumers" (HMLSA, § 1901). The prevention of "needless suffering" is the sole reference to animal welfare in the statute, and this requires only that animals are "rendered insensible" prior to killing them (§ 1901). Greater balance between human and animal interests is seen in state anti-cruelty laws pertaining to companion animals, though the laws often support a desire to break the chain of violence leading to human harm (Frasch et al. 1999, 70). Prosecuting crimes against animals creates a record of physical violence that identifies individuals posing a risk to humans and may deter violent individuals from committing future crimes (Animal Legal Defense Fund 2009).

Recent developments in animal law clearly are prompted by human need and are therefore also vulnerable to changing human uses of animals. For example, federal quality standards for pet food were not proposed until contaminated food killed beloved companion animals, entered the human food chain, and threatened a $16.9 billion industry (Human and Pet Food Safety Act of 2007, Sen. 1274, H.R. 2108, 110th Cong., 2007). Congress passed a law allowing pets in shelters during federal emergencies after people were killed during Hurricane Katrina when they refused to evacuate their homes without their companion animals (Pets Evacuation and Transportation Standards Act of 2006, Pub. L. No. 109–308, 120 Stat. 1725, 2006). Similarly, some shelters for human victims of domestic violence allow companion animals because studies indicate that one-quarter to one-third of abused individuals are reluctant to leave their animal companions behind (Hsu 2007). Haley's Act, named after a young woman killed by a Siberian tiger while posing for a high school senior photo, would ban the use of large cats outside sanctuaries and zoos because of their danger to humans, not because of the cruelty involved in keeping such animals outside their native environment (Haley's Act, H.R. 1947, 109th Cong., 2007). The Animal Fighting Prohibition Enforcement Act of 2007 (AFPEA) stresses the risk to public safety posed by animal fighting operations (especially dog fighting, where animals are bred and trained for aggression and violence), the propagation of crime, and the culture of violence that surrounds the macabre sport (AFPEA, Pub. L. No. 110–22, 121 Stat. 88, 89, 2007).

Even when animals are protected by law, many animal welfare laws contain exceptions for particular human uses of animals or deny protections for certain species altogether. The AWA and anti-cruelty statutes in most states exclude farm animals (Wolfson and Sullivan 2004, 228) because factory farms are the most efficient, and arguably the only, means to produce enough flesh food to meet existing consumer demand (Singer 2002a, 160). Factory farms could not comply with the minimum cage requirements of the regulations supporting the AWA, namely, room for each animal to stand up, turn around, sit, lie down, and walk normally. Companion animals, the most protected of all domestic animals, fare no better when their interests clash with human interests. For example, the US Supreme Court disregarded animal cruelty laws and struck down city ordinances targeting the religious sacrifice of animals by the Santeria and the Church of the Lukumi Babalu Aye as a violation of the First Amendment's Free Exercise Clause (Church of the *Lukumi Babalu Aye, Inc. v. City of Hialeah*, 508 U.S. 520, 1993). No restrictions were imposed on the method of sacrifice. Working animals such as police, war, and drug- and explosive-detecting dogs have limited protections from their handlers under state anti-cruelty statutes (Scheiner 2001, 144). They are routinely subjected to abusive negative reinforcement training practices such as shocking and prolonged muzzling, worked to the point of exhaustion and bodily degradation, and placed in life-threatening situations. These dogs are government property and may be categorized and treated as equipment. Legal protections for animals are weakened further, and legal inconsistencies are exacerbated, when animal laws are reinterpreted to support either emerging human uses of animals or existing uses threatened by law reform efforts.

2. Reinterpreting laws in light of human uses of animals   Animal protection laws are frequently reinterpreted to accommodate new human uses of animals or to maintain existing ones. This disrupts fundamental protections for animals based on their natural capacities and further weakens animal protections. For some animals, prohibitions against mutilation and intensive confinement are placed in jeopardy.

For example, when state anti-cruelty laws conflict with human interest in efficient flesh food production, the protections they contain are minimized. In one case, the Superior Court of New Jersey baldly and tautologically declared: "Routine husbandry practices are humane [under state anti-cruelty law] because of who teaches them and who may perform them" (*N.J. Socy. for the Prevention of Cruelty to Animals v. N.J. Dept. of Agric.*, 2007 WL 486764 at *14 (N.J. Super. Ct. App. Div. Feb. 16, 2007)). The court reasoned that close confinement (resulting in extreme stress, neurotic behaviors, and insanity) as well as de-beaking, toe trimming, and castration without anesthesia are warranted as a practical matter: "[I]t would be essentially impossible, and certainly impractical … to list every possible routine husbandry practice taught … and then create specific humane standards for every practice" (*14). While the New Jersey Supreme Court later overturned the holding that agricultural institutions (rather than the State Board of Agriculture) may determine whether their own practices are humane, the court indicated that all but one of the practices at issue (tail docking) could be humanely performed (*N.J. Socy. for the Prevention of Cruelty to Animals v. N.J. Dept. of Agric.*, 955 A.2d 886, 889, 905–07-9, N.J. 2008).

Similarly, animal protections were undermined by Congress after the US Department of Agriculture's (USDA) Animal and Plant Health Inspection Service (APHIS) proposed regulations to protect rodents under the AWA, which covers "laboratory" and "warm-blooded" animals (64 Fed. Reg. 4356–67, 1999). APHIS's interpretation of the AWA was strongly contested by the National Association of Biomedical Research (NABR) and other lobbies because most animal research involves rodents. A statutory amendment was ultimately passed *excluding* rodents and birds from the definitions of "laboratory" and "warm-blooded" animals, creating legal fictions (Farm Security and Rural Investment Act of 2002, Pub. L. No. 107–171, §§ 10301, 10304, 116 Stat. 134, 491–92, 2002).

Occasionally, evolving human interest in using animals overlaps with animal well-being. The strongest example is the common law affecting companion animals. Historically, recovery for harm to companion animals was limited to the animal's market worth, which for a shelter animal may be negligible. As the number of companion animals increases (71.1 million living within 63 percent of US households) and human reliance on them grows, the common law is evolving to recognize greater recovery for owners who are injured by loss of companionship due to negligence or intentional harm (American Pet Products

2009; Huss 2004, 526–7). In some jurisdictions, recovery for emotional distress is allowed in veterinary malpractice actions, and malicious injury to a pet may be considered when assessing emotional damages arising from intentional harm. Some companion animal guardians may even be eligible for "petimony," that is, money paid upon divorce by the noncustodial guardian to the custodial guardian for the care of a pet (Britton 2006, 8 n.44).

While these developments for companion animals may deter future veterinary or other harm, dangers exist. As the factory farm and laboratory contexts demonstrate, animals are rendered hyper-vulnerable to changing human desires, and their most fundamental protections may be undermined. The same concerns apply to the third area of interest-convergence, which occurs when human interest in using animals resolves conflicts between competing human legal rights.

3. Using human interest in animals to resolve legal conflict   Perhaps the best example of using animals to resolve legal conflict among humans arises in the housing context. In this context, human use of animals may be privileged over other property claims, with little or no regard for animal welfare. A case from California, *Auburn Woods v. Fair Employment and Housing Commission*, provides a salient example. *Auburn Woods* pitted the no-dogs policy within the covenants, conditions, and restrictions (CCRs) of a condominium association against the rights of a couple with disabilities to keep in their residence Pooky, a small terrier, as an accommodation for emotional support (18 Cal. Rptr. 3d 669, 671–72 (Cal. App. 2004)). Ed Elebiari, disabled from a car accident, was hydrocephalic and suffered from bipolar, obsessive-compulsive, and seizure disorders (673). His wife, Jayne, experienced major depressive episodes involving insomnia and acts of self-mutilation (ibid.). Allegedly, Pooky enabled the couple to leave their home and Jayne to maintain employment (ibid.). After the Elebiaris were forced to place Pooky in the care of a friend, Ed became homebound, Jayne abandoned her job, and their marital relationship deteriorated (ibid.).

The couple did not dispute knowledge of the no-dogs policy and ultimately moved to another state (676). Nevertheless, they filed suit under the California Fair Employment and Housing Act (CFEHA), arguing that Pooky promoted their psychological well-being and that the condominium association, Auburn Woods, should pay damages for failing to accommodate them (ibid.). Auburn Woods argued that the Elebiaris were reasonably accommodated under the terms of the CCRs, which allowed residents to house other companion animals, such as rabbits or cats, for emotional support (ibid.). While the lower court found this argument compelling, the appellate court determined alternative animal companions to be ersatz and held that the Elebiaris were entitled to compensation for emotional distress (682, 684).

This case is particularly interesting because the desired accommodation at stake for the Elebiaris was not a trained guide or service dog—an accommodation that would be upheld as a matter of civil right under the ADA—but rather a companion animal with no special skills. The court upheld the Elebiaris' accommodation under the CFEHA on the basis that Pooky enabled the Elebiaris to use and to enjoy their home (677–9). Further, by requiring a dog as a necessary accommodation, the decision expanded the range of required accommodations beyond that mandated by the ADA; that is, only a particular type of companion animal was recognized by the court as adequate to meet the Elebiaris' emotional needs (683). In fact, one could understand the opinion to say that only Pooky himself was a reasonable accommodation for the Elebiaris.

In cases of accommodation for impairments rising to the level of disability under the ADA, which informs CFEHA jurisprudence, accommodation from within a category of similar goods is sufficient (677–8). The ADA only requires that the accommodation is reasonable, not that it is what the plaintiff prefers (29 C.F.R. § 1630.9(d), 2008). Under this reasoning, it is likely that a rabbit or another companion animal allowed by the condominium association would be considered a reasonable accommodation for the emotional needs of the Elebiaris. This is significant because it demonstrates how deeply human use of animals is embedded in current law. Claims involving the use of animals to promote human well-being may be legally recognized as stronger than claims for the use of inanimate tools of assistance.

Protections for animals based on this type of interest-convergence are extremely narrow. For example, while Pooky would be entitled to continued indoor shelter if the Elebiaris had stayed at Auburn Woods, the court was silent about the ability of the Elebiaris, who were often housebound for long periods of time, to care for Pooky. The dog's needs were addressed only with regard to Jayne's well-being: "Jayne described how her depression and related symptoms improved after getting the dog. She no longer sat around the house brooding but instead paid attention to the dog's needs …" (*Auburn Woods*, 679). The CCRs' shelter exception would not apply to a dog whose life was in danger due to illness, inclement weather, or human abuse. Further, under *Auburn Woods*, if human emotional needs or disability are temporary, so too may be the companion animal's home (and, if taken to a shelter or abandoned, possibly her life).

Whether laws are directed at animals as primary or secondary subjects, their lives are controlled by human interests. Animals are afforded either no or limited protections, and exceptions are made to laws that purportedly protect animals in order to privilege human over animal well-being. Animals are protected only when human and nonhuman animal interests converge. When interests diverge, fundamental protections are disrupted, as seen in the factory farming, laboratory, working animal, and animal sacrifice contexts. Because animal law is defined by human interests, and humans use the same types of animals or animals with similar capacities in different ways, inconsistencies are created.

B. Creating Legal Inconsistencies

Inconsistencies created by interest-convergence undermine the form and function of the body of law pertaining to animals. Ignoring animal capacities, such as the ability to suffer, disrupts the foundations upon which fundamental legal protections for animals are premised and weakens the precedential value of animal law. Inconsistencies also frustrate expectations about the duties owed to animals, which makes compliance with and enforcement of animal laws difficult.

1. Animals sharing the same legal or species category   Animals within the same legal category, as well as animals within species categories, may be subject to differential treatment under law based on human use. Primary legal categories of domestic animals include: "companion animal," "laboratory animal," "livestock," and "warm-blooded animal." Animals within these categories may receive different treatment, even if they are of the same species.

Consider the legal class "companion animals." Animals who assist an individual with a disability may evade quarantine and are allowed in places of public accommodation, including housing that would otherwise prohibit them. Yet even animals within the subcategory of "service animals" may experience different treatment, depending on their owner's impairment and whether the animal is a reasonable accommodation in a particular context. Some individuals with service animals may lack impairments legally recognized as disabilities and not be entitled to an accommodation. For others, a service animal may fail to be a reasonable accommodation. For example, a seizure-alert dog for a chef may be viewed as a public health hazard in areas of food preparation. Further, some building CCRs privilege one species of companion animal over another with respect to support animals.

Similar inconsistencies arise under the AWA and state anti-cruelty statutes with respect to "companion animals." The AWA draws distinctions within the category of companion animals based on the party selling the animal. Companion animals who are sold in retail pet stores are not protected under the AWA, while animals originating from commercial breeders have protections concerning their confinement, care, and conditions of transportation (AWA, §§ 2132(f)(i)-(ii), 2133, 2143).

Under state anti-cruelty statutes, prosecution of animal abuse cases may depend on the well-being of the abuser. Cruelty associated with pet hoarding is often seen as the product of a human illness rather than as a crime, or as a combination of both, warranting a lesser charge than other circumstances where animals experience similar neglect and suffering. The legal focus in hoarding cases frequently is shifted from animal well-being and the consequences of human behavior to the current and future well-being of the human engaging in the behavior.

Additional inconsistencies are found within other legal categories of animals. The AWA applies to "laboratory animals" who are "warm-blooded animals," yet rodents and birds are excluded from the Act (AWA, § 2132(g)). This is a sizeable omission, as the NABR estimates that 95 percent of animal experimentation is performed on rodents, with rats and mice being used for experimentation more than all other vertebrate animals together (NABR 2009; OTA 1986, 25). While the exact number of rodents used is unknown, some studies place rat use alone as high as 23.6 million a year (Physicians Committee for Responsible Medicine 2009). Differential treatment also arises under the AWA with regard to laboratory animals of the same species. The Act applies only to animals used in university or industry laboratories (AWA, §2132(e)). Animals used in primary or lower secondary education experiments are not protected (ibid.). Thus, high school teachers may allow their students to confine and experiment on animals without restriction, while college professors may not.

Under the AWA, "livestock" of the same species are treated differently depending on their human use (§2132(g)). Transportation conditions of farm animals are regulated only for animals *not* used for flesh foods and clothing, which are the primary uses of such animals (ibid.). Similarly, the AWA governs use of farm animals for laboratory experiments but excludes "livestock or poultry used or intended for use for improving animal nutrition, breeding, management, or production efficiency, or for improving the quality of food or fiber" (ibid.). Thus, a cow at a university may be treated differently depending on whether it is housed in a laboratory or a university farm. Similar inconsistencies apply to horses (AWA, § 2132(g)(2)).

The HMLSA governs the slaughter of "livestock," but it does not apply to poultry or fish. As a result, birds and fish need not be rendered unconscious prior to dismemberment. Around 9 billion chickens, turkeys, and ducks are slaughtered per year, which is more than 98 percent of terrestrial animals slaughtered for flesh foods (USDA 2008). Under the HMLSA, animals of the same species may be slaughtered in different ways depending on the downstream consumer of the flesh food. The Act's requirement that covered livestock are rendered insensible prior to killing is usually met by "captive bolt stunning," a process approved by the USDA whereby a bolt applies force to or penetrates the head of the animal to render it unconscious (9 C.F.R. § 313.15, 2008). Exceptions exist for ritual religious killing and may entail animals having their carotid arteries slashed and being hung upside down to drain the blood from their bodies (HMLSA, § 1902(b)).

Interest-convergence creates inconsistencies when animals with the same capacities—including those within the same legal or species category—are treated differently. Two animals of the same legal class or species, with identical injuries, caused in the same manner and by the same person, may have different protections depending on the human interests at stake.

2. Animals of different species and legal categories with similar abilities
Inconsistencies also arise across legal classes of animals when animals of different species with similar abilities are treated differently. For example, a pig, who has similar or higher intelligence than a dog, legally may be immobilized and confined to a crate as "livestock" for the entirety of its life in almost every state, whereas like treatment of a dog as a "companion animal" would result in prosecution for animal cruelty. This is because the welfare of most livestock is legally relevant only during slaughter; protecting the well-being of livestock more robustly conflicts with the efficient mass production of flesh foods. As human interests are less detached from

companion animals, companion animal welfare is legally relevant throughout the life of the animal. These examples could be multiplied—as animals with like capacities are treated inconsistently not only with respect to their conditions of confinement but with regard to the consequences of their wrongful killing—but space here does not permit further elaboration of this troubling reality.

Ultimately, the only distinction between the legal treatment of the pig and the dog (and other animals) is human emotional attachment. The differential treatment has nothing to do with animal capacities or even property status. The latter point is worth emphasizing, as changing the property status of animals alone would not remedy the effects of interest-convergence. Rather, the differential treatment of animals mirrors social attitudes towards animals. Individuals who pamper their pets consume the flesh of equally or more intelligent animals suffering in factory farms.

Thus far the discussion has focused on the effects of interest-convergence on animal classifications and corresponding protections. The next section examines one response to the problems of interest-convergence: moral compromises giving rise to humane food labeling.

IV. Lessons from the Humane Food Movement and Other Moral Compromises

Daily consumer choices deny that the capacity of animals to suffer is morally relevant. The reason for this is obvious: If animal capacities are morally relevant, current use of domestic animals for food, experimentation, exhibition, entertainment, and some forms of service must end, or people must acknowledge engaging in daily, immoral practices. Flesh foods are undoubtedly the most contentious. According to the USDA's National Agriculture Statistics Service, in 2011, over 9.1 billion animals including cattle (34,087,000), chickens (8,683,067,000), ducks (24,472,000), hogs (110,860,000), sheep and lambs (2,164,000), and turkeys (246,844,000) were slaughtered for flesh foods; the average person consumes more than 298 pounds of flesh and 244 eggs per annum (Humane Society of the United States (HSUS) 2013).

While the cruelty of factory farms is well documented, flesh foods and eggs cannot be mass-produced without factory farming, and consumers are unwilling to abandon flesh and egg consumption. Given the schism between those who consider animal capabilities morally relevant and those who do not (or choose to ignore them), it is unsurprising that social practice and law reflect some element of compromise.

One notable example of a moral compromise arises in the context of factory farming and the emergence of "humane labels." These food labels, and the underlying reforms that accompany them, are an effort to respond simultaneously to animal advocates exposing the cruelty of factory farming practices and the demands of flesh food producers and consumers. The practices labeled as "humane" represent the least amount of suffering necessary to serve the economic goals of agribusiness and to fulfill human demand for flesh foods.

In practical terms, humane foods mean marginal space increases for animals intensively confined at a slightly higher cost to producers and consumers. The first shift came with regard to chickens, when some colleges and universities eliminated all or part of their egg purchases from farms confining chickens to battery cages (cages typically containing five to ten hens where each bird has space less than the size of a standard sheet of paper in which to live). Whole Foods and Wild Oats grocery chains followed suit along with Bon Appetit food service company, Wolfgang Puck restaurants, Omni Hotels, Ben and Jerry's ice cream, and Burger King (only 2–4 percent of the eggs used by the latter corporation) (HSUS 2009). In addition, California, Michigan, and some municipalities passed resolutions calling for an end to battery cages. Alternative methods of confinement provide two and a half to three times more space for hens, allowing them some room to move and to spread their wings. They remain densely penned, however, and may not have exposure to sun (or other light) or grass to engage in natural behaviors, and many are still de-beaked and subjected to forced molting (starvation to produce extra egg-laying cycles).

Similar compromises are seen in the pork industry. In addition to nine states, Smithfield Foods, the world's largest pork producer, agreed to eliminate gestation crates (two-foot-wide barred boxes with a concrete floor immobilizing pregnant sows weighing as much as 600 pounds) by 2017 and to require the farms with which it contracts to do so "eventually" (Kaufman 2007). In addition, fast-food corporations such as Wendy's and Burger King vowed to reduce their reliance on pork from farms using gestation crates (Martin 2007). Pigs will remain closely confined indoors, though not in crates (ibid.). Firms have long periods for compliance or are making only small reductions—such as Burger King, which will reduce purchases from farms using gestation crates by 10–20 percent—due to the current lack of supply of "cruelty-free" pork (ibid.).

Unfortunately, a partial boycott of flesh food consumption through purchase of "humane" farm products fails to address the legal and moral inconsistencies in the treatment of farm animals. As long as flesh foods must be produced on a large scale on factory farms, farm animals with the same capacities as other legally protected animals will continue to receive different treatment. At best, over ten or more years some farm animals will have slightly greater space in which to live before slaughter. At worst, the false perception that factory farming practices are humane will prevail, and the volume of flesh food consumption will remain the same or increase.

As the product of interest-convergence, the humane food movement relies on changes to farm practices that promote flesh food flavor, otherwise enhance marketability of flesh foods, or soothe the conscience of flesh food consumers. Thus, humane foods amount to a continuation of policies and legal structures that support human interests over animal well-being. If human interests in these aspects of food production wane, perhaps in the wake of rising food prices and a troubled economy, so too will the limited protections offered to animals by the humane food movement.

Similar conclusions may be drawn about other moral compromises that appear to protect animal well-being. Some animal research institutions voluntarily seek review of their practices from independent firms, allowing the institutions to claim a "gold standard" of care. Such inspections serve to quiet some opposition to experimentation, though these institutions are agreeing only to adhere to minimal legal protections for animals. In addition, when the institutions have foreknowledge of site inspections, observed laboratory practice may not represent usual procedure.

New racing track surfaces for horses provide another example of a false compromise. Costly polymer tracks are purchased to quell concerns about the cruelty of horse racing, as it is believed that these tracks cause fewer bone fractures. Yet racehorses remain subject to both breeding practices and training regimes that increase the propensity for fractures, including racing at a young age before their bodies are able to sustain the stress. Horses who are injured on the track are frequently killed on site or sent to slaughterhouses.

As these examples indicate, "humane" foods and other moral compromises will likely result in minimal improvements for some animals and abusive practices for most. Worse, such compromises may arrest larger social change required to eliminate the causes of the exploitation of animals for human use. A paradigm shift is necessary to promote animal well-being.

V. Critique of Other Legal Solutions

Legal scholars propose a number of solutions to address the dearth of protections for domestic animals. Proposals typically either suggest changing the legal status of domestic animals—from property to "living property" or "persons"—or altering allowable uses of animals regardless of whether they are classified as property. This part argues that current proposals cannot overcome deeply entrenched inequalities that result from interest-convergence or the hierarchy problem of human rights or interests being privileged over those of animals.

Gary Francione has long argued that, in a legal world divided between persons and property, nonhuman animals should be treated as persons (Francione 2000, 100–102; Francione 1996, 177–86; Francione 1995, 14). A "person," according to Francione, is one who has "morally significant interests" (Francione 1995, 100). The problem with the current legal treatment of animals, as he sees it, is that "we balance animal interests unprotected by claims of right against human interests protected by claims of right in general and, in particular, by claims of human property rights in those animals" (91). He argues that even under acts such as the AWA, which purport to support animal welfare, human property interests in laboratory and other animals covered under the Act result in animal exploitation (165–250).

A move toward personhood, as Francione suggests, would entail a dramatic departure from the current legal treatment of animals as property. While personhood certainly does not equate with being human, it usually requires the recognition of higher-order cognitive properties. As persons, animals would have legal rights to avoid suffering and to continued existence. Recognizing personhood could afford domestic animals something akin to Constitutional Equal Protection.

The personhood model has a number of limitations. The move to legal personhood simply pushes the issue of conflicting interests to a higher level, demanding resolution of the same conflicts among *persons*. Further, the exploitation of animals runs deeper than whether we legally call animals "persons" or "property." Animal use is entrenched in religious and philosophical thought and thereby embedded in social practice. It is possible to call animals "persons" and not to consider their capacity to suffer, when recognizing such a capacity conflicts with individual or state interests in animal use. For example, children are no doubt legal persons, yet their interests are routinely sacrificed by those with whom they have a dependency relationship. In addition, legal personhood does not equate with being a member, let alone an equal member, of a moral community; laws recognize corporations as persons, for instance. Lastly, for personhood status to be meaningful in Francione's terms, sentient animals of all abilities would have to be granted personhood under law, and lower-order animals, such as mice, are unlikely to receive this status.

One solution would be to develop a property model where the suffering of animals and their interest in continued existence are considered adequately. A proposal by David Favre advocates such a paradigm, whereby owners of domestic animals would retain legal title over animals who enjoy a form of "equitable self-ownership" (Favre 2000). Through self-ownership, animals could hold equitable interests in other property (such as the house in which they live) and have standing to sue on their own behalf (501–2). Equitable self-ownership recognizes that animals have intrinsic worth (495). In addition, it acknowledges that the dependency relationship between particular human and nonhuman animals imposes duties on human guardians to care for animals, as defined by existing anti-cruelty statues (497–51). In more recent work, Favre simplified this paradigm, treating animals as "living property" (Favre 2010). This creates the same duties of care on behalf of human guardians of animals, though it does not support animals holding equitable interests in property or having standing to sue (ibid.).

In response to such expanded property views, Francione argues—invoking slavery by analogy—that property status prevents the recognition of rights and results in devaluation and degradation (Francione 2000, 131–4). The analogy is at best a loose one, given that domestic animals are permanently and completely dependent on human care. Granting personhood status does not change the exceptional nature of domestic animal dependency. The expanded property approach faces other more difficult challenges, however. It is unlikely to resolve moral or legal inconsistencies resulting from the unequal treatment of animal suffering, as protection relies on a case-by-case assessment under current laws, which entrench unequal treatment. Further, recognizing animals as possessing intrinsic worth does not translate into equal treatment of their capacities, given the hierarchy problem of rights-based (and interests-based) approaches whereby human rights (or interests) always trump animal rights (or interests).

An alternative property approach is used in the wildlife context. Animal life is viewed as an intrinsically important part of the ecosystem. Under the Endangered Species Act of 1973 (ESA) and other statutes, animals are held in trust (ESA, §§ 1531–1544). The state controls access to wild animals, and individuals may not hold title to them. While animals are treated as nonpersons, a trustee or guardian has standing to seek protections on their behalf.

While this approach does not require a case-by-case analysis, the obvious limitation is that the ESA and other wildlife statutes do not speak to individual animals who may need protection. They do, however, embrace the intrinsic value of animals, which translates into the domestic animal setting. As under Favre's approach, individual domestic animals could be recognized as having intrinsic value rather than value relative to human interest. The problems of hierarchy and operating under existing laws that fail to consider equally animal capacities remain, however.

The legal personhood, expanded property, and trustee proposals rely on a change in legal status to generate greater animal protections. Granting animals personhood would give them access to existing legal protections for persons, but it is unclear how the human–nonhuman animal dynamic would change, given the hierarchy problem. Deeming humans trustees or other types of guardians for animals would allow greater enforcement of existing animal protections, which entrench inequalities.

Another approach is to argue for a more foundational legal paradigm shift that removes the presumption of animal use for human interest. Such an approach is based on both animals' rights to noninterference and affirmative obligations of care, stemming from the human–nonhuman animal dependency relationship. Taimie Bryant has moved the discussion in this direction. In "Animals Unmodified," Bryant appeals to a right to noninterference for all living animals, including bacteria, and argues that advocates should develop alternatives to animal use to meet human needs (Bryant 2006, 192–4). Bryant's approach encapsulates some elements of the wildlife paradigm, in the sense that humans live in an ecosystem where organisms are mutually dependent (ibid.), but it goes much farther in terms of imposing an obligation to noninterference. Under Bryant's view, every animal, even the nonsentient, is part of our moral community (ibid.).

Bryant argues that legal paradigms that afford animals protections based on certain properties or capacities should be abandoned (Bryant 2007, 211–26). Under the properties view, there is an inevitable hierarchy of interests, and some animals will always have fewer properties and be treated as inferior (216–20). Recall, for example, the problem with Singer's argument that all sentient animals require equal consideration of their interests to avoid suffering. Animals with higher-order capacities may suffer in greater ways than animals with lower-order capacities, which may prevent the recognition of the interests of the latter.

But it is difficult to know how Byrant's approach would operate in practice. If every animal has moral significance and one cannot create a hierarchy based on sentience, how are conflicts among interests resolved? Without criteria to resolve such conflicts, the default position has been to resolve them in favor of human interests. It seems that the recognition of animal capacities matters for meaningful and sustainable protections. Drawing on Byrant's arguments for a presumption against exploitation, it is possible to advance another framework that recognizes animal capabilities as morally relevant.

VI. Equal Protection of Animals Paradigm

This part advances a new paradigm to regulate human use of animals and to respond to animal suffering by combining vulnerability and capability theory with the principle of equal protection.

A. Equal Claims to Basic Capabilities

Many scholars argue that, since animals are part of our moral community, we should consider them equally on certain grounds. Recall that Singer's equal consideration of interests principle states that the interests of sentient animals in avoiding pain and suffering are to be considered equally with human interests stemming from the pleasure derived from animal use, while Regan's rights theory holds that animals should be protected universally because of their inherent value. The difference between these conceptions of equality lies with how the claims—interests or rights—are enforced. Singer's view is an outcome-oriented (consequentialist) view that weighs the interests of animals and humans. Regan's view is deontological and imposes on humans duties that prohibit using animals in certain ways.

This chapter invokes equality in a different manner. The proposed paradigm supports the view that animals have equal claims to basic capabilities based on their capacity to suffer and their status as vulnerable subjects. These basic capabilities are to be equalized to the greatest extent possible within a given population of human and nonhuman animals (Sen 1987, 369). This approach is outcome-oriented but not utilitarian; it focuses on maximizing basic capabilities (not utility) within a given population.

B. Capability Approaches and Equal Protection

The proposed paradigm is based on a capability approach to well-being that values what an individual can do or be in a lifetime. As recently recognized by Martha Nussbaum, capabilities are enabled by the equal protection principle. In the civil rights context, Nussbaum claims that courts essentially ask the question: "[W]hat are these people actually able to do and to be ... [in order to] unmas[k] [] device[s] for the perpetuation of hierarchy" (Nussbaum 2007). "Doings and beings" are how capabilities are generally defined (Sen 1993, 4).

Nussbaum and Amartya Sen each offer a capability approach. Though Sen's theory was developed first, I begin with Nussbaum's work, as Sen's theory is the one that informs my proposal.

1. Capabilities as dignity   Nussbaum's theory of capability equality has evolved over time (Nussbaum 2006, viii–ix). In one work, she describes her approach as based on the notion of human dignity (70). Capabilities are distributive units that contribute to human dignity by allowing people to realize what they "are actually able to do and to be" (ibid.). Nussbaum makes an analogy to human rights concepts and argues that there is a minimum level of capabilities that must be provided to all humans (ibid.). She identifies a working list of ten capabilities, including life, health, bodily integrity, "[s]enses, [i]magination, and [t]hought," emotions, "[p]ractical [r]eason," affiliation, other species relations, play, and "[c]ontrol over [o]ne's [e]nvironment" (political and material) (392–401).

Unlike Sen, Nussbaum applies her theory directly to animals (346–407). She argues that animals may be part of our moral community based on sentience or other morally relevant capacities, such as those for movement, emotion, or affiliation (351, 362, 392–401). Using "sympathetic imagining" of animal behavior, she applies her ten capabilities developed in the human context to nonhuman animals (354, 392–401).

One problem with Nussbaum's theory is that it is unclear how capabilities that support dignity are identified. She argues that relevant capabilities for animals are "important and good," but it is difficult to know what that means, since she rejects human or other animal nature as good (193, 347, 366–72). Singer rightly suggests that the difficulty of conceptualizing what is important and good under Nussbaum's theory tempts one to argue that what is good is "be[ing] able to satisfy some of [one's] strongest considered preferences," and this collapses Nussbaum's theory into utilitarianism (Singer 2002b).

The primary difficulty with Nussbaum's model, however, is that she recognizes species distinctions for flourishing (Nussbaum 2006, 362–6, 383–4). For this reason, it seems that her theory cannot avoid dominance of human over animal capabilities. Sen's theory of capabilities offers an alternative approach.

2. Capabilities as functionings   Sen's theory of basic capability equality, which he discusses in a variety of works, seeks to maximize capabilities across given populations (Sen 1999). Unlike Nussbaum, Sen does not aim to promote dignity through a set of capabilities believed to be universally significant, but rather to enable certain types of functional outcomes or "functionings" depending on an individual's biology and other limitations (Sen 1993, 31). As a result, individuals choose a capabilities set that speaks to their biological capacities as well as to external limitations, such as financial, legal, or other restrictions (Sen 1999,

6–11). The capabilities set chosen by a given population is maximized (ibid.). Basic capability equality is egalitarian, as members of a population have the same potential for having their chosen capabilities maximized (ibid.). The ability to consider various levels and means of functioning, as well as to provide equal chances that the valued capabilities of every individual will be maximized, is paramount to extending Sen's theory to nonhuman animals.

Sen expresses his model formally, and I interpret his theory in other work (Satz 2008). What is important for present purposes is that the model is flexible enough to consider a spectrum of basic capabilities. Capabilities may be general, such as the ability to have health or intellectual stimulation or to exercise. They also may be specific, like the ability to breathe freely, to metabolize food, or to sleep. The capabilities mentioned thus far may all be considered vital goods. Additionally, basic capabilities may include less significant goods, such as the ability to be entertained, to possess certain material goods, or to live in a particular location. Within a given population, then, basic capability equality may be applied to various levels of the functionings that individuals seek to maximize.

Sen does not apply his model to nonhuman animals. But it does not seem too much of a stretch to apply his theory in this way. Almost any population of human animals will be one in which nonhuman animals reside. Consider the national population, or populations of states or municipalities, universities, laboratories, farms, zoos, military or police units, or households. All sentient animals have basic capabilities pertaining to suffering and perhaps other higher-order capabilities as well. (While nonsentient beings (such as plants) might share capabilities with sentient animals, such as the ability to be nourished, I leave the possibility of extending Sen's theory in this manner to others. Like Singer, I draw a moral line at sentience, possibly somewhere in the animal kingdom "between a shrimp and an oyster" (Singer 2002a, 174).)

The egalitarian premise of basic capability equality—that the valued capabilities of every individual have equal potential to be maximized—could be extended to nonhuman animals. Human and nonhuman animals within a population would have equal chances to maximize their capabilities. Combined with the equal protection principle and vulnerability theory, this gives rise to the new proposed paradigm.

Sen's capabilities approach offers two significant benefits over Nussbaum's approach. First, it avoids species distinctions, which, as discussed below, allows for equal protection of animal capabilities at least at the most basic level. Second, it does not assume that all organisms will benefit from the capabilities Nussbaum identifies. Some human and nonhuman animals may not have these capabilities. These individuals have claims to maximizing other basic capabilities under the proposed approach.

C. Extending Capabilities to Nonhuman Animals

The proposed approach requires that human and nonhuman animals with like capacities must be treated alike. Under Sen's model, relevant capabilities depend on the abilities of a given organism to function in particular ways. For example, animals with higher mental capacities will have different capabilities than animals with lower intellectual abilities. These differences are not confined to species variations per se, but rather result from variations in human and nonhuman animal biology. This section focuses on the most basic capabilities important to human and nonhuman animals alike.

Consider the capabilities to be fed, hydrated, "clothed" (have bodily integrity, including avoiding bodily pain), and sheltered; to exercise and to engage in natural behaviors of movement; and to have companionship. Now contemplate the current legal treatment of factory farm animals. Nourishment and hydration of farm animals is at the discretion of the farmer. Veal calves are provided only milk until they are too anemic to stand, and chickens are starved to force molting to stimulate egg production. While nonhuman animals obviously do not wear clothes, they may have bodily integrity, giving rise to an analogy about maintaining animals' natural protective coverings. Farm animals experience tail docking, de-beaking, and mulesing (removal of the skin and flesh of the posterior of a sheep). Sheep may be sheared prematurely, a practice that ensures that their wool is collected before they start to shed, but which may result in death. Factory farm animals cannot exercise or engage in natural behaviors of movement, as they are confined to battery cages, gestation crates, or veal crates. They do not experience companionship.

The same exercise can be performed with regard to laboratory and companion animals. Minimal protections exist for laboratory animals regarding food, hydration, and shelter, but these capabilities are not maximized. There is a spectrum of well-being between not starving and being well-fed; similar arguments may be made about hydration and shelter. Having enough room to stand, to turn around, and to lie down does not constitute maximal shelter. Further, only dogs and primates have exercise requirements (AWA, § 2143(a)(2)(B), 2008; 9 C.F.R. § 3.8, 2008). As for bodily integrity, laboratory animals' natural coats are damaged during invasive surgical experiments, where portions of their fur and skin are removed for better observation or manipulation of their internal organs and tissues, and some experiments are directed at animals' skin, eyes, or nails. It is unlikely that many laboratory animals experience companionship, especially in light of government regulations limiting human handling of them for human safety.

Companion animals come closest to having these very basic capabilities maximized. A well-cared-for pet may have proper nourishment, hydration, exercise, and shelter; possess a healthy coat and nails; and have companionship. In fact, some companion animals may have higher-order capabilities maximized, like the capability to travel, to be educated through positive reinforcement training or other mental stimulation (compare this to "enrichments" for laboratory animals to keep them sane) (9 C.F.R. § 3.81, 2008)), and to have entertainment or the ability to play. Yet, as the common horrors of puppy mills, animal hoarding, and animal cruelty and neglect cases indicate, basic capabilities are not maximized by current legal structures. Animal cruelty statutes come into play only in the worst cases, and they may not be enforced when resources are devoted to solving other crimes.

Laws maximizing even the most basic capabilities of domestic animals, such as the ability to have nutrition, hydration, shelter, bodily integrity, companionship, and exercise and to engage in natural behaviors of movement, would reshape dramatically animal protections. Factory farms would be abolished, though one could imagine some small-scale farming operations. It is doubtful that most animal experimentation could continue. Certainly invasive procedures would interfere with one or more of these basic capabilities, and behavioral research involving intensive confinement fails to maximize the capability to exercise and to engage in natural behaviors of movement. Alternatives to invasive animal experimentation, such as research on nonsentient beings, computer or math modeling, chemical analyses, and consensual human experimentation could be employed. Behavioral research involving domestic animals would require significant alterations to confinement. Studies of wild animals, whose natural territory may span tens of miles, would likely take place through human observation of these animals in their native environments. Companion animals could be kept in certain conditions.

Since the populations at stake include humans who also have claims to the maximization of these basic capabilities, my arguments for nonhuman animals rest on a couple of key assumptions. First, humans do not need to consume flesh to have proper nourishment. Second, animal experimentation does not improve the enumerated basic capabilities for humans. These assumptions are disputed, though many compelling studies and reports support their validity. For decades, a vegetarian diet has been considered at least as healthy as a carnivorous one, and, for some medical conditions such as diabetes, it may be recommended (American Dietetic Association 2003). Further, more resources are consumed to raise flesh than grain for direct human consumption, and fewer people are fed as a result (Lappé 1991). With regard to animal experimentation, some studies suggest we gain little if any information that translates into clinical use (in part due to the difference between animal and human physiology), and information could be obtained by other means (Pound 2004). Animal experimentation also may not benefit the very basic capabilities we are discussing. However, even if one rejects these assumptions, maximizing human and nonhuman animal capabilities within the same population will require the abolition of many current practices, such as factory farming and animal research as it is currently performed in many contexts, because continuing them would ignore basic animal capabilities altogether.

VII. Implications of Extending Equal Protection

A nondiscrimination approach to animals like the one described in Part VI will likely meet criticism.

A. Inevitable Conflicts and the Need to Start with Basic Capabilities

Perhaps the greatest hurdle for any paradigm that recognizes certain capacities or properties of animals as morally relevant is the inevitable conflicts arising between the maximization of human and nonhuman capabilities within a given population. Conflicts arise when human capabilities are furthered by using animals, for example, when the ability to be entertained is supported by animal fighting, circuses, or zoos. Francione argues, with regard to domestic animals, that these are "false conflicts" (Francione 2006, 247). Humans create domestic animals for their use and control and then act is if they are balancing human with animal interests (ibid.). Remember that Francione argues that it is the property status of animals that causes the hierarchy problem. If animals are property, their interests and capacities always will be given less weight than human interests and capacities.

The solution to the issue, I believe, lies not in changing the property status of animals but in applying the capabilities model to them. First, while it is certainly true that most humans have more capacities for which to account, the capabilities involved in preventing animal cruelty and suffering—having necessary food and hydration, maintaining bodily integrity, being sheltered, and having the ability to exercise / engage in natural behaviors of movement and experience companionship—are universal and basic to life. Thus, it is likely these capabilities will be chosen by humans to be maximized within a given population of human and nonhuman animals. Second, the egalitarian principle embedded within Sen's model requires equal potential to realize these capabilities. Under the extended version of his framework, animals will have equal claims to having the six basic capacities maximized.

Third, under the capabilities model, the conflict between human interest in using animals to realize "higher" capabilities and very basic animal capabilities is a weak one. While maximizing the most basic capabilities of human and nonhuman animals will undermine some higher human capabilities—such as the ability to consume flesh foods, benefit from new beauty and household products tested on animals, and wear the skins of animals for fashion—the perceived conflict embodies a misperception. These capabilities currently are framed in terms of the use of animals to realize them, rather than the realization of the capabilities themselves. However, the capabilities to eat, clean, wear make-up, and dress fashionably need not require the use of animals. The same is true for entertainment, companionship, police work, medical and veterinary school training, some scientific research, and the many other contexts in which animals are exploited. In other words, capabilities may be realized in various ways.

Thus, it is possible to focus on maximizing the most basic capabilities associated with avoiding suffering across a population. Only after these capabilities are maximized does it make sense to discuss competing claims of human and nonhuman animals to higher-order capabilities. Accordingly, emphasis should be placed on shaping legal and social institutions to recognize animals as vulnerable subjects and to support alternatives to animal use in order to maximize basic capabilities across populations of human and nonhuman animals.

B. Equality and the Decline of Human Exploitation of Animals

The proposed paradigm is a nondiscrimination approach to animal welfare. Such an approach relies on a presumption against the use of nonhuman animals. Currently, the opposite is true, as animal use is presumed legal absent exception.

The paradigm has a number of advantages over other proposals. It moves beyond the historically paralyzing discussion about whether animals are persons or property and attacks the legal and social sources of animal suffering. It demonstrates that property status need not determine the level of protection for animals; animals experience equality in the consideration of their capabilities regardless of their legal characterization.

The proposed paradigm also avoids speciesism and other problems of hierarchy. Animals are included within our moral community based on their universal vulnerability with respect to their basic capabilities. This vulnerability is addressed under my extension of Sen's capabilities framework, when capabilities are maximized across populations inclusive of human and nonhuman animals. The basic capabilities of human and nonhuman animals are promoted on equal terms. As the capabilities at stake are the most basic to life, humans representing their own interests as well as those acting as advocates for animals will choose to maximize them across the relevant population. While including animals in this way may undermine some higher-order human capabilities focused on the use of animals, these human capabilities may be realized in other ways.

As addressed in Part VI, Section C, the proposed paradigm requires the end of many of the current uses of domestic animals. Factory farming and much laboratory experimentation infringe on a number of the six enumerated basic capabilities. In practical terms, the proposal requires that the laws affecting animals as primary subjects in these contexts (the laws addressed in Sections III.A.1–2 and B) are altered to account directly for these capabilities. For example, the AWA and HMLSA could be amended to mandate the maximization of the six enumerated basic capabilities. These laws might be applied to small-scale farming operations as well as to researchers conducting investigations of animals in their natural habitats. Enforcement mechanisms could remain the same, with the USDA providing oversight through on-site inspections of domestic operations and approval of research protocols for experimentation occurring overseas. Statutory violations could be subject to civil penalties, unless the deprivation of basic capabilities rises to the level of animal cruelty, in which case individuals would be subject to prosecution, and criminal penalties would apply.

Changes to laws affecting animals as secondary subjects are more complex. I discuss the use of domestic animals as service and emotional support animals under disability and fair housing statutes as well as police and military dogs. While the six basic capabilities at stake may be realized by some animals used for these purposes, they are not currently legally protected unless human behavior amounts to animal cruelty. Civil statutes could be created to protect these basic capabilities. Severe deprivations of basic capabilities could still be prosecuted under state animal anti-cruelty statutes.

VIII. Conclusion

When interest-convergence frames the laws affecting domestic animals, animals receive minimal protections and are rendered hyper-vulnerable to changing human use. Animals' inherent capacities may be ignored and their most fundamental protections against suffering are disrupted. Often animals within the same legal classes and species are treated differently, as are animals with the same capacities from different species and legal categories. This undermines protections and creates legal inconsistencies.

The proposed paradigm seeks to regulate human use of domestic animals in a legally consistent and ethical manner. The paradigm creates a presumption against animal use, with the goal of maximizing the basic capabilities of sentient beings—human and nonhuman—within a given population. Under this proposal, the basic capabilities of having necessary food and hydration, maintaining bodily integrity, being sheltered, exercising and engaging in natural behaviors of movement, and experiencing companionship are realized. Animal use is warranted only when it does not interfere with these basic capabilities.

Bibliography

Ackroyd, P. (1998). *The Life of Thomas More*. New York: Anchor Books.

Adams, W.W. (2007). The primacy of interrelating: practicing ecological psychology with Buber, Levinas and Merleau-Ponty. *Journal of Phenomenological Psychology*, *38*(1), 24–61.

AFP Wire Service (2005). New Orleans bar stayed open through Katrina and chaos that followed. breitbart.com (August 29, 2005).

Alcock, R. (2008, October 7). A matter of protocol. *The Guardian*. Retrieved from http://www.guardian.co.uk/money/blog/2008/oct/24/repossessions-mortgages

Aldrich, D.P. (2009). Social, not physical infrastructure: the critical role of civil society in disaster recovery. doi: 10.2139/ssrn.1349353

Aldrich, D.P. (2010). Fixing recovery: social capital in post-crisis resilience. *Journal of Homeland Security*. Retrieved January 29, 2012, from http://www. homelandsecurity.org/journal/Default.aspx?t=344

American Dietetic Association (2003). Position of the American Dietetic Association and Dietitians of Canada: vegetarian diets. *Journal of the American Dietetic Association*, *103*(6), 748–65.

American Pet Products Association (2009). Industry statistics and trends. Retrieved November 22, 2009, from http://www.amavreericanpetproducts. org/press_industrytrends.asp

Anghie, A., Chimni, B., Mickelson, K., and Okafor, O. (eds) (2003). *The Third World and International Order: Law, Politics, and Globalization*. Leiden: Martinus Nijhoff.

Animal Legal Defense Fund (2009). No boundaries for abusers: the link between cruelty to animals and violence toward humans. Retrieved November 22, 2009, from http://aldf.org/article.php?id=268

Arrow, K. (2000). Observations on social capital. In P. Dasgupta and I. Serageldin (eds), *Social Capital: A Multifaceted Perspective*, 3–5. Washington, DC: World Bank.

Assiter, A. (2009). *Kierkegaard, Metaphysics and Political Theory: Unfinished Selves*. London: Continuum.

Assiter, A. (2013a). Kant and Kierkegaard on freedom and evil. *Royal Institute of Philosophy Supplement - Phenomenology and Naturalism*, 72. pp. 275–296.

Assiter, A. (2013b). Kierkegaard and the ground of morality. *Acta Kierkegaardiana*. Retrieved from http://www.actakierkegaardiana.com

Baer, S. (2010). A closer look at law: human rights as multi-level sites of struggles over multi-dimensional equality. *Utrecht Law Review*, *6*(2), 56–76.

Bainbridge, S.M. (2002). *Corporation Law and Economics*. New York, NY: Foundation Press.

Bartlett, P., Lewis, O., and Thorold, O. (2007), *Mental Disability and the European Convention on Human Rights*. Den Haag: Martinus Nijhoff.

Battersby, C. (2008), *The Sublime, Terror and Human Difference*. London, Routledge.

Baxi, U. (2002 and 2006). *The Future of Human Rights*. New Delhi: Oxford University Press.

Beck, U (2005/6). *Power in the Global Age: A New Global Political Economy* (Cambridge, Polity).

Beckford, M. (2011, February 9). Health authorities warned not to cut IVF treatment. *The Telegraph*. Retrieved January 23, 2013, from http://www.telegraph.co.uk/health/healthnews/8304268/Health-authorities-warned-not-to-cut-IVF-treatment.html

Beiser, F.C. (1987). *The Fate of Reason: German Philosophy from Kant to Fichte*. Cambridge, MA: Harvard University Press.

Bell, D.A., Jr. (1980). *Brown v. Board of Education* and the interest-convergence dilemma. *Harvard Law Review*, *93*(3), 518–34.

Benkler, Y. (2004). Sharing nicely: on shareable goods and the emergence of sharing as a modality of economic production. *Yale Law Journal*, *114*(2), 273–358.

Bentham, J. (2001). *An Introduction to the Principles of Morals and Legislation*. Holmes Beach, FL: Gaunt.

Bergoffen, D. (2012). *Contesting the Politics of Genocidal Rape: Affirming the Dignity of the Vulnerable Body*. New York: Routledge.

Berlin, I. (1969). *Four Essays on Liberty*. London: Oxford University Press.

Berryman, J.C., Thorpe, K., and Windridge, K. (1995). *Older Mothers: Conception, Pregnancy, and Birth after 35*. London: Pandora.

Birth Summary Tables – England and Wales, 2011. (2012, October 17). Retrieved January 23, 2013, from http://www.ons.gov.uk/ons/rel/vsob1/birth-summary-tables--england-and-wales/2011--final-/index.html

Births to older mothers "treble" in 20 years. (2010, May 26). Retrieved January 23, 2013, from http://news.bbc.co.uk/1/hi/uk/8705374.stm

Bossuyt, M. (2010). Judges on thin ice: the European Court of Human Rights and the treatment of asylum seekers, *Inter-American and European Human Rights Journal*, 3, 3–48.

Boyle, N. (1998). *Who Are We Now? Christian Humanism and the Global Market from Hegel to Heaney*. Notre Dame: University of Notre Dame Press.

Brants, C. (2011). The reluctant Dutch response to Salduz, *Edinburgh Law Review*, 15, 298–305.

Brems, E. (ed.) (2012). *Diversity and European Human Rights: Rewriting Judgments of the ECHR*. Cambridge: Cambridge University Press.

Bright, S. (2011). Dispossession for arrears: the weight of home in English law. In O.L. Fox and J.A. Sweeney (eds), *The Idea of Home in Law: Displacement and Dispossession*. Farnham: Ashgate Publishing.

Britt, R. (2006, April 6). Steakhouse closing N.O. outlet: Report. *Marketwatch*. Retrieved January 29, 2012, from http://www.marketwatch.com/story/smith-wollensky-to-close-new-orleans-restaurant

Britton, A.H. (2006). Bones of contention: custody of family pets. *Journal of the American Academy of Matrimonial Lawyers*, *20*, 1–38.

Brooks, N. (2003, November). Vulnerability, risk and adaptation: a conceptual framework. *Tyndall Centre for Climate Change Research*. Retrieved from http://www.tyndall.ac.uk/sites/default/files/wp38.pdf

Bryant, T.L. (2006). Animals unmodified: defining animals/defining human obligations to animals. *University of Chicago Legal Forum*, *2006*, 137.

Bryant, T.L. (2007). Similarity or difference as a basis for justice: must animals be like humans to be legally protected from humans? *Law and Contemporary Problems*, *70*(1), 207–54.

Butler, J. (2004). *Precarious Life: The Powers and Mourning of Violence*. London and New York: Verso.

Buyse, A. (2010, 17 November). The Court's new priority policy. *ECHR Blog*. Retrieved from http://echrblog.blogspot.nl/(2010)/11/courts-new-priority-policy.html

Cahn, N. (2009). *Test Tube Families: Why the Fertility Market Needs Legal Regulation*. New York: New York University Press.

Cahn, N. (2010). Reproducing dreams. In M. Goodwin (ed.), *Baby Markets: Money and the New Politics of Creating Families*, 147–63. Cambridge: Cambridge University Press.

Calmore, J.O. (1999). A call to context: the professional challenges of cause lawyering at the intersection of race, space, and poverty. *Fordham Law Review*, *67*(5), 1927.

Cameron, C. (2010, November 3). Prime Minister's Questions. Retrieved from http://www.youtube.com/watch?v=DjzmvvozHuw

Carbone, J., and Gottheim, P. (2010). Ethics within markets or a market for ethics? Can disclosure of sperm donor identity be effectively mandated? In M. Goodwin (ed.), *Baby Markets: Money and the New Politics of Creating Families*. Cambridge: Cambridge University Press.

Carr, H. (2011). The right to buy, the leaseholder, and the impoverishment of ownership. *Journal of Law and Society*, *38*, 519–41. doi: 10.1111/j.1467-6478.2011.00557.x

Carr, H., and Hunter, C. (2008). Managing vulnerability: homelessness law and the interplay of the social, the political and the technical. *Journal of Social Welfare and Family Law*, *30*(4), 293–307. doi: 10.1080/09649060802580979

Centesimus annus. (1991, May 1). Retrieved from http://www.vatican.va/holy_father/john_paul_ii/encyclicals/documents/hf_jp-ii_enc_01051991_centesimus-annus_en.html

Chambers, R.W. (1992). The meaning of Utopia. In T. More (Author) and R.M. Adams (ed.), *Utopia: A Revised Translation, Backgrounds, Criticism*, 137–47. New York: Norton.

Chamlee-Wright, E. (2007). The long road back: signal noise in the post-Katrina context. *The Independent Review*, *12*(2), 235–59.

Change4Life. Retrieved January 20, 2012, from http://www.nhs.uk/Change4Life/ Pages/change-for-life.aspx

Chapman A.R. and Carbonetti B. (2011). Human rights protections for vulnerable and disadvantaged groups: the contributions of the UN Committee on Economic, Social and Cultural Rights, *Human Rights Quarterly*, *33*(3), 682–732.

Chartered Institute for Housing (2008). Rethinking housing, Coventry, CIH.

Chavkin, W. (2010). The globalization of motherhood. In W. Chavkin and J. Maher (eds), *The Globalization of Motherhood*, 3–15. London: Routledge.

Chavkin, W. (2008). Working women, the biological clock, and assisted reproductive technologies. In I. Bakker and R. Silvey (eds), *Beyond States and Markets: Challenges of Social Reproduction,* 159–69. London: Routledge.

Clements, L.J., and Morris, R. (1999). *Gaining Ground: Law Reform for Gypsies and Travellers*. Hertfordshire, England: University of Hertfordshire Press.

Code, L (2006). *Ecological Thinking: The Politics of Epistemic Location*, Oxford: Oxford University Press.

Cohen, I.G. (2011). Regulating reproduction: the problem with best interests. *Minnesota Law Review*, *96*(2), 423–519.

Cohen, I.G. (2012). *S.H. and Others v. Austria* and circumvention tourism. *Reproductive BioMedicine Online*, *25*(7), 660–62.

Cohen-Eliya, M., and Porat, I. (2011). Proportionality and the culture of justification. *American Journal of Comparative Law*, *59*(2), 463–90.

Committee of Ministers (2011). *Recommendation CM/Rec(2011)5 on reducing the risk of vulnerability of elderly migrants and improving their welfare.*

Cornelisse, G. (2011). A new articulation of human rights, or why the European Court of Human Rights should think beyond Westphalian sovereignty. In M.-B. Dembour and T. Kelly (eds), *Are Human Rights for Migrants? Critical Reflections on the Status of Irregular Migrants in Europe and the United States*, 99–120. New York: Routledge.

Costa, J.P. (2011, December 11). Current challenges for the European Court of Human Rights. Paper presented as the inaugural Raymond and Beverly Sackler Distinguished Lecture in Human Rights Series at Leiden Law School, Leiden, Netherlands. Retrieved from http://media.leidenuniv.nl/legacy/ current-challenges-for-the-european-court-of-human-rights--sackler-lecture-by-costa-doc.pdf

Cowan, D. (2011). *Housing Law and Policy*. Cambridge: Cambridge University Press.

Cowan, D., and McDermont, M. (2006). *Regulating Social Housing: Governing Decline*. Abingdon: Routledge-Cavendish.

Cowan, D., and Hunter, C. (2012), "Yeah but not but": Pinnock and Powell in the Supreme Court'. *Modern Law Review*, 75, 78–91

Cross, F.B. (2005). Law and trust. *Georgetown Law Journal*, *93*(5), 1457–546.

Csete, J., and Willis, R.A. (2010). Rights as recourse: globalized motherhood and human rights. In W. Chavkin and J. Maher (eds), *The Globalization of Motherhood*, 205–27. London: Routledge.

Culley, L., Hudson, N., Blyth, E., Norton, W., Pacey, A., and Rapport, F. (2011, June). *Transnational Reproduction: An Exploratory Study of UK Residents Who Travel Abroad for Fertility Treatment* (rep. No. ESRC Project reference: RES 000-22-3390). Retrieved http://www.rcn.org.uk/__data/assets/pdf_file/0005/420296/TRANSREP_summary_report_FINAL_June_2011.pdf

Curtler, W.H.R. (1920). *The Enclosure and Redistribution of Our Land*. Oxford: Clarendon Press.

DCSF: Department of Children, Schools and Families. (2010, February 23). *About the Teenage Pregnancy Strategy.* Retrieved January 23, 2013, from http://webarchive.nationalarchives.gov.uk/20100408095957/http://www.dcsf.gov.uk/everychildmatters/healthandwellbeing/teenagepregnancy/about/strategy/

De Sousa Santos, B. (1995). *Toward a New Common Sense: Law, Science, and Politics in the Paradigmatic Transition*. New York: Routledge.

De Ville de Goyet, C., and Griekspoor, A. (2007). Natural disasters, the best friend of poverty. *Georgetown Journal on Poverty Law and Policy*, *14*(1), 61.

Dean, J. (2009). *Democracy and Other Neoliberal Fantasies: Communicative Capitalism and Left Politics*. Durham, NC: Duke University Press.

Dembour, M.-B., and Kelly, T. (eds) (2011). *Are Human Rights for Migrants? Critical Reflections on the Status of Irregular Migrants in Europe and the United States*. New York: Routledge.

Department of Health. (2009, June 18). *Primary Care Trust Survey: Provision of IVF in England 2008*. Retrieved March 11, 2010, from http://www.dh.gov.uk/en/Publicationsandstatistics/Publications/PublicationsPolicyAndGuidance/DH_101073

Descartes, R. (1968). *Discourse on Method, and Other Writings*. Harmondsworth: Penguin.

Dillard, C., Favre, D., Glitzenstein, E., Sullivan, M., and Waisman, S. (2006). Confronting barriers to the courtroom for animal advocates: animal advocacy and causes of action. *Animal Law*, *13*, 87.

Dine, J. (2012). Jurisdictional arbitrage by multinational companies: a national law solution? *Journal of Human Rights and the Environment*, *3*(1), 44–69.

Donald, A., Gordon, J., and Leach, P. (2012). *The UK and the European Court of Human Rights* (Equality and Human Rights Commission, research Report No. 83, 2012).

Douzinas, C. (2000). *The End of Human Rights: Critical Legal Thought at the Turn of the Century*. Oxford: Hart Publishing.

Douzinas, C., and Gearey, A. (2005). *Critical Jurisprudence*. Oxford: Hart Publishing.

Dyal-Chand, R. (2011). Home as ownership, dispossession as foreclosure: the impact of the current crisis on the American model of "home." In O.L. Fox and J.A. Sweeney (eds), *The Idea of Home in Law: Displacement and Dispossession*, 41–54. Farnham, England: Ashgate Publishing.

Earle, S., and Letherby, G. (2007). Conceiving time? Women who do or do not conceive. *Sociology of Health and Illness*, *29*(2), 233–50. doi: 10.1111/j.1467-9566.2007.00546.x

Easterbrook, F.H., and Fischel, D.R. (1989). The corporate contract. *Columbia Law Review*, *89*(7), 1416–48.

Elliott, R.C. (1992). The shape of Utopia. In T. More (author) and R.M. Adams (ed.), *Utopia: A Revised Translation, Backgrounds, Criticism*, 181–95. New York: Norton.

Elster, J. (2007). *Explaining Social Behavior: More Nuts and Bolts for the Social Sciences*. Cambridge: Cambridge University Press.

European Council of Refugees and Exiles. (2012). *Research on ECHR Rule 39 Interim Measures*. Retrieved from http://www.ecre.org/component/content/article/56-ecre-actions/272-ecre-research-on-rule-39-interim-measures.html

European Court of Human Rights (2012), *Annual Report 2011*. Retrieved from http://www.echr.coe.int/NR/rdonlyres/77FF4249-96E5-4D1F-BE71-42867A469225/0/(2011)_Rapport_Annuel_EN.pdf

Favre, D. (2000). Equitable self-ownership for animals. *Duke Law Journal*, *50*(2), 473–502.

Favre, D. (2010). Living property: a new status for animals within the legal system. *Marquette Law Review*, *93*(3), 1021–70.

Federal Emergency Management Agency. (2010). *National Disaster Recovery Framework*. Retrieved January 29, 2012, from Federal Emergency Management Agency website: http://disasterrecoveryworkinggroup.gov/ndrf.pdf

Federman, C. (2003). Constructing kinds of persons in 1886: corporate and criminal. *Law and Critique*, *14*(2), 167–89.

Fenton, R.A. (2006). Catholic doctrine versus women's rights: the new Italian law on assisted reproduction. *Medical Law Review*, *14*(1), 73–107. doi: 10.1093/medlaw/fwi041

Fenton, R.A., Jane, D., Rees, V., and Heenan, S. (2011). Shall I be mother? In J.M. Jones (ed.), *Gender, Sexualities and Law*, 241–54. Oxon: Routledge.

Fineman, M. (1995). *The Neutered Mother, the Sexual Family, and Other Twentieth-century Tragedies*. New York: Routledge.

Fineman, M.A. (2004). *The Autonomy Myth: A Theory of Dependency*. New York and London: The New Press.

Fineman, M.A. (2008). The vulnerable subject: anchoring equality in the human condition. *Yale Journal of Law and Feminism*, *20*(1), 1–23.

Fineman, M.A. (2010). The vulnerable subject and the responsive state. *Emory Law Journal*, *60*(2), 251–75.

Fineman, M.A. (2012). "Elderly" as vulnerable: rethinking the nature of individual and societal responsibility. *The Elder Law Journal*, *20*(1), 101–41.

Fineman, M.A. (2013). Feminism, masculinities and multiple identities. *Nevada Law Journal*, *13*(101) (Symposium Issue on Masculinities).

Fligstein, N. (2001). *The Architecture of Markets: An Economic Sociology of Twenty-first-century Capitalist Societies*. Princeton: Princeton University Press.

Flint, J. (2003). Housing and ethopolitics: constructing identities of active consumption and responsible community. *Economy and Society*, *32*(4), 611–29.

Ford, J., Burrows, R., and Nettleton, S. (2001). *Home Ownership in a Risk Society: A Social Analysis of Mortgage Arrears and Possessions*. Bristol: Policy Press.

Fordham, M.H. (1998). Making women visible in disasters: problematising the private domain. *Disasters*, *22*(2), 126.

Forrest, R., and Murie, A. (1988) *Selling the Welfare State: The Privatisation of Public Housing,* London: Routledge.

Foster, M. (2009, January 12). New Orleans restaurants are back in business after Katrina. *USA Today*. Retrieved January 29, 2012, from http://usatoday30. usatoday.com/travel/destinations/2009-01-12-new-orleans-zagat-survey_N. htm

Foucault, M. (1975). *Discipline and Punish: The Birth of Prison* (trans. A. Sheridan). London: Penguin.

Francione, G.L. (1995). *Animals, Property, and the Law*. Philadelphia: Temple University Press.

Francione, G.L. (1996). *Rain without Thunder: The Ideology of the Animal Rights Movement*. Philadelphia: Temple University Press.

Francione, G.L. (2000). *Introduction to animal rights: Your child or the dog?* Philadelphia: Temple University Press.

Francione, G.L. (2006). Equal consideration and the interest of nonhuman animals in continued existence: a response to Professor Sunstein. *University of Chicago Legal Forum*, 2006, 231.

Fredman, S. (1997). *Women and the Law*. Oxford: Clarendon Press.

Fresch, P., Otto, S., Olsen, K., and Ernest, P. (1999). State animal anti-cruelty statutes: an overview. *Animal Law*, *5*, 69.

Gallagher, M. (2010). Why do parents have rights? The problem of kinship in liberal thought. In M. Goodwin (ed.), *Baby Markets: Money and the New Politics of Creating Families*, 164–76). Cambridge: Cambridge University Press.

Gatens, M. (1996). *Imaginary Bodies: Ethics, Power, and Corporeality*. London: Routledge.

Gerards, J., and Senden, H. (2009). The structure of fundamental rights and the European Court of Human Rights. *International Journal of Constitutional Law*, 7(4), 619–33.

Geuss, R. (2005). *Outside Ethics*. Princeton, NJ: Princeton University Press.

Gill, S. (1995). Globalisation, market civilisation, and disciplinary neoliberalism. *Millennium – Journal of International Studies*, *24*(3), 399–423. doi: 10.1177/03058298950240030801

Gill, S. (2002). Constitutionalizing inequality and the clash of globalizations. *International Studies Review*, *4*(2), 47–65. doi: 10.1111/1521-9488.00254

Goodchild, S., and Elliott, F. (2006). Fertility trap: the £500,000 question – should you gamble with your body clock. *The Independent*, 19 Feb. 2006 http://www.independent.co.uk/life-style/health-and-families/health-news/fertility-trap-the-163500000-question--should-you-gamble-with-your-body-clock-467067.html (accessed 26/06/2013)

Goodwin, M. (2005). Assisted reproductive technology and the double bind: the illusory choice of motherhood. *The Journal of Gender Race and Justice*, 9(2), 1–54.

Grant, E. (2007). Dignity and equality. *Human Rights Law Review*, 7(2), 299–329.

Grant, I.H. (2006). *Philosophies of Nature after Schelling*. London: Continuum International Publishing Group.

Grant, R.W. (2008). Passion and interest revisited: the psychological foundations of economics and politics. *Public Choice—"Homo Economicus and Homo Politicus," 137*(3/4), 451–61.

Gray, J. (1993a). *Beyond the New Right: Markets, Government and the Common Environment*. London: Routledge.

Gray, J. (1993b). *Post-liberalism: Studies in Political Thought*. New York: Routledge.

Gray, J. (1995). *Enlightenment's Wake: Politics and Culture at the Close of the Modern Age*. London: Routledge.

Grear, A. (2006). Human rights—human bodies? Some reflections on corporate human rights distortion, the legal subject, embodiment and human rights theory. *Law and Critique*, *17*(2), 171–99. doi: 10.1007/s10978-006-0006-8

Grear, A. (2007). Challenging corporate "humanity": legal disembodiment, embodiment and human rights. *Human Rights Law Review*, 7(3), 511–43.

Grear, A. (2010), *Redirecting Human Rights: Facing the Challenge of Corporate Legal Humanity.* Basingstoke: Palgrave Macmillan.

Grear, A. (2011). The vulnerable living order: human rights and the environment in a critical and philosophical perspective. *Journal of Human Rights and the Environment*, 2(1), 23–44.

Green, K. (1998). Citizens and squatters: under the surfaces of land law. In S. Bright and J. Dewar (eds), *Land Law: Themes and Perspectives*, 229–56. Oxford: Oxford University Press.

Green, R.M. (1992). *Kierkegaard and Kant: The Hidden Debt*. New York: State University of New York.

Grosz, E.A. (1994). *Volatile Bodies: Towards a Corporeal Feminism*. Bloomington: Indiana University Press.

Gurney, C.M. (1999). Pride and prejudice: discourses of normalisation in public and private accounts of home ownership. *Housing Studies*, *14*(2), 163–83. doi: 10.1080/02673039982902

Gürtin, Z. (2011). Banning reproductive travel: Turkey's ART legislation and third-party assisted reproduction. *Reproductive BioMedicine Online*, *23*(5), 555–64.

Gürtin, Z., and Inhorn, M.C. (2011). Introduction: travelling for conception and the global assisted reproduction market. *Reproductive BioMedicine Online*, *23*(5), 535–7.

Habermas, J. (2010). The concept of human dignity and the realistic utopia of human rights. *Metaphilosophy*, 41(4), 464–80.

Halewood, P. (1996). Law's bodies: disembodiment and the structure of liberal property rights. *Iowa Law Review*, *81*(5), 1331–94.

Hammarberg, T. (2011). *Human Rights in Europe: No Grounds for Complacency. Viewpoints by Thomas Hammarberg Council of Europe Commissioner for Human Rights.* Strasbourg: Council of Europe Publishing.

Hamnett, C. (1999). *Winners and Losers: Home Ownership in Modern Britain.* London, UK: UCL Press.

Hanley, L. (2007). *Estates: An Intimate History.* London: Granta.

Haraway, D.J. (2008). *When Species Meet.* Minneapolis: University of Minnesota Press.

Hardin, G. (1968). The tragedy of the commons. *Science*, *162*(3859), 1243.

Harloe, M. (1995). *The Peoples's Home?: Social Rented Housing in Europe and America.* Oxford: Blackwell.

Harris, A. (2002). Reforming alone? *Stanford Law Review*, *54*(6), 1458.

Harvey, D. (2005). *A Brief History of Neoliberalism.* Oxford: Oxford University Press.

Health Inequalities (rep.) (2009, February 26). Retrieved http://www.publications.parliament.uk/pa/cm200809/cmselect/cmhealth/286/286.pdf

Helfer, L.R. (2012, June 8). The burdens and benefits of Brighton. *ESIL Reflections.* Retrieved from http://esil-sedi.eu/node/138

Hexter, J.H. (1992). The roots of Utopia and all evil. In T. More (author) and R.M. Adams (ed.), *Utopia: A Revised Translation, Backgrounds, Criticism*, 147–54. New York: Norton.

Hills, J. (2007). *Ends and Means: The Future Roles of Social Housing in England.* London: CASE.

Hirschman, A.O. (1970). *Exit, Voice, and Loyalty: Responses to Decline in Firms, Organizations, and States.* Cambridge, MA: Harvard University Press.

Horwich, G. (2000). Economic lessons of the Kobe earthquake. *Economic Development and Cultural Change*, *48*(3), 521.

Horwitz, M.J. (1981). The historical contingency of the role of history. *Yale Law Journal*, *90*(5), 1057–9.

Horwitz, S. (2008, March). Making hurricane response more effective: lessons from the private sector and the coast guard during Katrina. In *Mercatus Policy Series.* Retrieved January 29, 2012, from http://mercatus.org/sites/default/files/publication/Katrina_MPS_MakingHurricaneResponseMoreEffective_Horwitz.pdf

Hsu, A. (2007, May 10). Groups move to protect women and their pets. *NPR.* Retrieved November 22, 2009, from http://www.npr.org/templates/story/story.php?storyId=10119810

Human Reproductive Technologies and the Law (House of Commons Science and Technology Committee). (2005, March 24). Retrieved from http://www. publications.parliament.uk/pa/cm200405/cmselect/cmsctech/7/7i.pdf

Humane Society of the United States (2009, September 1). The HSUS's campaign to ban battery cages. Retrieved November 22, 2009, from http://www.humane society.org/issues/confinement_farm/facts/cage-free_vs_battery-cage.html

Humane Society of the United States (2013). Farm animal statistics: slaughter totals. Available from http://www.humanesociety.org/assets/pdfs/farm/table_ us_per_capita_meat.pdf and http://www.humanesociety.org/news/resources/ research/stats_dairy_eggs.html

Huss, R.J. (2004). Valuation in veterinary malpractice. *Loyola University Chicago Law Journal*, *35*(2), 479.

Hyde, A. (1997). *Bodies of Law*. Princeton, NJ: Princeton University Press.

Ishay, M. (2004). *The History of Human Rights: From Ancient Times to the Globalization Era*. Berkeley: University of California Press.

Jackson, E. (2001). *Regulating Reproduction: Law, Technology, and Autonomy*. Oxford: Hart.

Jackson, E. (2002). Conception and the irrelevance of the welfare principle. *Modern Law Review*, *65*(2), 176–203. doi: 10.1111/1468-2230.00374

Jacobi, F.H. (1812), *Werke*, vol.1, ed. G.H. Jacobi and F. Köppen, Leipzig: Fleicher.

Jacobs, K., and Manzi, T. (1996). Discourse and policy change: the significance of language for housing research. *Housing Studies*, *11*(4), 543–60. doi: 10.1080/02673039608720874

Jamieson, D. (2002). *Morality's Progress: Essays on Humans, Other Animals, and the Rest of Nature*. Oxford: Clarendon Press.

Johnson, G. (2011, June). *Holding back the British IVF Revolution? A Report into NHS IVF Provision in the UK today* (rep.). Retrieved http://www. garethjohnsonmp.co.uk/uimages/File/appg_IVF_report.pdf

Jones, O.D. (2000). On the nature of norms: biology, morality, and the disruption of order. *Michigan Law Review*, *98*(6), 2072.

Jung, H.Y. (2002). Enlightenment and the question of the other: a postmodern audition. *Human Studies*, *25*(3), 297 306.

Kant, I. (1964). *Critique of Pure Reason* (trans. N.K. Smith). London: Macmillan.

Kant, I. (1979). *The Conflict of the Faculties* [= *Der Streit der Fakultäten*] (trans. M. Gregor). New York, NY: Abaris Books.

Kant, I. (1979). *Lectures on Ethics* (trans. L. Infield). London: Methuen.

Kant, I. (1987). *Critique of Judgment: Including the First Introduction* (trans. W. Pluhar). Indianapolis: Hackett.

Kant, I. (1993). *Grounding for the Metaphysics of Morals; with On a supposed right to lie because of philanthropic concerns* (trans. J.W. Ellington). Indianapolis: Hackett.

Kant, I. (1993). *Opus postumum* (trans. E. Förster and M. Rosen). Cambridge: Cambridge University Press.

Kant, I. (1998). *Groundwork of the Metaphysics of Morals*. In M.J. Gregor (ed.), *Practical Philosophy*, 37–108). Cambridge: Cambridge University Press.

Kant, I. (2002). *Critique of Practical Reason* (trans. W.S. Pluhar). Indianapolis: Hackett.

Kapur, R. (2006). Human rights in the 21st century: take a walk on the dark side. *Sydney Law Review, 28*(4), 665–87.

Kaufman, M. (2007, January 26). Largest pork processor to phase out crates. *Washington Post*. Retrieved November 22, 2009, from http://www.washington post.com/wp-dyn/content/article/2007/01/25/AR2007012501785.html

Kearney, R. (2004). *On Paul Ricoeur: The Owl of Minerva*. Aldershot, England: Ashgate.

Kennedy, R., Kingsland, C., Rutherford, A., Hamilton, M., and Ledger, W. (2006). Implementation of the NICE guideline—recommendations from the British Fertility Society for national criteria for NHS funding of assisted conception. *Human Fertility, 9*(3), 181–9. doi: 10.1080/14647270600908411

Kierkegaard, S. (1936). *Philosophical Fragments; or, A fragment of Philosophy* (trans. D.F. Swenson). Princeton, NJ: Princeton University Press.

Kierkegaard, S. (1980). *The Concept of Anxiety: A Simple Psychologically Orienting Deliberation on the Dogmatic Issue of Hereditary Sin*, ed. R. Thomte and A. Anderson. Princeton, NJ: Princeton University Press.

Kierkegaard, S. (1980). *The Sickness unto Death: A Christian Psychological Exposition for Upbuilding and Awakening*, ed. H.V. Hong and E.H. Hong. Princeton, NJ: Princeton University Press.

Kierkegaard, S. (1983). *Fear and Trembling/Repetition*, ed. H.V. Hong and E.H. Hong. Princeton, NJ: Princeton University Press.

Kierkegaard, S. (1985). *Philosophical Fragments, Johannes Climacus*, ed. H.V. Hong and E.H. Hong. Princeton, NJ: Princeton University Press.

Kierkegaard, S. (1987). *Either/or, part one*, ed. H.V. Hong and E.H. Hong. Princeton, NJ: Princeton University Press.

Kierkegaard, S. (1988). *Stages on Life's Way: Studies by Various Persons*, ed. H.V. Hong and E.H. Hong. Princeton, NJ: Princeton University Press.

Kierkegaard, S. (1990). *Eighteen Upbuilding Discourses*, ed. H.V. Hong and E.H. Hong. Princeton: Princeton University Press 1990.

Kierkegaard, S. (1992). *Concluding Unscientific Postscript to Philosophical Fragments*, ed. H.V. Hong and E.H. Hong. Princeton, NJ: Princeton University Press.

Kierkegaard, S. (1995). *Works of Love*, ed. H.V. Hong and E.H. Hong. Princeton, NJ: Princeton University Press.

Kierkegaard, S. (2009). *Two Ages: The Age of Revolution and the Present Age : A Literary Review*, ed. H.V. Hong and E.H. Hong. Princeton, NJ: Princeton University Press.

Kilkelly, U. (2010). Protecting children's rights under the ECHR: the role of positive obligations. *Northern Ireland Legal Quarterly, 61*(3), 245–62.

King, P. (2010). *Housing Policy Transformed: The Right to Buy and the Desire to Own*. Bristol: Policy.

Kirby, P. (2006). *Vulnerability and Violence: The Impact of Globalisation*. London: Pluto.

Kirby, P. (2011). Vulnerability and globalisation: mediating impacts on society. *Journal of Human Rights and the Environment*, *2*(1), 86–105.

Kirkman, R. (2007). A little knowledge of dangerous things: human vulnerability in a changing climate. In S.L. Cataldi and W.S. Hamrick (eds), *Merleau-Ponty and Environmental Philosophy: Dwelling on the Landscapes of Thought*, 19–35. Albany: State University of New York Press.

Kiviat, B. (2010, September 11). The case against homeownership. *Time*. Retrieved from http://www.time.com/time/magazine/article/0,9171,2013850,00.html

Lakoff, G., and Johnson, M. (1980). *Metaphors We Live By*. Chicago: University of Chicago Press.

Lappé, F.M. (1991). *Diet for a Small Planet*. New York: Ballantine Books.

Leonard, D. (2005, October 3). The only lifeline was the Wal-Mart. *CNNMoney*. Retrieved January 29, 2012, from http://money.cnn.com/magazines/fortune/fortune_archive/2005/10/03/8356743/index.htm

Letherby, G. (2002). Challenging dominant discourses: identity and change and the experience of "infertility" and "involuntary childlessness." *Journal of Gender Studies*, *11*(3), 277–88.

Letsas, G. (2013). The ECHR as a living instrument: its meaning and its legitimacy, in constituting Europe. In A. Follesdal et al. (eds), *The European Court of Human Rights in a National, European and Global Context*. Cambridge: Cambridge University Press.

Lord, B. (2011). *Kant and Spinozism: Transcendental Idealism and Immanence from Jacobi to Deleuze*. Houndmills, Basingstoke, Hampshire: Palgrave Macmillan.

MacCallum, F., and Golombok, S. (2004). Children raised in fatherless families from infancy: a follow up of lesbian and single heterosexual mothers at early adolescence. *Journal of Child Psychology and Psychiatry*, *45*(8), 1407–19.

Makkonen, T. (2002, April). *Multiple, Compound and Intersectional Discrimination: Bringing the Experiences of the Most Marginalized to the Fore*. Institute for Human Rights, Åbo Akademi University. Retrieved from: http://cilvektiesibas.org.lv/site/attachments/01/02/(2012)/timo.pdf

Malpass, P. (1990). *Reshaping Housing Policy: Subsidies, Rents, and Residualisation*. London: Routledge.

Malpass, P. (2003). The wobbly pillar? Housing and the British postwar welfare state. *Journal of Social Policy*, *32*(4), 589–606.

Marius, R. (1984). *Thomas More: A Biography*. Cambridge: Harvard University Press.

Marks, S. (2003). Empire's law. *Indiana Journal of Global Legal Studies*, *10*, 446–65.

Martin, A. (2007, March 28). Burger King shifts policy on animals. *The New York Times*. Retrieved November 22, 2009, from http://www.nytimes.com/2007/03/28/business/28burger.html?pagewanted=all

Martin, A. (2008, May 21). U.S. moves to prohibit beef from sick or injured cows. *The New York Times*. Retrieved November 22, 2009, from http://www.nytimes.com/2008/05/21/business/21beef.html

Martin, R. (2011). The local geographies of the financial crisis: from the housing bubble to economic recession and beyond. *Journal of Economic Geography*, *11*(4), 587–618.

Mathieson, S. (2011, January 13). DH doubled ad spending to £60m. *The Guardian*. Retrieved January 20, 2012, from http://www.guardian.co.uk/healthcare-network/2011/jan/13/department-health-doubled-advertising-spending-60m

McCrudden, C. (2008). Human dignity and judicial interpretation of human rights. *European Journal of International Law*, *19*(4), 655–724.

McKean, E. (2005). *The New Oxford American Dictionary*. New York: Oxford University Press.

McKendry, C. (2007, March). Disaster for sale: neoliberalism and the privatization of socionatural disaster relief. Paper presented at the 48th Annual International Studies Association Convention, Chicago, IL, 28 February – 3 March, 2007. Retrieved January 29, 2012, from http://citation.allacademic.com//meta/p_mla_apa_research_citation/1/7/9/2/0/pages179200/p179200-1.php

Meillassoux, Q. (2008). *After Finitude: An Essay on the Necessity of Contingency*. London and New York: Continuum.

Merleau-Ponty, M. (2002). *Phenomenology of Perception*. London: Routledge.

Meyers, D.T. (2001). The rush to motherhood – pronatalist discourse and women's autonomy. *SIGNS: Journal of Women in Culture and Society*, *26*(3), 735–74.

Morawa, A.H.E. (2003). Vulnerability as a concept of international human rights law. *Journal on International Relations and Development*, *6*(2), 139–55.

More, T. (1992). *Utopia: A Revised Translation, Backgrounds, Criticism* (trans. R.M. Adams). New York: Norton.

Morgan, J. (2010). Family intervention tenancies: the de(marginalization) of social tenants? *Journal of Social Welfare and Family Law*, *32*(1), 37–46.

Morton, J. (2011, September 7). Tuscaloosa Forward plan passes unanimously. *TuscaloosaNews.com*. Retrieved January 29, 2012, from http://www.tuscaloosanews.com/article/20110907/news/110909820

Mowbray, A. (2004). *The Development of Positive Obligations under the European Convention on Human Rights by the European Court of Human Rights*. Oxford and Portland: Hart.

Murphy, A.V. (2009). "Reality check": Rethinking the ethics of vulnerability. In R.J. Heberle and V. Grace (eds), *Theorizing Sexual Violence*. New York and London: Routledge, 55–71.

Meillassoux, Q. (2005). *After Finitude: An Essay on the Necessity of Contigency*. London and New York: Continuum.

Mutua, M. (2001). Savages, victims, and saviors: the metaphor of human rights. *Harvard International Law Journal*, 42(1), 201–45.

Naffine, N. (2003). Who are law's persons? From Cheshire cats to responsible subjects. *The Modern Law Review*, 66(3), 346–67.

Nahman, M. (2011). Reverse traffic: intersecting inequalities in human egg donation. *Reproductive BioMedicine Online*, *23*(5). doi: 10.1016/j.rbmo.2011.08.003

Nakagawa, Y., and Shaw, R. (2004). Social capital: a missing link to disaster recovery. *International Journal of Mass Emergencies and Disasters*, *22*(1), 5.

National Association of Biomedical Research (n.d.). Rats and mice: the essential need for animals in medical research. Retrieved November 22, 2009, from http://www.nwabr.org/research/pdfs/FBRRatsmice.pdf

National Audit Office, Department for Communities and Local Government (2011). *The Mortgage Rescue Scheme*. HC 1030: Session 2010–2012. 25 May 2011.

National Center for Social Research (2011). *British Social Attitudes 28*. Retrieved from http://ir2.flife.de/data/natcen-social-research/igb_html/index.php?bericht_id=1000001

NICE: National Institute for Clinical Excellence (2004). *Fertility: Assessment and Treatment for People with Fertility Problems* (Clinical Guideline 11). Retrieved March 11, 2010, from http://www.nice.org.uk/nicemedia/pdf/CG011niceguideline.pdf

NICE: National Institute for Clinical Excellence (2012, May 22). More to receive IVF under draft fertility guidelines. Retrieved January 23, 2013, from http://www.nice.org.uk/newsroom/news/MoreReceiveIVFUnderDraftFertilityGuidelines.jsp

Neal, M. (2012). "Not gods but animals": human dignity and vulnerable subjecthood. *Liverpool Law Review*, *33*(3), 177–200.

Neocleous, M. (2003). Staging power: Marx, Hobbes and the personification of capital. *Law and Critique*, *14*(2), 147–65.

Nettleton, S., and Burrows, R. (1998). Mortgage debt, insecure home ownership and health: an exploratory analysis. *Sociology of Health and Illness*, *20*(5), 731–53.

Nibert, D.A. (2002). *Animal Rights/Human Rights: Entanglements of Oppression and Liberation*. Lanham, MD: Rowman and Littlefield.

Nkrumah, K. (1965). *Neo-colonialism: The Last Stage of Imperialism*. London: Panaf.

Norrie, A.W. (2001). *Crime, Reason and History: A Critical Introduction to Criminal Law*. London: Butterworths.

Nussbaum, M.C. (2006). *Frontiers of Justice: Disability, Nationality, Species Membership*. Cambridge, MA: The Belknap Press.

Nussbaum, M.C. (2007). Foreword. Constitutions and capabilities: "perception" against lofty formalism. *Harvard Law Review*, *121*(4), 4–97.

Otto, D. (2006). Lost in translation: re-scripting the sexed subjects of international human rights law. In Anne Orford (ed.), *International Law and Its Others*. Cambridge: Cambridge University Press, 318–56.

Pande, A. (2009). Not an "angel", not a "whore": surrogates as "dirty" workers in India. *Indian Journal of Gender Studies*, *16*(2), 141–73. doi: 10.1177/097152150901600201

Parks, J.A. (1999). On the use of IVF by post-menopausal women. *Hypatia: A Journal of Feminist Philosophy*, *14*(1), 77–96. doi: 10.2979/HYP.1999.14.1.77

Pateman, C. (1989). *The Disorder of Women: Democracy, Feminism, and Political Theory*. Stanford, CA: Stanford University Press.

Peroni, L., and Timmer, A. (2013), Vulnerable groups: the promise of an emerging concept in European Human Rights Convention Law. *International Journal of Constitutional Law*, *11*(4) (forthcoming).

Perreau-Saussine, E. (2007). What remains of socialism? In P. Riordan (ed.), *Values in Public Life: Aspects of Common Goods*, 11–34. Berlin: Lit Verlag.

Pfeffer, N., and Woollett, A. (1983). *The Experience of Infertility*. London: Virago Press.

Philippopoulos-Mihalopoulos, A. (2012). *Law and Ecology: New Environmental Foundations*. London: Routledge.

Physicians Committee for Responsible Medicine (n.d.). *Rats: Test Results That Don't Apply to Humans*. Retrieved November 22, 2009, from http://www.pcrm.org/resch/anexp/rats.html

Pieper, T.M. (2007). *Mechanisms to Assure Long-term Family Business Survival: A Study of the Dynamics of Cohesion in Multigenerational Family Business Families*. Frankfurt: Peter Lang.

Pittman, T. (2011, April 2). Japan: post-tsunami, town wonders if to rebuild. *Associated Press*. Retrieved January 29, 2012, from http://www.boston.com/news/world/asia/articles/2011/04/02/japan_post_tsunami_town_wonders_if_to_rebuild/?page=full

Plato (1948). *Phaedo*, In *Plato in Twelve Volumes*, vol. 1 trans. Harold North Fowler and intro. W.R.M. Lamb. Cambridge, MA, Harvard University Press.

Pollard, S. (2012). Put Abu Qatada on a plane and quit the European Court, *Express*, April 20, 2012.

Pound, P. (2004). Where is the evidence that animal research benefits humans? *British Medical Journal*, *328*(7438), 514–17. doi: 10.1136/bmj.328.7438.514

Prasad, R. (2008, July 30). The fertility tourists. Retrieved June 26, 2013 from http://www.guardian.co.uk/lifeandstyle/2008/jul/30/familyandrelationships.healthandwellbeing

Probert, R. (2004). Families, assisted reproduction and the law. *Child and Family Law Quarterly*, *16*(3), 273–88.

Putnam, R.D. (2000). *Bowling Alone: The Collapse and Revival of American Community*. New York: Simon and Schuster.

Radhakrishnan, R. (2003). *Theory in an Uneven World*. Malden, MA: Blackwell.

Ravetz, A. (2001). *Council Housing and Culture*. London: Routledge.

Rawls, J. (1971). *A Theory of Justice*. Cambridge, MA: Belknap Press of Harvard University Press.

Regan, T. (2004). *The Case for Animal Rights*. Berkeley: University of California Press.

Rerum novarum. (1891). Retrieved from http://www.vatican.va/holy_father/leo_xiii/encyclicals/documents/hf_l-xiii_enc_15051891_rerum-novarum_en.html

Rhee, R.J. (2009). Catastrophic risk and governance after Hurricane Katrina: a postscript to terrorism risk in a post-9/11 economy. *Arizona State Law Journal*, *38*(2), 581.

Ronald, R. (2008). *The Ideology of Home Ownership: Homeowner Societies and the Role of Housing*. Basingstoke: Palgrave Macmillan.

Rosegrant, S. (2007, August 28). Wal-Mart's response to Hurricane Katrina: striving for a public–private partnership (rep.). Retrieved January 29, 2012, from Kennedy School of Government Case Study No. C16-07-1876.0 website: http://www.case.hks.harvard.edu/casetitle.asp?caseNo=1876.0

Runyan, R.C., and Huddleston, P. (2009). Small business recovery from a natural disaster. In R.P. Malloy (ed.), *Law and Recovery from Disaster: Hurricane Katrina*,127–40. Farnham, England: Ashgate Publishing.

Sakamoto, M., and Yamori, K. (2010). A study of life recovery and social capital regarding disaster victims: a case study of Indian Ocean tsunami and Central Java earthquake recovery. *Journal of Natural Disaster Science*, *31*(2), 13.

Satz, A.B. (2008). Toward solving the health care crisis: the paradoxical case for universal access to high technology. *Yale Journal of Health Policy Law and Ethics*, *8*(1), 93.

Saunders, P. (1990). *A Nation of Home Owners*. London: Unwin Hyman.

Scheiner, C. (2001). "Cruelty to police dog" laws update. *Animal Law*, *7*, 141–4.

Schelling, W.J. (1987). *Ideas on a Philosophy of Nature as an Introduction to the Study of This Science* (trans. E. Behler). In *Philosophy of German Idealism*, pp. 167–202). New York: Continuum.

Science and Technology Committee (2005, March 24). Human reproductive technologies and the law. HC 7-I 2004-05, para. 107

Schmittlein, D.C., and Morrison, D.G. (2003). A live baby or your money back: the marketing of in vitro fertilization procedures. *Management Science*, *49*(12), 1617–35. doi: 10.1287/mnsc.49.12.1617.25119

Sclater, S. (2002). Introduction. In A. Bainham, S.D. Sclater, and M. Richards (eds), *Body Lore and Laws*, 1–28. Oxford: Hart.

Searle, J.R. (1998). *Mind, Language, and Society: Philosophy in the Real World*. New York, NY: Basic Books.

Sen, A. (1987). Equality of what? In J. Rawls, S.M. McMurrin, A. Sen, and T. Schelling (authors), *Liberty, Equality, and Law: Selected Tanner Lectures on Moral Philosophy*. Salt Lake City: University of Utah Press.

Sen, A. (1993). Capability and well-being. In M.C. Nussbaum and A. Sen (eds), *The Quality of Life*, 30–53. Oxford: Clarendon Press.

Sen, A.K. (1999). *Commodities and Capabilities*. Delhi: Oxford University Press.

Shamir, R. (2005). Corporate social responsibility: a case of hegemony and counter-hegemony. In B.D. Santos and G.C. Rodríguez (eds), *Law and*

Globalization from Below: Towards a Cosmopolitan Legality, 92–117. Cambridge: Cambridge University Press.

Shenfield, F. (2009, September 1). BioNews: Is cross-border reproductive care a problem, and for whom? Retrieved from http://www.bionews.org.uk/page_47257.asp

Short, J.R. (1991). *Imagined Country: Environment, Culture, and Society*. London: Routledge.

Shorter Oxford English Dictionary (2007). Oxford: Oxford University Press.

Shughart, W.F., II. (2006). Katrinanomics: the politics and economics of disaster relief. *Public Choice*, *127*(1/2), 31.

Simmonds, N.E. (2008). *Central Issues in Jurisprudence: Justice, Law and Rights*. London: Sweet and Maxwell.

Simons, P. (2012). International Law's Invisible Hand and the Future of Corporate Accountability for Violations of Human Rights. *Journal of Human Rights and the Environment*, *3*(1), 5–43.

Singer, P. (1993). *Practical Ethics*. Cambridge: Cambridge University Press.

Singer, P. (2002a). *Animal Liberation*. New York: HarperCollins.

Singer, P. (2002b, November 13). *A Response to Martha Nussbaum*. Retrieved from http://www.utilitarian.net/singer/by/20021113.htm

Skinner, Q., Dasgupta, P., Geuss, R., Lane, M., Laslett, P., O'Neill, O., and Kuper, A. (2002). Political philosophy: the view from Cambridge. *Journal of Political Philosophy*, *10*(1), 1–19. doi: 10.1111/1467-9760.00140

Small Business Administration. (n.d.). *Economic Injury Disaster Loans*. Retrieved January 29, 2012, from http://www.sba.gov/content/economic-injury-disaster-loans

Smith, A. (1982). *The Theory of Moral Sentiments* (D.D. Raphael and A.L. Macfie, eds). Indianapolis: Liberty Classics.

Smith, A. (2003). *The Wealth of Nations* (E. Cannan, ed.). New York, NY: Bantam Classic.

Smith, F. (2011). Indigenous farmers' rights, international agricultural trade and the WTO. *Journal of Human Rights and the Environment*, *2*(2), 157–77.

Smith, K.E. (2008). The GO ZONE Act: an innovative mechanism for promoting economic recovery for the Gulf Coast. *Mississippi Law Journal*, *77*(3), 807.

Smith, N., and George, G. (1997). Introductory tenancies: a nuisance too far?' *Journal of Social Welfare and Family Law*, *19*(2) 307–19

Spar, D. (2010). Free markets, free choice?: A market approach to reproductive rights. In M. Goodwin (ed.), *Baby Markets: Money and the New Politics of Creating Families*, 177–90). Cambridge: Cambridge University Press.

Sperling, D. (2011). "Male and female he created them": Procreative liberty, its conceptual deficiencies and the legal right to access fertility care of males. *International Journal of Law in Context*, *7*(03), 375–400. doi: 10.1017/S174455231100019X

Spinoza, B.D. (1951). *The Chief Works of Benedict de Spinoza*, ed. R.H. Elwes. New York: Dover Publications.

Storrow, R.F. (2005). Quests for conception: fertility tourists, globalization and feminist legal theory. *Hastings Law Journal*, *57*(2), 295.

Storrow, R.F. (2010a). Medical conscience and the policing of parenthood. *William and Mary Journal of Women and the Law*, *16*(2), 369–93.

Storrow, R.F. (2010b). Travel into the future of reproductive technology. *University of Missouri-Kansas City Law Review*, *79*(2), 296.

Storrow, R.F. (2011). Assisted reproduction on treacherous terrain: the legal hazards of cross-border reproductive travel. *Reproductive BioMedicine Online*, *23*(5), 538–45. doi: 10.1016/j.rbmo.2011.07.008

Strawson, G. (2006). Realistic monism: why physicalism entails panpsychism. *Journal of Consciousness Studies*, 13(10–11), 3–31.

Sunstein, C.R. (2000). Standing for animals. *UCLA Law Review*, *47*(5), 1333–68.

Super, D.A. (2011). Against flexibility. *Cornell Law Review*, *96*(6), 1375.

Surface Transportation Extension Act of 2005, Part III, H.R. 3332, 109th Cong., 1st Sess. (2005).

Teenage pregnancy rate falls. (2010, February 10). Retrieved May 8, 2010, from http://news.bbc.co.uk/1/hi/education/8531227.stm

Templeton, S. (2010, 21 November). Clinic imports Russian eggs. *The Sunday Times*. Retrieved June 26, 2013 from http://www.thesundaytimes.co.uk/sto/news/uk_news/Health/article455197.ece

Thatcher, M. (1993). *The Downing Street Years.* London: Harper Collins.

Tsakyrakis, S. (2009). Proportionality: an assault on human rights? *International Journal of Constitutional Law*, *7*(4), 468–93.

Tuebner, G (2006). The anonymous matrix: human rights violations by "private" transnational actors, *Modern Law Review*, *69*, 327–46.

Tuhiwai Smith, L. (1999). *Decolonizing Methodologies: Research and Indigenous Peoples* (London, Zed Books).

Turner, B.S. (2006). *Vulnerability and Human Rights*. University Park: Pennsylvania State University Press.

Twain, M. (1909). *Letters from the Earth by Mark Twain: Letter II.* Retrieved November 28, 2012, from http://www.online-literature.com/twain/letters-from-the-earth/3/

US Congress Office of Technology Assessment (1986, February). *Alternatives to Animal Use in Research, Testing, and Education.* Retrieved from http://www.princeton.edu/~ota/disk2/1986/8601/8601.PDF

US Department of Agriculture (2008, December 29). *Poultry Slaughter.* Retrieved April 11, 2009, from http://usda.mannlib.cornell.edu/usda/nass/PoulSlau/2000s/2008/PoulSlau-12-29-2008.pdf

Vandenhole, W. (2008). Conflicting economic and social rights: the proportionality plus test. In E. Brems (ed.), *Conflicts between Fundamental Rights*. Antwerp: Intersentia, 559–90.

Vandenhole, W., and Ryngaert, J. (2012). Mainstreaming children's rights in migration litigation: *ECtHR, Muskhadzhiyeva and others v. Belgium*, 19 January (2010). In E. Brems (ed.), *Diversity and European Human Rights:*

Rewriting Judgments of the ECHR. Cambridge: Cambridge University Press, 68–92.

Vasterling, V. (2003). Body and language: Butler, Merleau-Ponty and Lyotard on the speaking embodied subject. *International Journal of Philosophical Studies*, *11*(2), 205–23. doi: 10.1080/0967255032000074190

Vincent, K. (2004, August). Creating an index of social vulnerability to climate change for Africa (Working Paper No. 56). Retrieved from Tyndall Centre for Climate Change Research website: http://www.tyndall.ac.uk/sites/default/files/wp56.pdf

Waldron, J. (2009, September). Dignity, rank and rights. Paper presented at the 2009 Tanner Lectures at UC Berkeley. Retrieved from: http://papers.ssrn.com/sol3/papers.cfm?abstract_id=1461220

Weil, F.D. (2007, February). Reconstituting community: varieties of social capital in disaster recovery. *Katrina's Jewish Voices*. Retrieved January 29, 2012, from http://katrina.jwa.org/content/vault/Weil_KatrinaSurveyResearchNSFPr oposalPublic_84af6e7d37.pdf

Westra, L. (2004). Environmental rights and human rights: the final enclosure movement. In R. Brownsword (ed.), *Global Governance and the Quest for Justice*, 107–19). Oxford: Hart Publishing.

Westra, L., and Lawson, B.E. (eds) (2001). *Faces of Environmental Racism: Confronting Issues of Global Justice*. Lanham, MD: Rowman and Littlefield.

Whitehouse, L. (2009). The Mortgage Arrears Pre-action Protocol: an opportunity lost. *Modern Law Review*, *72*(5), 793–814. doi: 10.1111/j.1468-2230.2009.00768.x

Whitney, S.Y. (2011). Dependency relations: corporeal vulnerability and norms of personhood in Hobbes and Kittay. *Hypatia*, *26*(3), 554–74.

Willse, C. (2010). Neo-liberal biopolitics and the invention of chronic homelessness. *Economy and Society*, *39*(2), 155–84. doi: 10.1080/03085141003620139

Winston. (2007). Lords Hansard of 4 Dec 2007, column 1614. *Lords Hansard of 4 Dec 2007*. Retrieved from http://www.publications.parliament.uk/pa/ld200708/ldhansrd/index/071204.html

Wintour, P. (2008, October 22). Brown pledges action to curb home repossessions. *The Guardian*. Retrieved from http://www.guardian.co.uk/money/2008/oct/23/gordon-brown-mortgages-home-repossessions

Wise, S.M. (2000). *Rattling the Cage: Toward Legal Rights for Animals*. Perseus Books.

Wolfson, D., and Sullivan, M. (2004). Foxes in the hen house: Animals, agribusiness, and the law: a modern American fable. In C.R. Sunstein and M.C. Nussbaum (eds), *Animal Rights: Current Debates and New Directions*, 234–50. Oxford: Oxford University Press.

Wood, E.M. (1999). *The Origin of Capitalism*. New York: Monthly Review Press.

Woodiwiss, A. (2005). *Human Rights* (Abingdon: Routledge).

Wright, P. (1991). *A Journey Through Ruins: The Last Days of London*. London: Radius.

Xenos, D. (2009). The human rights of the vulnerable. *The International Journal of Human Rights*, 13(4), 591–614.

Yoshino, K. (2011). The new equal protection. *Harvard Law Review*, *124*(3), 747–803.

Index